# Anti-Yankee Feelings

# in Latin America

An Anthology of Latin American Writings
from Colonial to Modern Times in Their
Historical Perspective

BY

F. TOSCANO

*Delaware State College*

JAMES HIESTER

*University of Delaware*

UNIVERSITY
PRESS OF
AMERICA

LANHAM • NEW YORK • LONDON

Copyright © 1982 by

**University Press of America,™ Inc.**

4720 Boston Way
Lanham, MD 20706

3 Henrietta Street
London WC2E 8LU England

**ISBN (Perfect): 0-8191-2146-0**
**ISBN   (Cloth): 0-8191-2145-2**

*To our wives, Margaret Nava and Francine, with love.*

iii

# Acknowledgements

The authors gratefully acknowledge the
contributions of the following people in translating,
proofreading, typing, and a myriad of other duties:
students like Shirley Dill, Susan Flores, Phyllis
Kohel, Joyce Mullins, Pedro Sanchez and colleagues
like William Marshall from The Tatnall School,
Robert Zaetta from the State Department of Education,
Jack Gardner and Charlotte Zaback from D.S.C. A
special thanks to Tom Lathrop from University of
Delaware for his most needed help in the making of
this book.

F.T.
J.H.
September, 1981.

# Table of Contents

# ❧ Introduction ❧

Latin America, since her early colonial period, has consistently produced a literature aimed at social problems. Several countries, some to a greater degree than others, have suffered political, economic, and military abuse by foreign powers. Most of the time, the only way they could protest was through writing. So they did.

To identify and isolate socio-political ideas in literary works has never been an easy task. Works judged as "literary" are usually subjected to analyses of linguistic import and aesthetics; intrinsic eschatological messages are considered secondary. It is for this reason that many critical studies dealing with literary topics fall short of their intended goals. Additionally, it is difficult to ignore the emotional charge that was precipitated, rightly or wrongly, by historical events in any selection of protest writing.

For this study, each writer surveyed represents an individual responding to his historical events. Therefore, these subjective responses cannot/should not be judged as historicity, but are presented as variations on a common socio-political theme. This book cannot offer a complete study of all literature in Latin America with an anti-American mood because of the prolific writing on the subject. It is intended (despite the subjectivity of the material analyzed) to be an objective survey of the many turbulent events that took place south of the border and their effects on the people who witnessed and felt their traumas.

Some readers, knowledgeable in Latin American affairs, might not give too much importance to this work because of its literary sources. Others, with experience in literature, will probably (for their purposes) find superficiality; but the intent of this work is to provide a literary perspective on the historical complexities and the effect of American aggression in Latin America.

Because it is essential to know the people of Latin America, their history and work, the format of this book will vary somewhat from the literary analyses which have gone before. In the presentation of each movement or personality, a solid foundation, based on the historical, social, and intellectual facets of the given society will be examined. Thus, every author represented will be viewed within the framework of his environment, his people, and, where relevant, his personal life. Rather than a mechanical presentation of factual material, the concerns here will be with the Latin American people - their emotions, feelings, and literary outpouring of expression. The reaction of these people to outside invaders, to foreign intruders, will be recorded no matter how they are named. "Yankee", "Gringo", whatever - they are all Protestants, they all speak English, they are all the same.

The Latin American society's political or military defense has often been less than effective. Of greater impact have been the emotional and often fearful writings of Latin Americans. In many cases, the only weapon of the nations of the south has been the pen.

J.E. Rodo published Ariel in 1900, in which he assumed the role of a retiring professor delivering a speech to his disciples. His speech is meant to be addressed to the young countries of Latin America and contains words of warning against the possible threats from the North Americans. At the time, his message was particularly timely because it coincided with the war of aggression by the United States against Cuba and with the defeat of the latter in 1898.

The mood of the people in South America was sad and fearful as they wondered which country would next be invaded. From this fear stemmed the anti-Yankee feelings of the people as they became more and more watchful of the subsequent abuses from the United States. Perez Petit was able, better than anyone else, to verbalize the thoughts of his people in his book on J.E. Rodo:

> The United States of North America,
> using the pretext of the mysterious

x

explosion of their battleship 'Maine',
directly intervened in the war that
Spain maintained with the last of its
colonies, the island of Cuba.  In a
few months the campaign was ended;
from April to the month of September,
1898, Spain made a final effort to
keep its pavillion filled with pride,
but its new enemy was powerful - and
the fight was useless and unequal.

The disaster of the fleet of Cavite
brought about the loss of the
Philippine Islands.  The heroic sacrifice of Admiral Pascual Cervera,
who, with a knightly gesture deserving
of the old Cids, left the port of
Havana with his ships, knowing that
he was sailing to his death, did not
prevent the defeat.  Thus, in less
than five months, 'the nation in
whose dominions the sun does not set'
yielded its proud pavillion over the
sea of Antilles.

This rough fight dispirited us; it
gave Rodo and me the greatest anxiety.
We wanted and craved the freedom of
Cuba, the last country of the
Americas to remain subject to the
yoke of Spain, notwithstanding the
virile fights for independence and
the glorious struggles of the
Martis and the Maceos.  But, we
desired equally that this liberty be
won by the sons of the subjugated
nation, as all South America had been
won, or, at the most, with the aid
of our brother countries.  A new
Bolivar would have filled us with
pride.  But what we could not accept,
in any way, was the intervention of
North America.  It was certain that
the liberation of Cuba was favored,
but we did not appreciate the
service.  What did this nation have
to do with the struggles of the
countries of another race?  In the
fight we were for Spain.  Free Cuba,
yes, but not in favor of North America.

It was a little complicated, obviously,
this method of reasoning, but that is
the way it was. In us, sentiment
predominated - with a better love,
perhaps, than that of many of her
sons who attacked her while we defended her. It was not impossible then
that her ruin echoed as our own in
our hearts. And we loved Spain as
much as North America disgusted us.
We cordially hated Dewey, his ponderous
'Iowa' and his invincible 'Massachusetts'.

Walking at night with Rodo, we
forgot Cuestas for this foreign war.
These were long and hearfelt chats
about our beautiful and idealistic
Latin race and this other, this
severe and utilitarian race of the
north.

'One should say all of this,'
exclaimed Rodo, 'one must say this
profoundly well, with much truth,
without hatred, and with the coldness
of a Tacitus.'

The inspiration for Ariel awakened
in his mind. But the vision was not
yet complete. He continued to
comment on the successes with me;
loving a free Cuba, by sympathizing
with Spain's disaster.

'Between us,' he said, 'we Latins,
with all that we desire, we can
break the bonds of brotherhood and
later return to embrace and be one,
with the same thoughts, the same
blood, the same traditions and habits
and the same tongue. But this other
calculating, cold, egotistic country,
whose god is the dollar, and who puts
self-interest before ideals; this
other country is our common enemy.
It is our future danger. And the
youth of Latin America who forget
the ideal in place of interest is in
danger of falling into their clutches.

One has to say all of this, don't
you think?'

This great book, this unfading work
of Jose Enrique Rodo, was germinated
in his  soul like a Eucharistic flower.
And because of this, because it was
from the heart, because it really
lived, because it translated a state
of spirit which had to be common in
its time in many South Americans,
because it was a cry for salvation,
because it preached the ideal of our
race against the egotism of the
other, distinctly different race,
because it enclosed in the most inti-
mate of its senses a salute to conquered Spain - it is in this direct
and thundering way that it came to the
heart of all South America. Conscious-
ly, they would see, and they did see,
the danger of the North. Afterwards,
the geniality of its conception, the
insurmountability of its realization,
the immortal beauty of the form, did
the rest.[1]

In 1925, a rather fantastic book was published
in Mexico, entitled The Cosmic Race, by a man called
Jose Vasconcelos (1882-1959). He was an active
member of a group of scholars called Ateno de la
Juventud. Other members interested in the intellectual
advancement of the country were: Pedro Henriquez
Urena, Alfonso Reyes, Antonio Caso, Gonzalez Martinez,
among other lesser known literary figures. The
intention of the author in writing this book was to
raise the morale of the Mexican people and to give
them hope and pride for the future. His thesis was
that, at the beginning, the Nordic people of Europe
advanced in civilization by conquering the cold, and,
now, natural cycle of history. The proud dolichoceph-
alous blonde would have stepped back to a new race,
formed on a natural selection of beauty, and they
would settle in the tropics. This means that all
people together would live in peace and harmony in a
Latin tropical atmosphere. Vasconcelos revised history
in his book (which in his later days wasn't taken too
seriously and was considered a juvenile impulse) and,
like Rodo, rejected all forms of utilitarianism
identified with the Anglo-Saxon culture. But, unlike

Rodo, he reached his anti-Yankee mood via experience
rather than through reading or literary clubs. His
experience led him to condemn the American ambassador,
J.R. Poinsett, who worked intensively to undermine the
social and racial Hispanic culture in his Mexico as
well as in other Latin American countries. Because
Poinsett was a Mason, committed to the destruction of
the power of the Roman Catholic Church, Europe openly
and severely criticized him, and he was known by his
contemporaries as "the abominable Poinsett, a political
fiend in human guise who plunged a gentle and brotherly
people into an abyss of discord, hatred, and revolution."[2]

In Latin America, as in no other geographical area,
there is a common cultural foundation. As such, the
literature of all the countries is based on the same
ideological base. Therefore, in each chapter of this
study, historical background will be presented so that
the most significant literary manifestations of a
society, inspired by specific historical events, will
be understood, both in the context of that particular
nation and as linked with similar events and works
in all of Latin America.

Delaware State College 1981

Americans, traditionally, love to fight. All *real* Americans love the sting of battle. When you were kids, you all admired the champion marble shooter, the fastest runner, the big league ball players, the toughest boxer. Americans love a winner, and will not tolerate a loser. Americans play to win all the time. They yell for a man's loss, and laugh. That's why Americans have never lost, and will never lose, a war. Because the very thought of losing is hateful to Americans.

PATTON

# ❧ 1 ❧

# The Colossus Threatens

Prior to the eighteenth century, the lands of Central and South America were, in many ways, the most advanced in the Western Hemisphere. These areas, which were under the control of Spain and Portugal, excelled in culture and education, for they were the heirs of the peak of Iberian civilization. In some important ways, Latin America preserved a high level of excellence in the intellectual realm even after Spain and Portugal had long since begun an irreversible decline. The early universities and Catholic grammar schools of the new world produced a small, but outstanding, group of scholars who became the historians, writers, and educators of the Latin colonies. Furthermore, these colonies also drew on this circle of intellectuals for their political leaders. Even to the present day, many Latin American heads of state have risen to prominence through a reputation as educator or writer.

When the Pilgrims landed in Massachusetts in 1620, there already existed numerous distinguished Latin American universities. The Colegio Santo Tomas in Santo Domingo was founded in 1538, and thirteen years later, major universities were founded in Lima, Peru and Mexico City. By 1600, Quito, Bogota, and Cuzco had also become university cities. So when Harvard was established as the first university in British Colonial America in 1636, the Latin American university system was nearly a century old. A similar chronology can be presented regarding the establishment of early printing presses in America. With the South once again taking the lead, there can be little question

1

that, even into the early years of the eighteenth
century, Latin America produced a more advanced
educational and literary culture.

The educational establishment in the South, however, showed a marked difference from that in the North.
In much of Europe as well as in North America, early
universities were associations of students.  As such,
they also served as the focal points of liberal
causes and new ideas.  In Latin America, as in Spain,
the universities were more a center of advanced
cultural and intellectual pursuits.  There was little
influence by students and a high degree of control
exercised by the Catholic Church.  These Latin universities attracted the cultural and intellectual leaders
of Latin society and also served the emerging nations
of the South by providing the politicians.  The weak
points of the Latin system can generally be traced
to the strong domination of all intellectual pursuits
by the Catholic Church, for this domination led to
stagnation in many areas of thought.  Culturally also,
Latin America lacked vitality.  This is, moreover,
unusual due to the rich variety which the lands of
the South show.  One would expect that the early
cultures of the colonies would be heavily influenced
by the varied Indian influences as well as by the
widely differing geographic settings, but the
opposite is true.  The colonial leadership was
adamantly unwilling to bend the culture of Iberian
Catholicism to fit the widely varied lands of the
New World.  These rigid influences were to have a
harmful effect on generations of Latin Americans,
who sought to find a new and separate cultural and
intellectual base which was not dominated by Spanish
Catholicism.

Despite these differences between North and
South, from the early eighteenth century, the course
which Latin American society followed was quite
similar to that of North American society.  In the
South, there occurred a lengthy period of colonial
domination, a growing dissatisfaction with the
"mother country", and a series of national uprisings
which eventually led to independence.  During this
period, the differences between North and South lay
not in these general matters, but rather in the
specific colonial influences in the cultural, economic,
and political spheres.  The political system of
Spanish colonialism, along with its religious and
intellectual influences, gave rise to a rigid

2

organization throughout Latin America. There was surprisingly little variance between territories separated by thousands of miles, a common national and religious bond linked the lands of the South. This bond was undoubtedly the reason for the strong influence of Spanish and Catholic ideas throughout Latin America.

The more varied nature of the national and geographic roots of North America, along with the wide diversity of religious and intellectual thought, gave rise to a less unified but more fruitious society. In the North, one finds vitality in educational establishments as well as in society as a whole, with a proliferation of newspapers and pamphlets, and an emerging school of "American" political philosophy. The northern colonists brought with them the theories of men such as John Locke (Two Treatises of Government, published in 1690) and Jean Jacques Rousseau, author of Social Contract (1762). Concepts of anti-absolutism were firmly rooted in North America and gave hope to even the lowest of economic groups. Town meetings and political clubs also inspired new governmental ideas, and the American system of politics which emerged in the 1770s and 1780s contained new theories of ruler and ruled, of human rights and justice.[1]

In the economic sphere, the United States was strongly influenced by the new theories of economists such as Adam Smith. Therefore, in areas both political and economic, the emerging nation was filled with new ideas, with vitality and liberal philosophy, there was a solid cornerstone upon which to build a nation. There existed also a handful of truly capable and creative men who were well-schooled in the theories of government, and these individuals provided the leadership for the first generations of the new nation. The new rulers were not kings, for there was little love of royalty. Those who would have made George Washington "king" were in the minority, and the absolutism which held Europe and Latin America within its grasp never truly took root in the North.

In the Latin sphere, similar conflicts led to the breaking of the bonds of colonialism, but the Spanish system had not inspired diversity in religious or political thought. Royal absolutism and the subservience of much of society to the ruling class assured that Latin America would have trouble making the

3

transition to a Republican or Democratic form of government. The concept of absolute rule was buried too deeply within the Latin psyche. Theories from France, England or North America had only limited influence. The American and French Revolutions made an impression on Latin America, but actually only scratched the surface of the civilization. While these revolutions gave hope to the nationalities of the South (and were, in part, responsible for the eventual independence of the Latin nations) they did little to change the centuries-old colonial foundations. As a result, the countries of Latin America achieved independence, but were, in virtually every case, unprepared to deal effectively with their own political destinies.

The ideal of national independence grew slowly among the Spanish colonies, and its growth was the result of widely diverse influences. The initial successes of the emerging United States were an important influence, but not in 1775 - or even 1789. It was not until the final days of the War of 1812 that the leaders of the independence movements in the South began to draw upon the example of the United States. Prior to this time, the prime motivation of their demands was the continuing intransigence of the Spanish colonial administration. Also of major influence, as the nineteenth century began, was the intervention of foreign powers in the affairs of Latin America.

As a result of the Spanish policy of Asientos (the granting of specific trade contracts to individual companies), the British, as well as other European nations, had been involved in trade with Latin America since the 1500s.[2]

This system generally meant profit for Spain and problems for the colonies, and led to further involvement of European powers in the South. By 1800, the British had designs on several valuable Latin areas, and the situation grew tense when local uprisings led to a lessening of Spanish influence. Only the Napoleonic Wars forced Britain to abandon plans to take over Venezuela. However, when the British government withdrew, a large number of British soldiers (who had already begun to exert influence over areas of the northeast coast of South America) moved southward to Buenos Aires where they occupied the city in 1806. Their motives were personal and inspired by greed, but some of them, Sir Home Popham in particular, were very influential with high British officials.

As a result, the British government became involved and aided in the occupation of Buenos Aires. This single act is often overlooked by some historians in discussing the early Latin independence movements. It is, however, significant, for although the British were expelled by the Spanish in little more than a year, this occupation by a foreign power inspired overwhelming feelings of nationalism throughout the South. Between 1809 and 1816, a series of revolutions swept through Latin America. These uprisings had in common their almost universal failure. In only one area, that of Buenos Aires, was there a successful outcome with the foundation of the independent provinces of the Rio de la Plata.

Despite the widespread failure of this first phase of revolt, the Latin peoples had finally acted; inspired by the marauding British and of Anglo-Saxons in general emerged at this time, and one finds in literature strong warnings against the North Americans as well as the British.

The second stage of revolutions followed immediately in 1816. Led by men such as Simon Bolivar, this phase was inspired by a growing realization of the successes of the United States, by the intellectual inheritance of the French Revolution, and by the rekindled nationalism which had been temporarily suppressed by Spain in the period prior to 1816. The Republicanism of the United States was highly respected, and the leaders of the uprising were liberal, educated, and nationalistic. They were not "political" in the North American sense, but were fervent in their desire for independence. The attempt to emulate the United States can be seen in the names and governments of the newly formed nations, but these also show the political immaturity of the South. Their leaders were, for the most part, educators or soldiers, and not politicians.

The revolutions of 1816-1825 were successful because they were attacking an outmoded, corrupt colonial network and a nation which was a quarter of the way around the world. The Spanish colonial system was far from orderly, but the new republican political systems which replaced it were, at best, chaotic.

Constitutions, republican ideas, and elections
went far to renovate the South, but the positive
influences were negated by the lack of a vital political
heritage, by an uninformed populace, and by an intellectual system that was firmly entrenched in absolutism
and Catholicism.  Royal institutions and the Catholic
Church came under attack, but almost as an afterthought,
and mostly because they represented the harsh
influences which Spain had had on Latin America.
Within a short period, the Church had regained most of
its prestige, and the leaders of the new nations
took on the character of Spanish kings, albeit at a
reduced level of importance.

Intellectuals and educators were called upon to
stabilize the new government, but they were ill-
prepared for their task in most cases.  Each new
country was different, with varying constitutional
bases and styles of leadership.  They were all similar
in that they could not, in a dozen generations, overcome the long and rigid inheritance from the colonial
era.  The Church and absolutism, although no longer
controlled by Spain, ruled the day.

As in all intellectual areas, the pre-revolutionary
literature of Latin America was strongly dominated by
Spanish influences.  There were a number of political
writers.  Both fiction and poetry were produced, but
there was little which was either original or
important.  With the nineteenth century and the
revolutions, there occurred surprisingly little
change.  There were more newspapers and several
isolated flashes of literary brilliance, but it was
not until the last decade of the century that Latin
American literature truly reached a high level of
influence and importance.

The influence of the French encyclopedists and
philosophes was quite strong in the South, and such
figures as Juan de Egana, J.M. Caballero, and Frutos
Joaquin Gutierrez were much influenced by the
literary forms and intellectual ideas of the French.
But, even Rousseau's Social Contract proved difficult
to apply to Latin society, because the rigid class
structure persisted and excluded large segments of
the population from participating in the government.
It was, rather, in the literary scene that new forces
were at work in Latin America in the first half of
the nineteenth century.  The old Spanish-inspired
neo-classicism gave way to the new literary school of

Romanticism. And while the Romantic authors were
significant, few of them had a lasting influence even
within their own countries. The obscure and idealistic
creations of these Romantics set the tone for much of
the century, but the writers whose words had the most
significance during this period belonged to no school.
They were the political writers who surveyed the
contemporary scene, and who wrote as individuals in
books and newspapers. Many of their words were most
assuredly lost, but several authors of this type were
among the first to show evidence of anti-United States
sentiments.[3]

Even in the pre-revolutionary period, there
occurred "anti-Yankee" diatribes, but most of these
were the work of the Spanish colonial government. This
is not surprising, for the Spanish clearly realized
the danger which the new ideas from the North could
have on the colonial system. Thus, among conservative
Spanish authors, men such as Fray Melchor Martinez,
strongly defended both the king and the cross.

They also warned the peoples of the South to be
wary of the "Boston revolutionaries" whose only
interests in Latin America were economic and selfish.
In the late eighteenth century, these views were perhaps unpopular with most of the population, but
within fifty years they proved to be all too accurate.[4]

Even after the Latin countries had gained their
independence, literary figures continued to perceive
a threat from the North. In some instances, these
perceptions were precursory and stemmed more from
the authors' personal convictions than from historical
objectivity. Jose Maria de Salazar (1785-1828), a
Columbian, was both poet and statesman. He warned
in 1823 that the Latin countries should not try to
imitate the United States because he believed that
the policies and ideologies that were beneficial for
the North could spell disaster for the South.

Lucas Alaman (1729-1853), throughout his life
defended everything Spanish and denounced the United
States. A Mexican, Alaman saw first-hand the growing
attempts by the United States to control the lands
to the South. Based on his fear and hatred of
imperialism (he had lived through Mexico's struggle to
shed the European form of domination), he decried in
his Semblanzas e ideario the expansionist motives of
United States foreign policy in the 1820s and 1830s.

These authors, and others who wrote political literature during this period, were important for their
ideas.  Their styles or literary talents are
secondary.[5]

There was also Francisco Bilbao (1823-1865), a
Chilean, who at mid-century responded to a decade of
North American atrocities in his La America en peligro.
His work, better than any other, sums up the state
of Latin political literature prior to the 1880s.
Bilbao was violently opposed to U.S. actions in
Mexico and Central America, and he correctly assessed
the motives behind the heinous activities, but his
words were little known by his contemporaries.  He
was one individual writer, little known, and without a
coherent or creative style.  He was, however, an
accurate and astute observer, and as such was a
pivotal figure in the history of anti-Yankee literature.[6]

It is important to be aware of the conditions
affecting the relationships between North and South,
because virtually every literary outcry in the course
of anti-Yankeeism was inspired by some U.S. action or
policy.  The threat of a Northern power emerged
only after 1815.  Prior to this time, the United
States was fighting hard for its own survival.  It was
not until the U.S. fought long and well against
Britain in the War of 1812 that the world community
admitted a new power, and an observant Latin America
viewed, with some alarm, the new "colossus to the
North".

During the time that a series of successful
revolts was sweeping through Latin America, the U.S.
was emerging from the War of 1812, chartering the
Bank of the United States, and electing James Monroe.
Northern troops were expected to help in Bolivar's
campaigns, but the U.S. was busy stabilizing its
economy and expanding through the purchase of Florida
and through treaties with Britain.

The first steamship had crossed the Atlantic and
slavery was becoming an issue in North America.  By
1823, most of the Latin states had gained independence,
and toward the end of the year, on December 2, the
most important document in the history of American
relations was issued.

President Monroe had been re-elected in 1820 and had been faced with problems in foreign affairs for much of his administration. The Holy Alliance of European nations threatened to intervene and restore Spain as the "legitimate" power in Latin America. Russia and, to a lesser extent, Britain were pursuing aggressive policies on the northwest coast of North America. Within this atmosphere, Monroe was determined to ensure and maintain the independence of the Latin republics, and at the same time, assist his nation's newly-recognized position in the world diplomatic community. This he accomplished on December 2, 1823, when he addressed Congress and leveled a challenge to the world with the Monroe Doctrine.[7]

The Doctrine's basic tenets are well-known. The United States agreed not to interfere in the status quo of Latin America, but maintained the right to oppose any other power which attempted such intervention. The implication was that the Doctrine would keep Europe out of Latin America and that the United States would stay clear of European entanglements. Also, the U.S. proclaimed itself a champion of republicanism versus the absolutism of Metternich's Europe. The Doctrine also implied, however, that the United States might be forced to intervene in Latin America when it was deemed necessary. This interpretation was to be important within twenty years, and was to prove a tool of imperialism again and again during the next hundred years.

The fears of Latin Americans regarding the colossus were first proved well-founded in the area of Mexico. The United States sent, as their first representative to the new nation, Joel R. Poinsett, a career diplomat and amateur botanist. He is probably best known for giving his name to the poinsettia. He was a key figure in the early history of U.S.-Latin American relations. On the surface, he appeared to be a good choice in 1825. President John Quincy Adams saw him as a fine diplomat, a man of Latin heritage, and someone who had spent time in Mexico. A novice or blunderer he was not, as some critics have suggested; but he was a liberal, a staunch Mason, and an Anglophobe. These qualities quickly entangled him in the tense Mexican political situation.

For Mexico, the period from 1821 to 1855 was a difficult one. Although independent from Spain, the country was still run by the social nobility through a series of military caudillos. An effective form of government was being sought, and there had been little success. An empire was instituted for a time, was replaced by a federal system, which finally led to a centralist regime. There was much strife during this period. When Poinsett arrived in 1825, President Guadelupe Victoria was in power. His administration strongly supported the Church and the privileges of birth. As a Protestant and liberal, Poinsett hardly fit into this setup.

It is also interesting to note that the Masonic movement was strong in much of Latin America during this period, certainly as a reaction against the power of the Church, and perhsps due to a prepossession with things Anglo-Saxon. In the 1820s the politicians of the South were the guardians of privilege and often emulated British and North American politicians.

In Mexico, two parties emerged in the political arena: the yorkinos and escoceses. These parties were Masonic in origin, and in fact, the Spanish names are directly from the English; "Yorkists" and "Scots", for the Yorkist and Scottish Masonic rites. The former was the more liberal party and was supported and advised by Poinsett. In 1826, when the yorkinos won the congressional elections, the opposition rose in revolt, calling for the suppression of secret societies; especially the Yorkist Masons; the immediate resignation of the liberal government, and the expulsion of Poinsett.

The minister found himself at the center of a serious political situation, but he continued to stir up trouble by championing the cause of the lower classes and by denouncing the Catholic Church. His strong attacks on the Spanish were one of the reasons for their expulsion in 1827. One thing is certain, Poinsett was controversial and belligerent and his personality did little to help the cause of U.S.- Latin American relations. As an expert on Poinsett, Justin Harvey Smith states, "He considered it a part of his duty to work actively for the overthrow of aristocracy and hereditary privilege and priesthood."

The course of Mexican history after 1828 was not to change for the better and the Church was to continue to play a vital role in the nation. Thus, Poinsett's expulsion when the escoceses came to power was an

indication of the future course of events. Internal
stability was still a long-range goal, and anti-
Yankee sentiments grew stronger.

A major figure in Mexico in 1830 was not a
politician, but an intellectual: Lucas Alaman. He
was an aristocrat, a Catholic, and a prime opponent
of Poinsett. Alaman was also a major political
power. He engineered the election of various candidates, including President Bustamante in 1830. But
even Alaman's abilities could not bring an end to
constant civil war. Many figures rose and fell as
the assassin's and the executioner's bullets flew.
But between 1832 and 1855, one man dominated the
Mexican political scene. He was Antonio Lopez de
Santa Anna. His character tells us much of Mexico
during this period.

Santa Anna was corrupt and incompetent, and one
wonders how such a blunderer could remain in power.
He attempted to end civil strife by issuing a
Centralist Constitution in 1836, which provided that
all officials were directly responsible to the central
government. This attempt to "tighten the reins" of
government seemed to have the opposite effect, as
some outlying territories which had been relatively
quiet began to cause problems.

In 1836, an area of the state of Coahuila, known
as Texas, seceded and declared its independence on
March the second of that year. Santa Anna could not
accept this situation and so led an army against
Texas. He found a handful of the Texas leaders in
San Antonio at the Alamo and managed to defeat and
kill all of them.

Santa Anna was to pay for this - for in April,
at San Jacinto, a U.S.-Texas force crushed the
Mexicans and captured the president. Santa Anna was
returned to Mexico, and Texas was lost, claimed by
the United States. These problems were minor when
compared to the next northern challenge which Mexico
had to face.

The isolation which the U.S. had followed after
the War of 1812 turned in the 1830s and 1840s into a
new spirit of expansionism. Financial problems,
conflicts with Canada, and debates over slavery led
politicians to seek another rallying point to muster
support. "Manifest Destiny" emerged. It was

11

theorized by President James Polk and his advisors that the United States had a right, in fact, a "destiny", to expand in North America - to Texas, California, Oregon, and so on. Polk was willing to negotiate for the desired lands, and even sent John Slidell to Mexico in 1845 to arrange for the purchase of New Mexico. In early March, 1846, the Mexicans gave their final refusal, and in April, an American army arrived in Texas.

The Mexican War which ensued was hardly a major international conflict; the only matter in question was who would fire the first shot. This question was answered on April 26 when Mexican troops fired on U.S. troops along the Rio Grande. The U.S. followed this incident by returning Santa Anna to Mexico. The deposed president had been exiled to Cuba in 1845, and the U.S. hoped that by returning him to power, he would side with the United States. He did not; rather, he formed a new Mexican government which lasted until September, 1847, when General Winfield Scott led a victorious army into Mexico City.

The United States occupied northern California and New Mexico, and the Guadalupe-Hidalgo treaty which followed (February 2, 1848), recognized all of the United States' demands.[8] Mexico lost Texas, New Mexico, and the northern portion of California. In return, the U.S. paid 15 million dollars and agreed to recognize Spanish land grants in New Mexico. With the stroke of the pen which signed this treaty, Mexico lost more than one-half of its land area. A period of instability followed the war because the Yucatan had also declared its independence from the central government and had to be rejoined to the nation. Within this chaotic atmosphere, Santa Anna again returned to power in 1853. He felt that he needed financial backing to remain in power, and so sold La Mesilla to the United States in the Gadsden Purchase for the sum of ten million dollars. Santa Anna was permanently exiled in 1855.[9]

The entire course of events from 1820 to 1855 set the stage for future relations between the U.S. and Mexico. Even into the twentieth century, Mexico felt little love for its neighbor to the north. Mexican literature was consistent in its attacks on the United States.

Mexico was not the only area which witnessed U.S.
imperialism during the early and mid-nineteenth
century.  In 1848, the U.S. needed a quick route to
its new lands in the west.  This need led to discussions
of the building of a railroad or canal across Central
America; it also brought North Americans in close
contact with the South as many travellers made the
voyage around the cape to reach California.  Thus, U.S.
influence can be seen even in Chile and Argentina.
American financial interests believed that the
immediate solution to the transportation problem lay in
a railroad across Nicaragua, but this move was strongly
opposed by the nations of Central America.

As a result, the railroad tycoon and financier,
Cornelius Vanderbilt, hired the adventurer-mercenary,
William Walker, to lead an expedition to take over
Nicaragua.  Walker landed in 1855 and managed to
force his control over much of the nation.  He
engineered the election of his own candidate as president and became commander of the army.  Despite these
seeming successes and the beginnings of construction
on the railroad, Walker faced great opposition from
within Nicaragua and from the surrounding nations.
But it was a quarrel with the U.S. transit company
which forced his flight to a United States man-of-war
in 1857.  Walker made a brief return in 1860, but was
captured and shot in Honduras before he could mount
an offensive.[10]

Central America thrived economically during this
period; great strides were made in transportation and
building.  The effect that Walker's excapades had on
Latin America as a whole was, however, more important.
The nations of the South greatly feared the presence
of the United States because they did not welcome rape
and plunder within their borders.  The great fear of
the "Colossus to the North" is clearly stated by the
words of the Chilean, Francisco Bilbao (1823-1865).
Although he was not a first-hand observer  of the
Central American incursions, Bilbao was afraid for the
entire Latin American world.  With this era, we see
the beginnings of eloquent cries of fear from the
writers of the South.  And while the United States
had long been admired by the Latin Americans in
general, this feeling of friendship was changing to
one of alarm.

These works by Latin writers, which so clearly
show the shift in attitudes, arrived on the literary

13

scene at a time when there was little real creativity in literary style or topics.

But with the events of the early republican period, men such as Lucas Alaman wrote harsh criticism of the United States. Moreover, armed with ammunition gathered during the American aggressions of the 1830s, forties, and fifties, writers such as Bilbao produced some extraordinarily astute attacks upon U.S. aggression. By 1860, a new literary movement had not yet emerged, but within the old framework, new literary topics had been elevated to a position of importance.

The following section will reproduce some of the important words of the era prior to 1860. The writings which will follow this and each succeeding chapter are those which most clearly elucidate the growth of "Anti-Yankee" sentiments.

# FRANCISCO BILBAO

## *Chile*

## (1823-1865)

Francisco Bilbao was born in Santiago, Chile. In 1839 he enrolled in the Instituto Nacional to study law. As a student he participated in several cultural movements such as Sociedad Literaria (1842). He was very active; his publication shows in newspapers such as El Siglo and Crepusculo. He always kept close contact with his academic world; his book La America en Peligro (1856) was dedicated to his teachers Michelet and Quinet. This book deals with an old and familiar theme: religion and politics, which should work hand in hand, should complement and re-inforce each other. When they oppose each other the result is almost always anarchy.

Parenthetically, Bilbao asks whether the people should be blamed for the government's foreign policy. Should the people be responsible for the action of their free elected leaders? After all, it is the people that have put the president where he is, and if he should perform infamous deeds, the people that he represents should be equally blamed.

# America in Danger

Today we see empires that seem to be reviving the old idea of global domination. The Russian Empire and the United States, two powers situated at geographical and political extremes, aspire to this end. The one to extend Russian serfdom under the mask of Pan-Slavism, the other to secure the domination of Yankee individualism. Russia is very far away; the United States is nearby. Russia sheathes its claws, trusting in its crafty snares; but the United States, daily, extends its talons in a hunting expedition that it has begun against the South. Already we see fragments of America falling into the jaws of the Saxon boa that magnetizes its victims as it unfolds its tortuous coils. Yesterday it was Texas, then it was northern Mexico and the Pacific that greets a new master.

Today the guerillas of the North are arousing the Isthmus with thier shots, and we see Panama, the future Constantinople of America, doubtfully suspended over the abyss and asking itself: Shall I belong to the South or to the North?

There is the danger. He who doesn't see it renounces his future. Is there so little conscience in ourselves, so little faith in the intelligence of the Latin American race, that we must wait for a foreign will, a different intellect, to organize us and decide our fate? Are we so poorly blessed with the gift of personality that we must give up our own initiative and create our identity from the outsider, who is hostile and overbearing? I don't believe it; the moment of truth is now.

This is the historic moment of South American unity; the second campaign has begun which will add the association of our peoples to winning of independence. Its motive is the danger to our independence and the threat of our race's loss of initiative.

The peril to our independence and the disappearance of initiative is one motive. The other motive that I invoke is no less important. We have pointed out the stupidity of the world in our time. History vegetates, repeating essays, renewing mummies,

unearthing cadavers.  We only see one political
science:  despotism, the sabre, the Machiavellian,
the conquest, the silence.  European science reveals
to us the secrets and the strength of creation in
order to better dominate:  but, strange phenomenon!
in any phase of history, personality has appeared
small in the midst of so much splendid intelligence.
It seems that science cooperates to sink in the
torrent of destiny the noble cause of the freedom of
man.  Matter obeys, time and space are conquered.
Enjoyment and well-being are understood, but spontane-
ity is forgotten.  Originality disappears and the
spirit of creating flees.  It seems that the old
world worked at digging a grave and raised a mausoleum
to personality in order to present the development of
the centuries as a new species of the animal kingdom.
Masses, government, appear nowadays in harmony and
the universal suffrage of the old Europe consecrates
an alliance created on the abdication of the
sovereignty of the people.  But America lives - Latin
America, Saxon and native, protests, and charges
itself to represent the cause of man, to renew
faith in the heart, to produce, at last, not repeti-
tions of the pseudo theatricalism of the Middle Ages
with the servile jester of the nobility, but enduring
actions of the citizens, and the creation of life
justice in the fields of the republic.

The son of America who circuits the view, at
any point of the horizon, will not only see America
in the attitude of spreading her wings to sail the
red sea of history.  We receive the breath that will
thrust us forward.  We understand the starting momentum
that the new world presents.  We are "independent by
reason or by strength" ("independientes por la razon y
la fuerza").  We depend on nobody to be great and
happy.  We must wait for no one to start the march
when conscience, nature, and duty say to the American
world; the hour of your great days has arrived.  When
the world abdicates, you do not despair of the politics
of justice.  In spite of your faults, you have never
denied the responsibility of a free people.  Purify
your soil of the legacy of conquest.  There are no
more slaves in the republics of the South.  Tear to
pieces the cape of Loyola.  Break down the barriers
that separate the people.

The word spreads in your valleys, visits the
banks of the great rivers and shines in the Andes to
contemplate the sky, full of the words of God.  Forward,

world of Columbus, America of the Maipu, of the Carabobo, and the Ayacucho!

But to uproot from the conscience of a continent its secrets, to the future her mysteries, to create our destiny, union is necessary; unity of ideas and association as a means. Allow me to insist. We must develop independence rather than preserve the natural and moral frontiers of our country. We must perpetuate our Latin American race rather than develop the republic, to make vain the petty personal things in order to elevate the great American nation, the confederation of the South. We must prepare the field with our institutions and books for our future generations. We must prepare this revelation of freedom that must produce more homogeneity in the nation, more new, more pure, extended to the Pampas, plateaus, and plains watered by the Amazon and the Plata, shaded by the Andes. None of this can be accomplished without union, without unity and without association.

All of this; borders, races, the republic and a new moral creation; everything is in danger if we sleep. The United States of South America has sighted the smoke of the campfires of the United States. We start to hear the footsteps of the young colossus, that without fearing anybody, every year, with its diplomacy, with its seeding of a crop of adventurers who scatter with its influence and its growing power, that magnetizes its neighbors with confusion in our cities, with new treaties, mediations, and protector-ates, with its industry, its navy, its enterprises, spying our faults and our weariness, taking advantage of the division among our republics, every year more impetuous, more audacious, this young colossus that "believes" in its empire as Rome believed in hers, infatuated already with a series of her successes, advances like a growing tide that falls like a cataract upon the South.

Already it echoes in the world, this name, the United States, our contemporary, but one that has left us so far behind. The children of Penn and Washington opened a new historical era when, assembled in Congress, they proclaimed the greatest and most beautiful of all existing constitutions, even before the French Revolution.

Then they caused rejoicing on the part of sorrow-ing humanity, which from its torment hailed the Atlantic

19

Republic as an augury of Europe's regeneration. Free
thinking, self-government, moral freedom, and open
land for the immigrant were the causes of its growth
and glory. It was the refuge of those who sought an
end to their misery, of all who fled the theocratic
and feudal slavery of Europe; it provided a field
for utopias, for experimentation; in short, it was
a temple for all who sought free lands for free souls.

That was the heroic moment of its annals. All
grew; wealth, population, power, and liberty. They
destroyed the forests, peopled the deserts, pirated
the seas. Scorning tradition and systems, and creating a spirit that devours space and time, they formed
a nation, a particular genius. And turning upon
themselves and contemplating themselves so great,
they fell into the temptation of the Titans. They
believed they were the arbiters of the earth, and
even the rivals of Olympus.

Personality infatuated with itself degenerates
into individualism; exaggeration of personality turns
into egotism, and from there to injustice and callous-
ness is but a step. They pretend to concentrate the
universe in themselves. The Yankee replaces the
American; Roman patriotism, philosophy, industry,
charity; wealth, morality; and self-interest, justice.
They have not abolished slavery in their states; they
have not preserved the heroic Indian races - nor have
they made themselves champions of the universal
cause, but only of American interests, of Saxon
individualism. They hurl themselves upon the South,
and the nation that should have been our star, our
model, our strength, daily becomes a greater threat
to the autonomy of South America.

Here is something providential that spurs us to
enter the stage of history, and this we cannot do if
we are not united.

What shall be our weapons, our tactics? We, who
seek unity, shall incorporate in our education the
vital elements contained in the civilization of the
North. Let us strive to form as complete a human
entity as possible, accepting all the good qualities
that constitute the beauty or strength of other
peoples. They are different, but not antagonistic
manifestations of man. To unite them, associate them,
to give them unity, is our duty.

Science and industry, art and politics, philosophy and nature, should march together, just as all the elements that compose sovereignty should live inseparably and indivisibly in a people: labor, association, obedience, and sovereignty.

For that reason let us not scorn, let us rather incorporate in ourselves all that shines in the genius and life of North America. We should not despise under the pretext of individualism all that forms the strength of the race.

When the Romans wished to form a navy, they took a Carthaginian ship for their model; they replaced their sword with a Spanish one; they made their own the science, the philosophy, and the art of the Greeks without surrendering their own genius; they opened a temple to the gods of the very peoples that they fought in order to assimilate the genius of all races and the power of all ideas. In the same way we should grasp the Yankee axe in order to clear the earth; we should curb our anarchy with liberty, the only Hercules capable of overcoming that hydra; we should destroy despotism with freedom, the only Brutus capable of extinguishing all tyrants. All of this is possessed by the North because it is free, because it governs itself, because above all sects and religions there is a single common and dominant principle; freedom of thought and the government of the people.

Among them there is no State religion because the religion of the State is the State; the sovereignty of the people. That spirit, those elements, we should add to our own characteristics. This is how the ideas, these divinities without conscience that wander about the woods and the mountain ranges of America will appear one day in the forum of the republic of the south.

Let's not fear movement. Let's breathe in the virile sura that emanates from the resplendent star-spangled banner; let us feel our blood seething with the germination of new enterprises; let us hear our silent regions resounding with the din of rising cities, of immigrants attracted by liberty; and in the squares and forests, the schools and congresses, let the cry be repeated with all the force of hope; forward, forward!

Quicker than a railroad or the electric telegraph,
the thoughts of the children of the South, in unison
in its ruins, thrum harmoniously in our cities so as
to give a center a capitol, a heart to this world
upon which heaven has given so many blessings.

It is to reach this end that I have convened you.
Let's not believe ourselves so barren in virtue that
we are discouraged by the limitations of our deeds.

We know the glories and even the superiority of
the North, but we too have something to place in the
scales of justice.

We can say to the North:

Everything has favored you.  You are the sons of
the first men of modern Europe, of those heroes of
the Reformation who crossed the great waters, bringing
the Old Testament, to raise an altar to the God of
conscience.  A knightly though savage race received
you with primitive hospitality.  A fertile nature and
an infinite expanse of virgin lands multiplied your
efforts.  Foolishly you were cast in the primitive
forest with the enthusiasm of a new faith, illuminated
through the press of the freedom of the word and
recompensed with abundance.

You received a matchless education in the theory
and practice of sovereignty, far from kings (being
yourselves all kings), far from the rachitic castes of
Europe, far from their habits of servility and their
domesticated manners; you grew with all the vigor of
a new creation.  You were free.  You wished to be,
and so you were independent.  Albion fell back before
the Plutarchian heroes that made of you the greatest
federation in history.  It was not so with us.

Instead, there came the men of Philip the Second,
under the authority of the Council of Trent, who
crossed the ocean to conquer races and nations with
the sword and leave the land barren as a desert.  The
thoughts and ideas of those explorers delineated our
cities.  The flames of orthodoxy eclipsed the splendor
of the mountain ranges, and those men, tempered in the
slaughterhouses of Granada and in the thickets of the
Low Countries, and converted on the gallows of
heretics, became the legislators and bureaucrats of
South America.  Our cradle was of iron, and the blood
of nations was our baptism.  A battle hymn of terror

22

was the lullabye that nurtured our first steps.

Isolated from the universe, with no other light
than that granted from the graveyard of the Escorial,
with no other voice than that of blind obedience,
spoken by the militia of the Pope (the friars) and
by the militia of the kings (the soldiers); such
was our education. We grew in silence and saw one
another with fear.

A gravestone was placed over the continent, and
upon it was laid the weight of eighteen centuries of
slavery and decadence. And in spite of this, there
was word; there was light in those gloomy depths; and
we shattered the sepulchral stone, and cast those
centuries into the grave that had been destined for us.
Such was the power of the impulse, the inspiration or
revelation of the Republic.

With such antecedents, this result merits being
placed in the balance with North America.

We, immediately, had to organize everything. We
have had to consecrate the sovereignty of the people
in the womb of theocratic education.

We have had to struggle against the sterile
sword that, infatuated with its triumphs, believed
that its tangent of steel gave it a claim of the
title of lawmaker. We have had to awaken the masses,
at the risk of being suffocated by the fatality of its
weight, in order to initiate them in a new life by
giving them the sovereignty of suffrage.

We who are poor have abolished slavery in all the
republics of the South, while you who are rich and
fortunate have not done so; we have incorporated,
and still do, the primitive races, which in Peru, form
almost the totality of the nation, because we regard
them as our flesh and blood, while you, with the
byzantine logic of the Jesuits, exterminate them.

In our regions there survives something of that
ancient and divine hospitality; in our hearts there
is room for the love of mankind. We have not lost the
tradition of the spiritual destiny of man. We believe
and love all that unites; we prefer the social to the
individual, beauty to wealth, justice to power, art
to commerce, poetry to industry, philosophy to textbooks,
pure spirit to calculation, duty to self-interest. We

side with those who see in art, in enthusiasm for beauty for its own sake, and in philosophy, the splendor of the highest good. We do not see in the earth, or in the pleasures of the earth, the definitive end of man. The Negro, the Indian, the disinherited, the unhappy, the weak, find among us the respect that is due to the name and dignity of man!

That is what the republicans of South America dare to place in the balance opposite the pride, the wealth, and the power of North America.

But our inferiority is latent. We must develop it. That of the North is present and is growing. This means that time strikes our borders to call the nationalities to action.

Just as Cato the Censor ended all his speeches with the destructive phrase, Delenda est Carthago, thus, at the end of all argument only one creative idea presents itself; the necessity of an American Union.

What nation shone more brilliantly in history than Greece? Possessing in the highest degree all the elements and qualities that man can display in the plentitude of his powers, united for the full development of personality, she succumbed through internal division, and that division quenched the light that her heroism had maintained. We are newly born, and in our cradle, snakes attack us. Like Hercules, we must strangle them. Those serpents are anarchy, division, national pettiness. The battle summons us to perform the twelve symbolic labors of the hero. In the forest of our prejudices, monsters lurk, spying upon the hour and the duration of our lethargy. Today, the columns of Hercules are in Panama. And Panama symbolizes the frontier, the citadel, and the destiny of both Americas.

United, Panama shall be the symbol of our strength, the watchman of our future. Disunited, it will be the Gordian knot cut by the Yankee axe, and will give the possession of empire, the dominion of the second focus of the ellipses described by Russia and the United States in the geography of the globe.

Furthermore, the interest that we have in being united to develop the Republic, and give a normal progress to the nations, besides the glory that waits

24

for us, the initiative in this historical moment exhausted the liberty in the Old World, the geographical, territorial interests, the property of our races, the theatre of our genius; all of this will push us into unity, because all of this is threatened in the future, not so remote from the invasions of the Jesuits of yesterday, by the impudence of the United States today.

Walker is the invasion. Walker is the conquest. Walker is the United States. Do we wait for the balance of strength to tilt in such a way to the other side that the vanguard of adventurers and pirates of the territories arrive to situate themselves in Panama to unite us against a common front?

# ✌ 2 ✌

# The Condor Counterattacks

After the middle of the nineteenth century, a
new phase of U.S.-Latin American relationships began
to emerge.  The obvious imperialism of the Mexican
War and of Walker's campaigns were over.  This new
phase was characterized by an increasing concern in
the United States with the Caribbean and Panama, and
with the feeling in the north that the U.S. should
act as the "big brother" of the Latin nations.  This
big-brother attitude was not without justification,
because the Latin republics were immature and generally
unstable during this period.  Dozens of internal
rebellions and many international conflicts swept
through Central and South America.  The United States
may not have had the highest motives for intervention,
but there was cause for concern because the stability
of the entire hemisphere was threatened.

The United States and Europe took an early
interest in the Isthmus of Panama.  In fact, as early
as the sixteenth century, plans for an interoceanic
canal route had been proposed.  These plans became
technologically possible, however, only in the nineteenth century when canal building had become quite
advanced.  It came as no surprise in 1850 when the
United States and Great Britain signed the Clayton-
Bulwer Treaty, in which the signatories agreed that
neither should obtain or maintain control of an isthmus
canal, and that such a canal would always be neutral.

Walker and Vanderbilt were involved in Nicaragua
because a railroad and canal route was proposed for
this area, but with the exception of some railroad

construction in southern Panama and Nicaragua, little
was accomplished. One reason that plans were put
aside was the outbreak of the Civil War in the U.S.[1]

The health of the Monroe Doctrine seemed good
in 1860. Despite some problems with Britain, France,
and Spain, the United States' protectionist policies
in the hemisphere had been little challenged. But
by early 1861, the nation of Monroe was no longer
able to back up its decrees. While the United States
was torn by internal strife, Europe took advantage
of the situation in Mexico. The internal strife
which Mexico endured throughout the 1850s ended with
the victory of the liberal forces of Juarez in 1860,
but the nation was financially and politically bank-
rupt. Spain and England, encouraged by France and its
ruler, Napoleon III, signed the Treaty of London in
1861, by which document they agreed to occupy
Mexico to ensure debts owed to European nations. The
three powers occuped Vera Cruz, and it quickly became
apparent that Napoleon was manipulating his allies.
His plan was to establish a Catholic Empire in Mexico,
under tight French control, and when his allies
realized this in early 1862, they withdrew their
support and troops.[2]

In 1863, French soldiers occupied Mexico City
with the support of the conservative, anti-Juarez
forces, and in 1864, an Austrian archduke, Maximillian,
was named emperor of Mexico.

In a strange historical twist, however, Maximillian
proved to be a champion of reform and liberal causes.
As such, he alienated first his Mexican allies and
then his imperial mentor, Napoleon III. His position
thus weakened, Maximillian was deposed and executed
with the aid of the United States and the Juarez
forces in the year 1867.[3]

Also during the period of the U.S. Civil War,
Spain attempted to expand in America by seizing the
Chincha Islands off the coast of Peru. Peru, with
the aid of Chile and Ecuador, repulsed the Spanish
fleet, which had also attempted to take the cities
of Valparaiso and Callao. A formal end to hostilities
did not occur until 1871, however, when the United
States intervened, imposed the Monroe Doctrine,
and supervised the terms of peace.

After 1865, the United States once again became
the "protector of the South", and despite much opinion
to the contrary, this protection was welcomed in many
areas.  In this same period, every Latin nation was
involved in conflict with its neighbors.  Alliances
were formed and renegotiated regularly and scores of
minor wars occurred.  The U.S. intervened on a regular
basis, dictating terms of peace, even choosing rulers
of nations.  The maintenance of peace and stability
in Latin America became a nearly impossible task,
but one which the U.S. found profitable, because as
more and more political intervention took place, the
U.S. was becoming more involved in the economy of
the south.  This involvement bred resentment among
the Latin peoples, and despite the possible good
intentions of the United States, intervention instilled
fear throughout the continent.

In Chile, the United States not only aided negotiations with surrounding nations regarding border
disputes, but also became involved in internal
politics during the civil war in the 1880s and early
1890s.  This involvement led to an attack on the crew
of the U.S.S.Baltimore by the citizens in Valparaiso,
an attack which caused a severe controversy and for
which Chile was forced to pay an indemnity.  The
United States was closely involved in the internal
problems of Paraguay from the 1840s, and in 1878,
President Rutherford B. Hayes arbitrated a border
dispute.  The U.S. was drawn into this area because
of extreme political and geographic instability.
Involvement occurred in Uruguay as well, and in each
nation, the "colossus" made clear its intent to
exert economic control.  Railroads, mines, and other
industries came under the control of the North
Americans, and while much good was done for the
developing nations, there was also widespread resentment.

In the War of the Pacific (1879-1884), involving
Chile, Peru, and Bolivia, the United States sought
repeatedly to end hostilities, but with little success.
The belligerents showed a growing resentment toward
North American attitudes and involvements.  A close
analysis of this war seems to lead to the conclusion
that a major reason for the duration of fighting was
that the participants rejected any settlement dictated
by the U.S.  In Ecuador, this intervention continued,
but was entirely unwanted, especially after the 1860s
when the nation underwent a return to strong

29

Catholicism, which also led to a rejection of republican ideas.

The United States was only welcomed as a protector
when European powers threatened Latin America, as in
the case of Venezuela.

In this area, a border dispute with Britain flared
up in the mid-1890s, and the U.S. was a welcome
participant to ensure Venezuelan sovereignty. Again,
in 1902, an international dispute arose as the British,
German, and Italian governments threatened to send
troops into Venezuela to protect their nationals from
possible harm during a period of instability. The
United States, once again, was able to convince these
nations that the Monroe Doctrine was still in force.
Despite the relative success of the U.S. in its
defense of Venezuela, the people of the nation, as
well as the government, began to take a dim view of
the United States' intervention. In fact, the
Venezuelan treatment of U.S. citizens became so poor
that the U.S. broke relations with Venezuela. This
turn of events clearly shows the growing dissatisfaction with U.S. policies, even in an area where its
actions appear to be justified. Throughout the
South, by the last decade of the nineteenth century,
the United States was feared and resented.

In Central America, U.S. intervention was common,
and its inspiration was almost exclusively economic.
This intervention reached its peak during the events
surrounding the building of the Panama Canal. The
incidents leading up to the opening of the canal
show an attitude which is typical of U.S. policy
during the second half of the nineteenth century:
everything which the United States wanted, it got;
whether by treaty, unilateral agreement, or outright
force.

The Clayton-Bulwer Treaty was signed in 1850
between the United States and Great Britain, but in
1878, Colombia granted the rights to build a canal to
France. Under Ferdinand de Lesseps (1805-1894), who
had directed the Suez Canal construction, a sea-level
canal was begun in 1879.

Weather, disease, administrative and topographical
problems spelled disaster for this effort, and the
company failed in 1887. Another French company took
over in 1894, but it also failed within the next five

years. At the same time, the U.S. Congress decided to actively pursue the construction of a canal. It was first necessary to get the approval of Britain, due to the terms of the Clayton-Bulwer Treaty. This approval was received in the second of two Hay-Pauncefort Treaties in 1901, and Colombia agreed to lease a Canal Zone to the United States in the Hay-Hessan Treaty of 1903, but the Colombian senate never ratified this agreement.[4]

Faced with this political barrier in Central America, the United States sought an alternative approach, and decided to plan and back a Panamanian revolution against the Colombian government. With the aid of U.S. warships and money, the revolution was quickly successful in 1903. Colombia was extremely distressed and it was not until many years later that U.S.-Colombian relations regarding Panama were settled. Once Panama had proclaimed its independence, approval for a U.S. Canal Zone was rapidly given in the Hay-Bunau-Varilla Treaty. This treaty gave the U.S., in perpetuity, the use and jurisprudence of a zone, five miles wide on either side of the canal. The U.S. agreed to pay ten million dollars and a yearly rent of a quarter million dollars to Panama. The U.S. also guaranteed the independence of Panama, which implicitly gave the U.S. the right to intervene in Panamanian politics. Thus, the United States got exactly what it wanted and began the construction of the canal, which was completed in 1914 and formally opened in 1920.[5]

The other area of great concern for the United States in the late nineteenth century was the Caribbean. It represented one of the last strong-holds of Old World influence in the Americas, and as such, was a problem area for the U.S. As early as 1854, the U.S. foreign ministers to England, France, and Spain met at Ostend and drew up the Ostend Manifesto, which declared that the United States should annex the island of Cuba, and if Spain would not agree to sell the island, the United States should take it by force. Cuba was a threat to the U.S. as a colonial territory, and since Cuba was a slaveholding territory, pro-slavery factions in the U.S. believed that the annexation would be a great aid to their cause. There was actually talk of Cuba being made a state of the United States. The Civil War put these notions aside, but even in the years immediately after the war, there was much public opinion in favor of a U.S.-controlled Cuba.[6]

From 1868 to 1878 and again from 1895 to 1898 there occurred popular uprisings in Cuba. The rebels demanded reform and independence and were supported by the United States. Spain attempted to assuage the rebels by granting a high degree of autonomy to Cuba and Puerto Rico in 1897, but Cuba was not placated. This was the situation in February, 1898. Cuba wanted independence and was supported in this by the U.S.; Spain was unwilling to grant full independence, and public opinion in the U.S. was strongly in favor of helping Cuba at any cost. It should be noted that it was not sensationalist journalism that precipitated war, but rather, public opinion.

On February 15, 1898, the U.S. battleship Maine was blown up in Havana harbor. The blame for this event is difficult to place, but it was most likely to have been the work of Cuban revolutionaries. They certainly realized that bringing the United States into their fight would spell doom for Spain. Other theories for the Maine disaster exist. Many observers claimed that Spain or Spanish soldiers had set the explosives. There was even the suggestion that U.S. industrialists had paid for the deed in order to realize wartime profits. There is also the chance that the explosion was accidental, due to a boiler failure. A survey of the most influential newspapers shows that they did not unanimously demand war, but the American people did! Public outcry reached the politicians as well as the press, and a little over two months later, war was declared.

The specific events of the Spanish-American War are generally of little importance, but several factors are worth discussing. Most U.S. troops were poorly trained and supplied; for example, some of the rations sent to Cuba were Civil War surplus, even the salted meat! Also, most of the troops were equipped with Arctic uniforms, despite the tropical heat of the summer of 1898. Cavalry divisions were shipped out to Cuba without their horses, and few people realize that the cavalry attack on San Juan Hill, led by Teddy Roosevelt, was carried out without benefit of horse, and without much resistance from the Spanish.

The war was important because Roosevelt emerged as a political force, and because Spain was effectively pushed out of the Americas after 406 years.

This era was also the beginning of a new orientation in U.S. policy toward the South, because after 1898 most involvements in Latin America occurred for economic reasons. This economic imperialism of the United States continued through World War II, and continues, in some ways, to this day.[7]

Spain lost the war, the United States won, and Cuba, Puerto Rico, the Philippines, and Guam became pawns in the U.S. strategy of world politics. Guam and Puerto Rico became U.S. possessions. The Philippines also became a possession, but was officially purchased from Spain with guarantees of eventual independence. Cuba became an independent nation under U.S. guardianship and was occupied by U.S. troops. General John R. Brooke became the first military governor of Cuba, and as such, he initiated many important administrative reforms. He was replaced within the year (1899) by Leonard Wood, who was to oversee the transition to a native Cuban government. Wood proved to be an excellent choice because he made strides toward stabilizing the administration and led the battle against yellow fever. Sanitation and public health measures were carried out, schools were established, and legal reforms were begun. Wood also arranged for elections to a constituent assembly, which provided for the election of a president and a Congress with two houses.

With the adoption of the new Cuban constitution, however, the U.S. demanded that an addition be added to the document. This was called the Platt Amendment. Its articles contained evidence of the U.S. attitude toward Cuba.

Cuba was not allowed to enter into any treaties which threatened its sovereignty. Excessive foreign debts could not be contracted, and the United States could intervene at any time to maintain Cuban independence or to preserve a stable government. The U.S. also received leased lands for use as coaling stations. The provision for intervention was effectively a "blank check" to let the U.S. into Cuba with troops just about any time, as Cuba was soon to find out.[8]

The first Cuban president, Estrada Palma, was elected in 1902 with little opposition, and he

followed the constructive policies which had been laid
down by Leonard Wood. He was also associated with
the pro-U.S. and conservative political elements on
the island. This was to prove problematic because by
1906, many factions opposed the U.S. domination and
the policies of Roosevelt. Estrada Palma was re-
elected in that year, but a liberal revolt surfaced
and the government appealed to the United States.
Roosevelt sent William H. Taft and Robert Bacon to
stabilize the situation, which they failed to do. In
fact, Estrada Palma was forced to resign, and the
Cuban Congress was unable to choose a successor. At
this point, Taft set up a provisional government and
called for the occupation of the island by U.S. troops.
Charles E. Magoon replaced Taft, and the occupation
continued until 1909. The island was finally
pacified and a new president, Gomez, was chosen, but
severe criticism of the Platt Amendment emerged
during the occupation. Roosevelt's policies brought
fear to the Cubans, and this fear spread throughout
Latin America as the Latin peoples saw the possibility
of U.S. intervention, at any time, and in any area.

During these same years, Puerto Rico became a
U.S. possession. The population seemed to welcome
the United States as many improvements were promulgated
in the areas of public health, education, the judicial
system, and agricultural production. In this period,
however, there were two trouble spots in U.S.-Puerto
Rican relations. First, the Puerto Ricans were not
United States citizens, and thus, had none of the
rights and privileges which citizenship provided.
Second, although the wealth of the island increased
through better means of production and an expanded
system of trade, more wealth became concentrated in
fewer hands. The small landholders decreased by over
one-third during the first years of U.S. control.
These two factors caused a long-term opposition to
U.S. treatment of the island. This opposition, led by
Luis Munoz Rivera, opposed the United States and
called for more fair treatment of the Puerto Rican
people.

In both Santo Domingo and Haiti, the U.S.
became involved in the early 1900s due to the
financial instability in these nations. In 1905,
Roosevelt responded to European intervention in Santo
Domingo by taking control of that nation's customs.
This action was unilateral and without congressional
support, but by 1907, Dominican finances were firmly

in the hands of the United States through a series of treaties. The Dominican economy was substantially improved through these actions, but its national sovereignty was also threatened because the United States could intervene at any time to protect its rights. A similar course was followed in Haiti a few years later when, in 1915, the U.S. occupied the nation to restore order and keep out European powers. They also aided in the choice of a president and set up both a political and financial protectorate which continued until 1936.

In this view of U.S. policy in Latin America, it has seldom been necessary to analyze the specific policy-makers or their motivations, but in the case of one such man, a closer view is in order. Theodore Roosevelt was a man of the "new imperialism", a follower of Kipling, a lover of adventure, and a believer in the theories of Social Darwinism.[9] He felt a responsibility to bring the civilization of North America to the world, a responsibility which he had a chance to realize in his dealings with Latin America. As a military leader in the Spanish-American War, he gained a prominence which made him a national figure and the vice president in 1901. When McKinley died of an assassin's bullet in September, Roosevelt became the youngest president in the United States' history. His colonial policies came to the fore in his administrations. The Supreme Court upheld Roosevelt's view that lands such as Puerto Rico could belong to the U.S. while at the same time not offering citizenship to its inhabitants. The viewpoint which is clearly expressed through these policies is that the United States has an obligation as a "white colonial power" to take care of the "backward natives" of the countries of Latin America, or Africa, or the Far East.

A straightforward policy was shown in 1904 in the Roosevelt Corollary to the Monroe Doctrine. This statement said that if chronic wrongdoing occurred in any nation of America, the United States must intervene as a sort of "international policeman" to protect the sovereignty of the nation and to protect against European intervention. Less than a year later, Roosevelt moved into Santo Domingo to "forestall European intervention".

With this corollary, U.S.-Latin American relations entered into a new period characterized by the United

States acting as a "white, wealthy policeman", and the nations of Latin America as the "poor, helpless Indians" who were uneducated and in need of constant protection against themselves and their neighbors.[10]

In the intellectual realm, the second half of the nineteenth century was a period of old traditions and new foundations. As discussed in the first chapter, the early Republican period in Latin America was typified by a carryover from the colonial era. The literature of most of the early years of the century was essentially "neo-classical" with a few exceptions, namely those essayists and journalists such as Bilbao and Alaman. There were several significant, purely literary figures such as Jose Maria Heredia (1803-1839) and the poet Andres Bello (1781-1865), both of whom brought a degree of recognition to Latin literature, but the real flowering of literature was to wait another fifty years.[11]

After 1830, some changes took place as a result of European contacts, and Romanticism replaced the neo-classical. But, especially in this hemisphere, Romanticism failed to meet the needs of the intellectual population. Thus a new form and a new synthesis were sought, and a new force emerged in the literary world in the last years of the century.

Several important authors set the stage for the new movement in literature which came to be called Modernism. The first was one of the foremost political writers of the century, the Argentine, Domingo Faustino Sarmiento (1811-1888). He was a familiar figure in Latin American history, the intellectual who was drawn from the university environment into the political arena. He travelled in the United States and in Europe and recognized the need for the modernization of the Latin countries. He saw much to praise in the U.S., and eventually tried to bring these things to Argentina as he became a politician and, later, president. He also became the first Latin American literary figure to gain fame in the United States and Europe, through his books and essays. Interestingly, his death occurred at almost the precise time when the new literary movement was being born.[12]

Another key figure after mid-century was the Cuban, Jose Marti (1853-1895), who is often called the "Apostle of Cuban independence". He spent time in jail as a youth and became a prolific writer of both poetry

and prose.  He travelled both in Europe and the United
States, afterwards returning to Cuba to fight for independence where he was killed at the age of forty-two.
Perhaps his most important role was as political journalist, and as such he expressed fears that the United
States might become imperialistic and a threat to the
South.  In Nuestra America (1891), he further explained
his feelings toward the U.S., saying, "The United
States is a nation that is beginning to regard liberty
as its sole privilege, and invoke it to deprive other
nations of theirs."13  He saw that the U.S. was becoming a powerful colonial and imperialistic power and
eloquently expressed this fear.

Marti was a great literary figure for many reasons,
not the least of which was his poetry, which gained him
a world-wide reputation.  His literary work was Romantic
in tone, but he was not guided by the conventions of
Romanticism.  His subject matter was not Romantic, but
realistic, politically inspired and purposeful.  As
such, he laid much of the groundwork of Modernism.  He
also saw clearly the threat from the North.  While not
blatantly anti-Yankee, he expressed fear at what the
United States could become, and it was this fear which,
in turn, spread through the Latin intellectual community.  The threat of the "colossus" was evoking an
emotional outcry, and Marti led the chorus.

Modernism can best be examined through the
analysis of a handful of authors.  Ruben Dario (1867-
1916) and Jose Santos Chocano (1875-1934) were the two
most important Modernist writers.  They were, however,
not part of a school or movement, but rather were
individuals who manifested the realities of Modernism.

Modernist works began to appear between 1880 and
1885 when a fresh desire to renovate literature began
to surface as a reaction against the old Latin American
literary styles.  All over the Western World, in this
period, new expressions, values, and styles emerged,
in society as a whole and also in the intellectual and
artistic realms.  One sees the pessimistic philosophy
of Schopenhauer, the existentialism of Kierkegaard,
and the neo-Christianism of Tolstoy.  In music, the
symbolic nationalism of Wagner took over, and in the
theatre, Ibsen and others participated in the fervor
of renewal - artistic, philosophical, and spiritual.14

In literature and the arts, all the "-isms" began
to dominate the scene with:  Symbolism, Cubism,

Impressionism, and Parnassianism. This last -ism
dominated the first period of Modernism. This single
most important influence during this early developmental stage was the Parnassian poetry of France. The
Parnassians rejected much of Romanticism and turned
their backs on the society from which they emerged.
They rejected social commentary and elevated the principle of "art for art's sake".

The principles of the Parnassians were established
by Flaubert and Baudelaire, but the Parnassians carried
these to an extreme level. Led by Leconte de Lisle,
Francois Coppee, and Theodore de Banuille, the
Parnassians sought perfection in the form of poetic
communication. They withdrew from commonplace themes,
and produced poems which could be understood only by
other poets. This poetry was cold and sterile, and can
best be explained through the poem, "El Cisne" (The
Swan) by Dario, in which the poet locks himself in an
"ivory tower" and rejects the whole world.[15] He can
communicate only with other poets who have assumed the
same lofty position. In seeking this escape many
Parnassians found the route through drugs and alcohol.
The Parnassian imagery depended upon the repeated use
of the symbols of the long-necked white swan, the
peacock, the fleur-de-lis, and the colors blue and
white. These images were drawn from the pre-revolutionary French period, from the elegance of Versailles,
but became nearly standard in all Parnassian poetry.
These same evidences are also seen in the first phase
of Modernism in Latin America. As such, this phase had
little influence on society as a whole and did little
to provide Latin America with a true literary style.

Symbolism was an integral part of Parnassianism
because poets found that direct uses of words could not
fulfill the promise of communication they envisioned.
Emotion could best be communicated through an image or
symbol, through a picture which told more than the words
it used of the story. A good example is "Nocturno III"
by Jose Asuncion Silva (1865-1896), in which two shadows
projected by the rays of the moonlight symbolize the
tender and romantic feelings between two lovers.[16]
Symbolism became more subjective as poets wrote only
for other "ivory tower" dwellers.

The elements of Parnassianism and Symbolism were
combined in the individual Modernist writers. The
first and most important was Ruben Dario, who began his
literary life in the ivory tower milieu, writing of

swans and past glories.  The second, more important
phase of Modernism began as Dario took on an intense
concern for his own people and his country.  He turned
the creativity of Parnassianism and Symbolism to
express these new-found concerns.  He descended from
the ivory tower and replaced the "swan" with the
"condor", the Roman gods with Cuahutemoc, the figures
of classical mythology with Latin American heroes.
With this symbolic descent from the ivory tower, Dario
initiated what was later on called "Mundonovismo", or
"New Worldism".[17]

This renewed concern with Latin America and her
peoples led Dario to produce a vicious attack on
Theodore Roosevelt in the form of a brief, but profound,
poem.  Dario felt that the chief enemy of the emerging
nations of the South was the United States, and he
warned of impending danger from the North, as he stated:
"You are the United States, future invader of our native
America, that has indigenous blood, that still prays to
Jesus Christ and still speaks Spanish."[18]  The swan's
neck had become a question mark about the future of the
Latin world, for Dario communicated to all Latin peoples
a deep-seated fear of Northern aggression.  As he said
of the U.S., "though you had everything, you are lacking one thing:  God!"[19]

At a time when the United States was deeply
involved in Panama and Cuba, Dario descended to the
real world and took up the cause of Latin America.
Where armies could only fail, words might succeed.

Dario was an educated man, a world traveller, and
a diplomat.  He first gained prominence with his book,
Azul, which, when published in 1888, marked the beginnings of Modernism.  But, even in his second great
work, Lay Hymns (1896), Dario was still in his poetic
tower.  The Modernist synthesis emerged full-blown in
his third work, Songs of Life and Hope (1905).  In
this work he showed his great concern for his people
and left behind the swan and the lily.  The U.S.
aggression at the turn of the century did much to
inspire fearful works in the Modernist mold.  Dario's
"To Roosevelt" was, perhaps, the most eloquent and
fearful cry from the South because it showed the feelings of a Latin citizen with his gaze turned northward.
The futility, fear, and confusion which can be seen in
the South were mirrored in Dario's life.  The destiny
of the Latin peoples, the lack of strength, the seeming
impossibility of facing up to this aggression, led to

severe anguish among Latin Americans, and Dario was no
exception. He was racked by depression, and found comfort only in alcoholism which hastened his death from
pneumonia and complications in 1916.

Modernism was a unique synthesis of Parnassianism,
Symbolism, and "New Worldism" which were blended with a
genuine concern for the social and political dilemmas
of the South. This union really began and ended with
Dario because he was responsible for the synthesis and
with his death, the most eloquent voice for this expression was silenced. While Chocano and others may be
called Modernists, they were mostly followers of Dario
in the area of socio-political commentary.

The actions of the United States and its Latin
policies inspired other writers to a high level of
creativity. After Dario, Jose Santos Chocano was the
most prominent Latin writer of the early twentieth
century.

While influenced by French writers such as
Victor Hugo, and by Dario, Chocano was most influenced
by his overwhelming concern for the political and
social future of Latin America. As a political
activist, he spent time in jail, and he was a staunch
supporter of Spain in the Spanish-American War. He
was anti-Yankee, pro-Latin, and a supporter of his
native country, Peru. His Alma America (1906) was a
world-wide success for its emotional verses singing
the praises of Peru, the condors, and the Andes. He
even praised the conquering Spanish conquistadors and
the elegant viceroys of the colonial period. He became recognized in Spain and France, as well as in
Latin America, as one of the great national poets of
his age. His Fiat Lux! (1908) also met with resounding acclaim as he continued to forward the hope for a
Latin culture, for a politically strong South, and for
resistance to U.S. aggression.

Although his work was imbued with symbolism,
Chocano's use of it was different from the Parnassian
obscurity. Not for Chocano was the weak and graceful
swan or the images of medieval France, but rather the
breastplate of Pizarro, the feathery helmets and powerful swords of the conquering Spanish legions. His
political activism led to much trouble as he was imprisoned for inciting revolt in Guatemala in 1920 and
was released only because of the intervention of the
King of Spain. He was crowned poet laureate of Peru

40

in 1922 and was killed over some business dealings by a partner in 1934. Chocano lived as he died, adventurously, full of conflict and vitality. The condor reached its soaring peak in the lines of Chocano.[20]

In the works of Dario and Chocano, words carry more meaning than a cursory examination reveals. Not only does symbolism expand the meaning, but if one seeks to understand the motivation for most of the Modernist movement, one finds the historical events of the late nineteenth and early twentieth centuries as the underlying framework and inspiration. These inspirations may be seen in the instances of U.S. imperialism in Panama, in Cuba, in Puerto Rico, and throughout South and Central America. It is no coincidence that Northern incursions in the late 19th and early 20th centrues led to the production of significant literary works in these same years. Perhaps Latin American literature owes a greater debt than ever realized to the United States, for it appears that the writers of Latin America emerged from behind the walls of their "ivory towers" in order to meet the challenges of U.S. aggression.

# RUBÉN DARÍO

## *Nicaragua*

## (1867-1916)


Ruben Dario was of Spanish-Indian-Negro extraction. He was born in Metapa (Nicaragua) in 1867, in a remote and insignificant place of the Latin American world. His birthplace was poor, and his family was poor, not only in wealth but in educational and spiritual enrichment. He was raised by an aunt in a gloomy house where he learned to be alone and experienced pain all through childhood.

His real name was Felix Ruben Garcia Sarmiento, but his poetic instincts guided him in assuming the more rhythmic name of Ruben Dario. This choice was explained later by the fact that one of his past relatives was called Don Dario. His style more than anything else represents the apex of Modernism. He studied with the Jesuits in the Instituto Nacional and from an early age he showed a great interest for the classic Spanish studies to a point that he earned the title of "poeta nino" (boy poet) at the age of 13 for writing some poems. At the age of 15, he was in El Salvador where the poet Francisco Gavida exposed him to French literature, particularly to Victor Hugo and the French Alejandrino.

He served as a journalist in several countries, and in 1892 he left for Spain where he became the friend of important authors and critics. Dario served as a consul from Colombia to Buenos Aires. He liked to travel, and he did travel a great deal. In New York, in 1893, he met Jose Marti; in Paris, the same year, he met Verlaine. A newspaper from Buenos Aires sent him as a correspondent to Europe; he was Nicaraguan consul in Paris and in Madrid he was plenipotentiary minister. Everywhere he went he was acclaimed for his literary work. On his way back home he suffered an attack of pneumonia in New York, to die a year later in his country in 1916. With him, Modernism died, after having been started with the publication of his book, Azul, in 1888.

Azul came out as the result of the material already published in the periodicals of Chile. This book showed a distaste for the common and trivial people whom Dario always considered dull and prosaic. A copy of Azul reached the desk of the great Spanish critic Juan Valera who was so impressed that he dedicated to Dario two of his "Cartas Americanas" (American letters), giving to Dario his full support. Dario's book was frivolous, but because of its innovative style was considered the start of Modernism. The stories are of Parisian type; although the author himself had never been in Paris, he earned the title of the most French of Spanish writers. His collection was considered important because he abandoned the conventional cliches for the use of adjectives used by the French Parnassian writers.

In 1896 a new work came to light. Its title was Lay Hymns (Prosas Profanas) which firmly established Modernism in Latin America. Here, Dario had a particular taste for luxury; his work is full of gold, oriental silk and rare marble. He chose the French lily as his symbolic flower; the swan was his symbolic bird. (The prologue was written by Jose Enrique Rodo, one of the best essay writers of that time.) The book had a strong Parnassian influence, particularly from Gautier and Verlaine. The only criticism that the book was to receive was the lace of Americanism illustrated by Darío's third publication, Songs of Life and Hope (1905). In his opinion, if there was any poetry in America it would be found in its past Indian legends of the Incas and in the great Montezuma for "the rest is yours, democratic Walt Whitman."

In 1905, the poet was ready to come down from his fantastic ivory tower and started to be concerned with great and small things that happened about him. He was now a man among men, he felt as few did at the end of the century, the flood of dehumanizing perils moving upon him and them. He also realized that this century would see the end of great historical aristocracies. He saw the end of one era and the beginning of another, the pragmatic Yankee and the English stockbrokers.

The Latin Americans were divided by the harsh
reality of geography and the political subdivision of
the continent; in other words, they were isolated not
only from the world, but also among themselves. It
was Dario's generation which recognized this fact, and
it was then that they changed to a denunciation of the
U.S. imperialism, in the moment when it was rampant.
Politics was not Dario's strong point; in fact, he was
bored, but like others he felt that he had to defend
and speak out for his people: a reaction to the
American "big-stick" and Pan-American diplomacy.
Songs of Life and Hope can be considered a natural
development of his earlier style, full of rhythmic in-
novations and brilliant words with the rhythms more
daring and more secure.

Ruben Dario was not an atheist. He found atheism
repugnant, and in his own way he was religious and, at
times, even superstitious. He feared death and the
unknown after death. He was born in a Christian world,
but practiced no faith. His disorderly life and his
anxieties resulted in a crisis of lethargy, attributed
to his lack of Christian eschataology, in which he
felt as though he were in a bottomless well. He saw
the ignorance of our end, and the reason for our birth
as a "dark terror", which compelled him to alcoholic
excesses. In later years, Dario would consider death
as a serene happiness that brings rest to the body and
to the soul. He does not give death any particular
name or face, but only a pronoun: "she". In this
regard, life was a nightmare to Dario. A collection
of grotesque and terrible moments in which silence is
broken only by the thumping of the heart and the
breathing of men, where a prayer becomes a blasphemy
in an anguished city of the night.

45

## THE SWAN

It was a divine hour for the human race.
Before, the Swan sang only at its death.
But when the wagnerian Swan began to sing,
there was a new dawning, and a new life.

The song of the Swan is heard above the storms
of the human sea; its aria never ceases;
it dominates the hammering of old Germanic Thor,
and the trumpets hailing the sword of Argentir.

Oh Swan! Oh sacred bird! If once white Helen,
immortal princesss of Beauth's realm, emerged
full of grace from Leda's sky-blue egg, so now,

beneath your white wings, the new Poetry,
here in a splendor of music and light, conceives
the pure, eternal Helen who is the incarnation
of the Ideal.

# TO ROOSEVELT

The voice that would reach you, Hunter, must speak
in Biblical tones, or in the poetry of Walt Whitman.
You are primitive and modern, simple and complicated;
you are one part George Washington and one part Nimrod.

You are the United States,

You are the future invader of the native America
that has indigenous blood, an America that still
prays to Jesus Christ and still speaks Spanish.
You are a proud and strong specimen of your race;
you are cultured and skillful; you oppose Tolstoy.
In breaking horses and murdering tigers,
You are an Alexander-Nebuchadnezzar.
(You are a Professor of Energy,
as the current lunatics say.)
You think that life is a fire,
that progress is an eruption,
that the future is wherever
your bullet strikes -

No.

The United States is grand and powerful.
Whenever it trembles, a profound shudder
runs down the huge spine of the Andes.
If it shouts, the sound is like the roar of a lion.
And Hugo said to Grant: "The stars are yours."
(The dawning sun of the Argentine barely shines;
the star of Chile is rising...) You are rich,
joining the cult of Hercules to the cult of Mammon;
while Liberty, lighting the path
to easy conquest, raises her torch in New York.
But our own America, which has had poets
since the ancient times of Netzahualcoyotl;
which preserved the footprints of great Bacchus,
and once learned the Panic alphabet
and consulted the stars; which also knew Atlantis
whose name comes ringing down to us in Plato,
and has lived, since the earliest moments of its life,
in light, in fire, in fragrance, and in love -

the America of the great Moctezuma, of the Inca
Atahualpa, the perfumed Moctezuma America of
Columbus, Catholic America, Spanish America,
the America where noble Cuauhtemoc said:
"I am not on a bed of roses" - our America,
trembling with hurricanes, that lives for love:
O men with Saxon eyes and barbarous souls,
our America lives. And dreams. And loves.
And vibrates. And it is the daughter of the Sun.
Be careful. Long live Spanish America.
A thousand cubs of the Spanish lion are roaming free.
Roosevelt, you must become, by God's own will,
the deadly Rifleman and the dreadful Hunter
before you can clutch us in your iron claws.
And though you have everything, you are lacking
one thing:
       God!

# José Santos Chocano

*Peru*

## (1875-1934)

Jose Santos Chocano was born in Lima, Peru on
May 14, 1875. His father, Jose Felix Chocano de Zela
was an officer of the army and his mother was Maria
Aurora Gastanodi de la Vega. As a child he did not
receive any humanistic culture nor did he study any
foreign languages. Since he knew only Spanish, he had
to read all his books in translation. He lived a very
adventurous type of life; he was of violent nature and
restless. As other poets in Latin America, Chocano
served in many diplomatic posts in America and Europe.
In Spain, because of the sympathy that he gave to the
mother country after the war with the United States,
he received the title of "poeta de la raza" (poet of
the race).

At the age of 19 he was imprisoned for taking
part in a local revolution. In 1920 he was captured
and imprisoned in Guatemala, soon to be executed while
there by the revolutionists who overthrew the government. He was saved by a plea coming from all over the
world; even the King of Spain begged his captors not
to kill the poet of America. When released, he went
back to his native Peru where he received a triumphal
welcome and it was there on November 5, 1922, that he
was crowned Poet Laureate of Peru. Chocano formed a
business for the search of hidden treasure. On
December 13, 1934, while travelling in a streetcar
with his partner, who felt he had been cheated, the
partner stabbed Chocano to death.

Chocano received the title of Poet of America
after the triumph of his Alma América (Soul of America)
(1906) which is a flow of verses acclaiming the past
glories of Peru. He focused his attention on the
Incas and their greatness, the magnificence of the

51

landscape of the Andes, the majestic condors that now
have taken the place of the weak and sophisticated
swan so much used and abused in the previous poems.
Chocano never evaded the world and secluded himself
in the ivory tower like other modernistic writers.  He
sings directly to Americans' nature, to the soil of
the Spanish race.  He praises all the beautiful symbols
of the American landscape and culture, including in his
work the symbols of the glorious past from the shining
conquerors with bright breastplates, flags, feathery
helmets, and powerful swords to the great Andean peaks,
alligators, boas, tropical forests and elegant viceroys.

Chocano started his early poetic work under the
influence of the French writer Victor Hugo, but he
knew how to perfect and polish his poems like Ruben
Dario and other modernists and still present his preoccupation and concern for the political and social
future of his so much beloved continent.  His fame was
so great that he was accepted as a friend in the
company of great thinkers of Spain such as Miguel de
Unamuno, Marcelino Menendez y Pelayo, Perez Galdos,
Benavente, Valle Inclan, Pio Baroja, and the Countess
Pardo Bazan, to mention but a few.  In 1908 he published Fiat Lux (Let There Be Light) in Madrid and
Paris.  Needless to say, this work reached the same
popularity of his previous Alma America.

# BLASON

I am the singer of the savage and autochthonous America
my lyre has a soul, my song an ideal.
My verse does not swing hanging from a limb
with the quiet sway of a tropical hammock...

When I feel myself an Inca, offering myself like a
vassal to the sun, who gives me the scepter of its
royal power;
when I feel myself Hispanic and I evoke the Colonial,
m- stanzas seem like crystal trumpets.

My fantasy comes from Moorish ancestry:
The Andes are made of silver, but the lion is of gold;
and the two races I fuse with one epic clamor.

My blood is Spanish and Inca is my pulse;
and if I were not a poet, maybe I would have been
a white adventurer or an indian emperor.

## THE EPIC OF THE PACIFIC
### (Yankee Style)

The United States, as a bronze pillar,
against a nail torture America's foot;
and America must, since it longs to be free,
imitate them first and equal them later.
Let's imitate, oh muse, the creaking stanzas
that move in the North with the grace of a train;
and let the rhymes whirl as swift wheels;
and let the verses fall as railroad beams.

Let us not trust the man with blue eyes,
when he wishes to steal the warmth of our homes
and with buffalo skins a tapestry gives
and nails it with discs of sonorous metal,
although fleeing is futile, if they wish not to
imitate him those that ignore, wasting themselves in
belligerent zeal that work is not the blame of an
already lost Eden, but the only means to obtain
its delights.

But let no one ache in fear of future conquests:
our jungles know no better race,
our Andes ignore the importance of being white,
our rivers disdain the worth of a Saxon;
and, thus, the day that a people of another race dare
to explore our nations, they will shout with horror,
because miasma and fever and reptile and swamp
will crush them to the ground under the fiery sun.

It won't be the race with blonde hair
that finally breaks the Isthmus...It must be broken
by twenty thousand Antillians with dark heads
that will boil in the breach as a gloomy throng.
Race of the Pyramids, race of wonders,
Beacon of Alexandria, Temple of Jerusalem;
Race that poured blood at the Roman Circus
and poured sweat at the Suez Canal!

When they cut the knot that Nature has formed,
when they half-open the gullet of the thirsty canal,
when the strike of the rod of a Moses in the rocks
solemnly cast one sea against another,
in the only instant of the titanic encounter,
let it rise in the air in the form of a toast

as the striking of two glasses of melodious crystal...

The canal will be the blow that will open the seas
and take away the keys of the great river from Brazil;
because our mountains will pay their tribute
to the vessels that happily arrive at the port,
when then from Paita, with energetic sketch,
the Amazonian margin solicits the railroad
and the Pacific unites with the epic River,
and the trains gallop, shaking their manes.

Oh, the crowd that, afterwards, from the vibrant ports
of Latin Europe will arrive in that region!
Barcelona, Le Havre, Geneve, in thousands of hands
they will see the handkerchiefs displaying a farewell
and the Latin that feels from the lively noon tide
that Sun in the blood resembling this Sun,
will inhabit our forests and will come from Europe
by the same road that the Saxon prepared (for him)!

Proclaim, oh muse! your songs, as waters that run
and pretend while running to be like the miraculous
Jordan, where America may redeem her sins,
refresh her fatigues, her miseries wash;
and, after the bath has freed her from guilt,
rinse the waters and wrap herself, perhaps, in pure
sheets that spread out in the wind,
as white flags of Work and Peace!

# JOSÉ JULIÁN MARTÍ
## *Cuba*
### (1853-1895)


Jose Julian Marti was born on January 28, 1853 in Havana, Cuba. He was educated in San Anacleto and San Pablo, and, with the help of the poet, Rafael Maria de Mendive, he continued his education in the Instituto Segunda Ensenanza de la Habana. In addition to being Marti's teacher and benefactor, Mendive became his main source of inspiration.

In 1869 Marti and Mendive participated in an uprising at the Teatro Villanueva, and after Marti served six months of hard labor, he was deported to Spain on January 15, 1871.

In Spain, continuing his education, he received his law degree and an M.A. from the University of Saragossa in 1874.

Between 1874 and 1877, Marti went from France to Mexico City, then to Cuba, and finally to Guatemala. In Guatemala he taught literature and achieved fame as an orator. In December of 1877 he married the daughter of a Cuban exile, Carmen Zayas Bazan.

Guatemala was then ruled by Justo Rufino Barrios, and Marti and his wife moved to Cuba in 1878, where he was once more expelled to Spain because of his political activities. He remained in Spain only two months, then went to France, and on to New York City.

Marti went to Venezuela in 1881 where he founded the Revista Venezolana. His articles, however, were disapproved by Venezuela's dictator, Antonio Guzman Blanco, and Marti was forced to return to New York after less than five months. He remained in New York (except for occasional trips to the Caribbean and Florida) until his death.

While living in New York, Marti continued to write for Latin American periodicals. His articles in <u>La Nacion</u> (Buenos Aires) made him famous in Latin America.

Due to a disagreement with some Cuban revolutionaries, Marti withdrew from politics for three years until 1877, when he returned to the fight for Cuba's independence.

In 1892, the Partido Revolucionario Cubano was formed with Marti as its leader. From New York, he made plans for the invasion of Cuba.

In 1895 the attack was begun. On May 19, Marti was killed in a skirmish on the plains of Dos Rios, Oriente province.

# THE MENACE OF UNITED STATES IMPERIALISM

From

## El Partido Liberal

...It was at night, as is usual in these cases, when in a conference room in one of New York's leading hotels the directors of the American Annexation League and the delegates from its numerous branches met in solemn conclave to make an inventory of their forces and show their power to the mysterious representatives sent to the League by the annexationist territories of Canada. They were also there to honor the president of the Company for the Occupation and Development of Northern Mexico, a Colonel Cutting. Presiding was Colonel Gibbons, a well-known lawyer. Many Canadians were present, in addition to the delegates of the League - whose immediate objective is "to take advantage of any civil strife in Mexico, Honduras, or Cuba in order to act quickly and assemble an army." But no one was there from Honduras, Cuba, or Mexico. "The occasion may soon come", said the president, "it is certain to come at any moment." "Honduras too?" asked a novice. "Oh yes; look at Byrne's map. Honduras has a lot of mines." "Don't let them underestimate us", said a speaker, "we know what we have behind us; Walker started with less thirty years ago! All we must do is be careful not to end the way he did."

The Annexation League was established nine years ago, and today, with branches in several states of the Republic, it numbers over ten thousand members ready to "march to the colors." "Good people", says one of the reports, "and hard to restrain, but the times are not yet ripe for an isolated and independent attack." Delegates from each of the American Annexation League's many branches read this report, and these documents, together with the delegates' verbal comments, give the League confidence in that heavy shouldered cur who is so impatient for war and plunder. There is always such a man springing up in strong and densely populated nations, just as poisonous mushrooms spring up in the choicest trees. The people feel duty bound to run to the first powerful voice. Far from lacking members, the League's branches have too many, it is said, and they are organized like a reserve army.

59

Special delegates have come for this important gathering from all of southern and eastern Canada - delegates of no little note, since two of them are deputies in the Dominion's parliament. And how can one take the League's endeavors entirely lightly, at least in regard to what it is doing in Canada, when at the same time as a special convention is being held to declare its relations to the neighboring country, and to confer with its representatives, the Democratic newspapers the Sun and the World are asking the party to add to its platform the League's plans for annexing Canada to the United States? And other newspapers are not even raising their eyebrows. In New Brunswick not a single citizen wants to be English, according to one of the deputies, and all of Manitoba is annexation-minded.

"Why not Mexico", another newspaper asked of the Sun, "since it is so close and just as necessary to us as the Dominion of Canada?"

"We must not covet Mexico", the Sun answered, "for its annexation would be violent, immaterial, and contemptible. Furthermore, we would find it cumbersome because Mexico's institutions, language, and race are not ours, and there would be no way of arriving at a beneficial assimilation. In Canada, on the other hand, the people come from the English, like ourselves; they speak English, like ourselves, and the country desires fusion with our Republic, as do we with it." That very statement was made by the Canadians at the meeting - the Canadians, who are known by number instead of name so their native government will not accuse them of treason.

But regardless of the importance of this matter, the conference considered it less so than the presence of Colonel Cutting. "He is coming", it was whispered, "to unite the forces of the Annexation League with those of the Company for the Occupation and Development of Northern Mexico." "Yes, that's why; he's working hard on the project. The two associations are going to hold one meeting." "Where?" "In Niagara Falls." "Oh, on the Canadian border?" "Then what is the first thing on the agenda, Canada or Mexico?"

And in the midst of these comments, all true and to the point, and after Cutting had tried to stir up hatred with the treacherous picture he painted of his imprisonment in Mexico - which hardly managed to give the invading company a good pretext - he began explaining to the meeting how the "company's forces" were organized. The meeting lent him a responsive ear. His statements should be repeated, and all the newspapers are printing them. He said that the company's soldiers belong to different states, but that more of them come from the South because it is nearer to them; that fifteen thousand of them are now mobilized; that the company's objective is to dispossess Mexico of its northern states, especially Sonora, California, Chihuahua, and Coahuila; that 'its people' are tried and true, strong and fearless, adventurous and already embarked on such undertakings. In short, he said what cannot be so, that Nuevo Leon and Tamaulipas - like a son who has just killed his mother because she insisted upon making him go of his own free will - are prepared to be taken over by the United States. And he made the idiotic statement that if the government were overthrown, many Mexicans would lend their support to the invasion in spite of their hatred for the North. He is about to call a general preparatory meeting in New Orleans.

A Niagara Falls hotel has already been selected for the general meeting. Cutting looks out for his personal comfort. Now he insists on publicizing and disseminating everything favorable to Mexico, so that when these bandits raise their heads in either place, people will be neither indifferent nor inclined in his favor, but will feel that his restraint comes from his conscience; all of which cannot succeed without quickly seizing every occasion to inspire respect in anyone who, with his efforts or his purse or his indifference, can be antagonistic. Are not Lincoln's historians this very minute recounting how turbulent spirits from the frontier have been stirring up the fire year after year, making scattered forays, and how they have finally brought about the war between South and North, of which they were the whip and the vanguard? Poisoned arrows are only arrows, but they can kill. And it is good to recognize them and take precautions against their use...

## ✌ 3 ❧

# Between the Two Roosevelts

In the early decades of the twentieth century, there was political instability throughout much of Latin America, especially in Mexico, Central America, Cuba, and Paraguay. In these areas there was widespread political turmoil, social upheaval, and even full-blown revolutions. The United States was deeply involved in many areas, notably in Panama, Mexico, Cuba, Haiti, and the Dominican Republic. Problems between the U.S. and Colombia and Venezuela continued into this century, although after 1915 relations with Colombia had improved.

On the surface, the United States appears to be less involved with the major nations of the South such as Argentina, Bolivia, Chile, and Ecuador, but this is probably due to the relative stability of these countries. The United States was becoming involved in many areas in less political and less obvious ways - economic imperialism was spreading in the South. This involvement in Latin America was, for a brief time, totally overshadowed by the events of the first World War, and with the presidency of Woodrow Wilson, the orientation of U.S.-Latin American relations changed. In the days of Teddy Roosevelt, the U.S. was acting as the white, wealthy protector of the South, as the right-wing imperialist center of Kipling's and Roosevelt's "protectorate of the colored". By 1912, the forces of liberalism were evident. This liberalism was, however, all too similar in practice to the theory of "The White Man's Burden".[1]

Since U.S.-Latin American relations were greatly

63

varied from area to area in the early 20th century, each country involved will be reviewed separately, beginning with pre-war Mexico.

For most of the period from 1870 to 1911 Mexico was in the hands of Porfirio Diaz. He made many improvements throughout the country, and this era is accurately seen as a time of enormous influence by the United States in the financial realm. Although invited into the country by the ruling powers, the U.S. was seen by the lower and middle classes as the main cause of social, economic, and political problems; it is true that, despite general stability and prosperity, the lower classes suffered during this time. Schools and the level of education declined among the poor, and the wealthy classes became more prosperous as the majority suffered deprivation. By 1911, the nation was ripe for revolt, and revolt came on May 15 of that year, when Francisco Madero, a liberal, took over the government. Although a seemingly capable politician, Madero appears to have totally misunderstood the social and political situation. He was overthrown and succeeded by Victoriano Huerta, a crude, but astute, soldier. The ill-fated regime of Huerta was plagued with great problems from the outset because much of the country was not under the president's control, but was held by revolutionaries such as Venustiano Carranza and Francisco (Pancho) Villa.[2]

There was a major crisis during Huerta's presidency - a crisis which shows quite clearly many of Mexico's problems, as well as the state of affairs between the United States and Mexico.

Interestingly, until 1912, most of the aggression which was aimed by the U.S. at Mexico was directed by a series of conservative, racist theories. There was "Manifest Destiny", "Social Darwinism", and the "White Man's Burden". Needless to say, the actions carried out in the name of these concepts were opposed by the Latin nations. They refused to accept American aid in the name of a "white man's philosophy", and they correctly saw greed and self-indulgence at the root of most of U.S. policies. But U.S. motives were somewhat altered after 1912 because liberalism and the causes which it espoused had replaced 19th century ideas. The rugged individualism of Roosevelt was replaced by the democratic liberalism of Wilson. In practical terms, the major change of policy lay in the diminished concern with things purely political, while the economic motivation for U.S. intervention changed little.

In April, 1914, Wilson was president and his Secretary of State was William Jennings Bryant. They supported the causes of liberalism and human rights. They sought to maintain peace in the world, and to free all nations from the forces of dictatorial absolutism. Unfortunately, they knew nothing of Latin America. Although a scholar and educator, Wilson was almost totally ignorant in the area of Latin American affairs. Bryant's contribution in international affairs was, effectively, non-existent. Furthermore, in April, 1914, Wilson's abilities were further diminished due to his concern and depression over his wife's serious and eventually terminal illness. The deficiencies of the administration in Latin American affairs and Wilson's personal depression played a part in explaining what has come to be known as the Veracruz Incident.[3]

In early April, a U.S. diplomatic messenger was taken into custody for a short time in the Mexican coastal town of Tampico. This was not unusual, considering that Huerta's troops in the town feared a rebel uprising, and everyone was suspect. The incident meant little, but was followed some days later by the equally brief detainment of several U.S. sailors. They were released and sent on their way and an apology was issued by those responsible. Admiral Henry Thomas Mayo, who was in command of the United States naval contingent at Tampico, was not satisfied. He demanded that Huerta give a written apology, that the officer responsible be severely punished, and that the Mexicans raise an American flag over Tampico and salute it with twenty-one guns. When Wilson was informed of the incidents (with what may have been exaggerated accounts) he supported Mayo. There may also have been a conflict in personalities because Huerta was a stereotypical "strongman" that Wilson found to be the antithesis of the liberal and just ruler. Huerta refused the demands.

Wilson, Bryant, and Mayo seemed to have believed that Huerta would consent to whatever they suggested; they had absolutely no conception that a Mexican held any self-respect or felt any national pride. The idea of raising and saluting a U.S. flag over Mexico seemed quite normal to the Americans, but was far from normal to the Mexicans. The only hope for a quick solution to the crisis lay with the United States'

charge d'affaires in Mexico, Nelson J. O'Shaughnessey.
He was an acquaintance of Huerta and as such was nearly
able to convince the Mexican president to accept the
terms, but a third incident added fuel to the fire.

An American sailor was detained in Veracruz due
to a case of mistaken identity, and although the authorities apologized, the event brought the situation
to a head. At this point, O'Shaughnessey arranged for
Huerta to apologize according to Mayo's terms, and
Huerta sent his letter to the Americans. He included,
however, a brief statement that he acted as the recognized ruler of Mexico. Wilson flatly rejected any attempts at apology at this point, and three small events
blown out of proportion by a group of uninformed
Americans led to an incident which could have become
a full-scale war.[4]

Tampico's harbor was protected by a sandbar. The
United States decided to shell the city, but the city
had no shore batteries, and by international law could
not be shelled. Therefore, the U.S. decided to attack
Veracruz since that city had batteries and did not
have a sandbar. Mayo was reinforced with fresh detachments led by Rear Admiral Frank Friday Fletcher. On
April 21 the city was taken, but not as the Americans
had expected.[5] Wilson believed that the Mexicans had
no heart to resist. He felt certain that there would
be no bloodshed and that the invaders would be greeted
as liberators by the populace for freeing them from
Huerta. Nothing went as expected. The troops in the
city did fight back, and when they finally fled, so
did all the public officials. The populace was in
turmoil and it took thousands of American troops to
bring order. Wilson had won a town full of hostile
citizens with no local authorities at all. The troops
were poorly equipped, and disease and deplorable conditions led to terrible morale. Veracruz was put
under martial law, and at great expense to the U.S.
(both in men and dollars) the city was cleaned, re-
built, and disinfected. Water, sewage, and garbage
problems were alleviated. The prison was improved,
malaria was successfully combatted, and criminal activity was curtailed.

Despite these beneficial results, the occupation
was totally unwanted by the residents. They feared,
even more, the time when the Americans would leave,
for they believed that the Mexican government would
punish them for cooperating with the "Yankees". The

occupation never went beyond Veracruz, and it ended in July.

Huerta resigned and was replaced by Carranza, who was Wilson's favorite candidate for the job.  Carranza's army "liberated" the city as the United States withdrew, and within six months Veracruz was just like before, except that the citizens had had a taste of foreign domination.  The ill feeling of the Mexicans about this incident had a ripple effect, as fear of the U.S. swept across Latin America.  Wilson's policies did not improve, and his support of Carranza proved to be disastrous.  Mexico embarked on a policy with the United States based on mistrust; an attitude that is still a part of U.S.-Mexican relations today. Significantly, the Mexican people, in general, feared their neighbor to the north.  Having experienced invasion and occupation, they would not easily accept the hand of friendship from the U.S.[6]

World War I kept the United States busy until 1919, and Mexico was supportive of the Germans for much of the time.  In 1917 a new constitution was chartered, a constitution which was liberal in tone, but which showed the growing strain on U.S.-Mexican relations.  Foreign ownership of land, money, and oil fields was attacked and severely curtailed.  Carranza was overthrown and killed in 1920 and was replaced by Alvaro Obregón.  He was supported by the United States and remained in power for four years, largely due to this support.

Under both Carranza and Obregon, the Minister of Public Education was Jose Vasconcelos, the renowned scholar and writer (see page #83).  Mexican reaction to the Veracruz incident and to U.S. economic infiltration was clearly shown in the writings of Vasconcelos.  In 1922 and 1923 he invited the Chilean poetess, Gabriela Mistral, to cooperate with his cabinet in the education reform that was in process at that time.  This experience greatly improved her reputation at national and international levels.  Prior to her contact with Vasconcelos, Mistral was noted primarily for her poetry in Chile, and would eventually become world famous as a poet.  During her two years with Vasconcelos in Mexico, her writing changed dramatically.  Exposed to his antiYankee diatribes, she produced work for the first time in her career that reflected political and social concern for Latin Americans in opposition to North American attitudes

and intervention.  She wrote <u>Desolacion</u> in 1922 while
in Mexico, and began her major work, **Paginas** en Prosa.

From 1924, until 1938, a series of presidents
ruled Mexico and maintained an anti-U.S. policy.  By
this time, U.S. holdings in Mexico had been nationalized and Mexico refused to compensate the United States.
Since 1933, when Franklin Roosevelt instituted the
"Good Neighbor Policy" throughout Latin America, Mexico
resisted this overture and made it difficult to be a
good neighbor.  Under President Lazaro Cardenas, many
demands were made on foreign nations which had economic
interests in Mexico.  Higher wages were demanded for
Mexican workers employed by U.S. companies; imports
from the Unites States into Mexico were curtailed by
high tariffs, and Mexican courts prosecuted foreign
companies for exploiting Mexican workers.  These situations culminated with the total takeover of U.S.
and British oil properties.  The United States demanded compensation, but no settlement to the problem was
rapidly forthcoming.

As a new world war brewed in Europe, Roosevelt
did not abandon the Good Neighbor Policy, but tried to
unify the South against totalitarianism.  This effort
was rewarded by several successful Pan-American conferences in the late 1930s, as even Mexico realized
the threat of a totalitarian takeover.  Minor differences were put aside, but they did not disappear.[7]

Between 1900 and 1940, the United States was
closely involved in Central American internal affairs.
In general, these policies can be summed up as
"Dollar Diplomacy" as U.S. companies and bankers dominated the economic and financial scene.  As a result,
many U.S. citizens resided in Central America.  With
financial interests, as well as American lives, at
stake the United States found numerous opportunities
to intervene in Central American affairs.  This situation was made even more precarious by the highly unstable political situations throughout this area.[8]

In Panama, the United States continued its close
involvement because of the canal.  The sovereignty of
Panama, which had been in question due to the unusual
circumstances of the nation's establishment, was
solidly maintained, and a very strong spirit of nationalism grew among the Panamanian people.  This
nationalism, although evident since the 1840s, grew
dynamically after the United States aided in the

establishment of the nation of Panama. This same
nationalism led to serious attacks on the U.S., its
treaties with Panama, and its policies with regard to
Latin America. Prior to 1920, most Panamanian difficulties were caused by Colombia because that nation
demanded payment and compensation for the loss of
Panama. A series of never-finalized treaties emerged
in the period from 1909 until 1920, and a final treaty
was ratified by both sides in 1921. This was the
Thomson-Urrutia Treaty, which marked the end of U.S.-
Colombian conflicts over Panama.[9]

The U.S.-Panamanian situation was not so rapidly
settled. Panamanian nationalism and the unstable political situation caused the Canal Treaty with the
United States to be questioned almost from its initial
passage. The situation came to a head in 1926, partly
due to a series of political uprisings, and partly due
to dissatisfaction with the original treaty. The major points of concern were that the U.S. should not
have full sovereignty over the Canal Zone, nor should
the U.S. be allowed to unilaterally intervene in
Panama, nor should the U.S. create commercial establishments to the detriment of Panama. Another treaty
in 1926 was also deemed unsatisfactory because the
United States refused to give up sovereignty in the
Zone, and demanded the right to do anything to defend
Panama or the Canal. The nation of Panama was so
angered by the U.S. position that an appeal was made
to the League of Nations. The League, however, with
all too typical indecisiveness, failed to make a
ruling. Only when the new president, Harmodio Arias,
visited the United States in 1933 was any compromise
worked out. Roosevelt and Arias negotiated the terms
of the treaties ratified in 1936 and 1939. These
treaties upheld the Panamanian position in most areas:
the U.S. agreed to pay the rent on the Canal Zone, not
in dollars, but in balboas, the currency of Panama;
the Panamanians were allowed full sovereign commercial
rights in the zone; and the U.S. agreed not to intervene unilaterally in Panama. Despite the solution of
these U.S.-Panamanian disputes, Panama's internal
crises continued as each government fought to survive
against serious opposition, an opposition often based
on anti-U.S. feelings.[10]

The remainder of Central America was also, for
the most part, tied to the United States in the years
between the two world wars. The nations between
Panama and Mexico attempted to unify into a federation

of states, but with little success. Constant internal strife and border disputes brought unstable conditions. In Costa Rica, the United States landed marines in 1919 "to protect American interests", and these interests were constantly expanding because U.S. dollars and companies were Costa Rica's main imports. Again, in 1932, the U.S. intervened to restore political stability. These examples of intervention may have been justified, but they were received with apprehension by nations of the South. The United States had some interests in every Latin nation, and thus could find cause to intervene almost at will, even in a period of "good neighbor" policy.[11]

In Nicaragua, the U.S. obtained rights to a canal and lands for naval bases as early as 1914. Between 1917 and 1924 a financial commission led by the U.S. took over Nicaraguan finances and brought stability. Political problems led to the intervention of American troops in 1926, an intervention which continued openly for eleven years, and which was carried on thereafter by the American-supported Somoza regime. Nicaragua became one of the most U.S.-dominated nations of the South, due mostly to its strategic location. Nicaragua's economic wealth has never been great, and the U.S. gained little economically, except for some profits from coffee exports.[12]

El Salvador, Honduras, and Guatemala are quite dissimilar nations which show a broad variation in the degree of U.S. involvement in their affairs. Only in Honduras did the United States intervene frequently, and only in Honduras did U.S. companies become dominant. This is especially true of the banana and fruit companies which came to control the national economy during this period.[13]

In Guatemala there was little U.S. intervention, very little economic progress, and a large, mostly Indian, population which struggled for mere survival. There were many uprisings, but the United States generally maintained a healthy disinterest. Guatemala is, for the purpose of this book, important as the homeland of the author Miguel-Angel Asturias.

In El Salvador the political situation was quite stable, the leanings were liberal, and the United States had accepted most political developments with a grudging realization that intervention in El Salvador was worthwhile in neither the political nor the economic spheres.[14]

In the Caribbean, the major area of concern was Cuba, although the U.S. was also involved in Haiti, the Dominican Republic, Puerto Rico and the Virgin Islands. During the World War I era Cuba was swept by prosperity due to its booming sugar industry and the export trade with the United States. But, by 1920, a reversal had occurred; the economy was depressed, and politically, the nation was in turmoil. The U.S. sent General Enoch Crowder to supervise elections, but the anti-U.S. candidate, Alfredo Zayas, was elected. The U.S. agreed, in principle, to a hands-off policy regarding Cuba, and there was no intervention during the remainder of the 1920s, but in 1930 a series of revolts hit the island. In 1933 the situation worsened when the army revolted and chose Manuel de Cespedes as president. The United States then sent in warships, and when the conflict ended a new power had emerged in the person of Fulgencio Batista. He was the real power in Cuba even before he became president for life in 1940. During the 1930s Cuba gained much in its relationship with the U.S. The Platt Amendment was abrogated in 1934, and a reciprocal trade agreement in the same year was good for Cuba, even though it favored the United States. After Batista took power, relations with the U.S. were both open and friendly.[15]

Haiti was a virtual U.S. protectorate during the period between 1915 and 1934. U.S. marines occupied the nation to protect American interests and to stabilize the political situation. There occurred, however, much national opposition to these actions. An all-out revolt by Charlemagne Perlate almost succeeded in driving out the Americans, but was finally defeated in 1919. In the 1920s, anti-American sentiment became increasingly evident until, in 1929, a special investigative committee led by W. Cameron Forbes was sent to Haiti. This had a stabilizing effect and also brought about administrative reform and the election of a new, pro-American president, Stenio Vincent. The Haitians, however, continued to demand an immediate end to United States occupation, an end which came about only with the Roosevelt administration in 1934. A continuing U.S. interest was shown in a mutual trade agreement with Haiti in 1935, but the people of Haiti seemed to hold little love for the nation which had occupied their land for almost twenty years.[16]

The Dominican Republic was dominated by the U.S. throughout this period. From 1905 to 1940 the U.S. controlled Dominican customs, and played a major role in the republic's political and economic life. Instability and the threat of European intervention led to the occupation of the Dominican Republic by the marines in 1905, and until 1922 the nation was run as a military protectorate by the United States Naval Department. Full-scale occupation ended with the year 1922, but American troops were still present, and the U.S. was still in control of finances throughout the 1920s. The presidency of Rafael Trujillo, from 1930 to 1938, set the stage for the total withdrawal of U.S. troops. Trujillo undertook many reforms to strengthen the country and was also a "strongman" who effectively dealt with any opposition.

By 1940 the United States was able to totally withdraw and return Dominican finances to the Dominicans. Although some benefit can be attributed to the U.S. involvement in the area, popular sentiment rigorously opposed what was perceived as American imperialist manipulation of the Dominican Republic.[17]

The status of Puerto Rico up to 1940 can be explained in a word: undefined. The U.S. owned the island, but could not decide what status it should have, or what title the Puerto Ricans should carry. In 1917 the Jones Act made the island a "territory" and the people "citizens', but with varying rights and privileges. Puerto Ricans were drafted into the service in World War I and in 1924 a U.S. delegation visited the island to prepare for the admission of Puerto Rico as a state.

The Puerto Rican legislature petitioned President Coolidge for "autonomy" without statehood. As Franklin Roosevelt took office, Puerto Rico was a seriously depressed area, and the new administration gave much aid to the island in the form of relief for the poor. From this period, there have been two opposing forces in Puerto Rico; one has demanded statehood, the other independence. As a result, neither movement has realized its goal, and an elective governor has run the island since World War II.[18]

The United States had an excellent chance to practice its administrative policies in the Virgin Islands. In 1916, an American-Danish treaty transferred the islands to the U.S. They were run as a military protectorate, and theoretically, American policies could be put into effect with little local opposition. The outcome, however, was not positive because the poor of the islands had a very difficult time since the U.S. aided the large farmers and the sugar mills. The world-wide depression which struck in 1929 was extremely severe in the islands. By 1930, over ninety percent of the population was surviving totally on U.S. relief. A civil government was set up in the islands with universal suffrage and the tourist trade began to expand prior to 1940. Despite these factors, little opposition and a free hand to make policy, the United States was unable to improve living conditions for the poor and uneducated populace. Even Franklin Roosevelt could do little to improve the lot of the islanders. In 1940 they were surviving mostly on welfare and were only slightly better educated than they had been a generation before.

In the literary and intellectual realms, most of the true anti-American attacks came from the far South. This is incongruous for it is evident that the United States was most vigorously involved in the nations north of the Equator. Why then should most of the literary manifestations of anti-Yankeeism emerge from those nations far removed from the Caribbean?

During the period from 1900 to 1940, several general trends emerged throughout South America. First, trade and economic growth were greatly accelerated, at least until 1929. The U.S. made enormous capital investments in the South as American corporations and engineers led the expansion of Latin American industrial growth. Also, both the lower and middle classes became stronger and gained political importance. Many of the conceptions of socialism, communism, and trade unions reached the continent around the turn of the century. As a result, social legislation was enacted in most nations, and demands were constantly made by the rural and urban lower classes for things such as higher wages, better working conditions, and the redistribution of land. In general, the nations of South America continued to be afraid of the U.S., and of American intentions. In seeming opposition to this, more than a dozen Pan-American conferences were held during this period with the United States playing a major role. Especially under Franklin Roosevelt, the U.S. displayed a renewed friendship and a policy of lessened intervention. The key to understanding the Latin American attitude towards the U.S. lies in the perception of the United States as a dominating and subjugating giant. This may not be based on reality in all cases, but the perception is present in virtually every Latin American nation.[19]

As a prosperous nation which has always been largely independent politically and has been populated mostly by European people, Chile has never been occupied or invaded by the United States. Chileans have had, however, cause to fear the "Colossus" because the industries of Chile have been dominated by U.S. financial interests. The United States, at times, has been in almost complete control, especially in the profitable copper industry. It has also been heavily involved in the mining of nitrates and in the production of iodine. Workers in these industries have made demands for improved conditions since the beginning of the century. They saw accurately that their bosses were mostly Americans, and that the companies subjugated the workers in pursuit of high profits.

These feelings were reinforced by the popular writings of Chileans, particularly the works of Baldomero Lillo, whose books Sub Terra and Sub Sole presented an accurate view of the conditions of the workers in the mines. Nationwide strikes led to bloodshed and economic trouble as early as 1907, and as a result, the government passed legislation to improve the lot of the workers. By 1920, the work week had been cut to six days and there was compensation for injured workers. Despite these improvements, the workers continued to view their companies, the government, and the United States as their enemies.

In the political arena, U.S.-Chilean relations were generally good during this period and many of the leaders of the nation admired and respected the stability and prosperity of the U.S. In fact, the Constitution of 1925 drew heavily upon the American model. After this, Chile's political system was influenced by the nation's close ties with Europe as socialist and communist ideas became widespread. It was from these ideologies that many attacks were leveled against the U.S.[20]

Chile did not have a completely stable government during this era, but the nation managed to avoid major turmoil at a time when many of its neighbors did not. In 1929, the close connection between the U.S. and the Chilean economies took its toll as the

worldwide depression hit Chile very hard. The government tried to reorganize the industries, but this was
a hopeless task without foreign capital. The left-
wing leaders came to the fore in this era and formed
a radical coalition which brought some relief to the
workers and farmers, but in 1940, an earthquake hit
the nation and toppled the improving economy. Chile
turned to the United States and received over twelve
million dollars in loans.

To the outside observer, it appears that between
1900 and 1940 the U.S. went from being the exploiter
of Chile to its savior. This may be true, but the
Chilean people continued to fear the U.S. because of
its involvement in the economy, and the forces of
socialism furthered the impact of the estrangement.[21]

The course of history in Uruguay was unlike that
of any other Latin nation because from early in the
century until 1940 there was in that nation peace and
prosperity. A series of able leaders and a profitable
meat packing and wool industry continued through this
era. U.S. involvement was, perhaps, less than in any
other nation of the South, although there were some
U.S. financial interests. It is interesting that this
relatively peaceful and prosperous era produced the
foremost anti-Yankee writer, Jose Enrique Rodo. Rodo
was not a politician, historian, or economist, but,
rather, a philosopher. As such, he was less inspired
by events than by the feelings of the Latin American
peoples. Rodo spoke for all of Latin America and
eloquently expressed the feelings of all who feared
the United States. He was from Uruguay, but his
works were international in scope.[22]

As the twentieth century began, U.S.-Venezuelan
relations were strained. This state of affairs was
due, in part, to the fear which many Venezuelans had
of U.S. aggressiveness. Venezuela has always been,
in many ways, a Caribbean nation, and as such, the
events in the island did not pass unnoticed. Under
the rule of Juan Vincente Gomez, however, things
changed, especially in the formal relations between
Venezuela and the U.S. Gomez ruled from 1908 until
his death in 1935. Although not loved by the
populace, he maintained order and a reasonable level
of prosperity. He cared little for human rights or
for the plight of the lower classes, but in major
policy, particularly the encouragement of foreign

investors, he was successful.

The United States and other nations invested
heavily; especially in the oil industry; and the
majority of the population resented this foreign
intervention. The nation grew to hate Gomez and his
policies, and the lower classes associated the evils
of the regime with the U.S. oil companies, American
banks and financiers. They greatly feared the course
of events which they felt was leading them to an ever
more miserable existence. These fears were expressed
strongly in the works of Romulo Gallegos, the
Venezuelan author who also became a political leader.
His pro-worker, anti-U.S. position made him a popular
figure, but in general, had little impact on U.S.-
Venezuelan relations which continued to be good both
during and after the presidency of Gomez. By 1940,
however, large segments of the population were demanding the nationalization of foreign companies and the
expulsion of their workers from the country.[23]

Argentina is somewhat unusual in South America.
It has always been closely linked with Europe, both
intellectually and economically. The nation produces
much wheat and meat, but has never served as the
continent's break basket, but rather as the chief
exporter to Britain, Italy, and the U.S. The country
has never had many problems with the U.S. and has
generally been stable. In fact, Argentinians seem
to have recognized the advantages of being friends
with Europe and the United States. It has had a
high standard of living since 1900 and has enjoyed
relative peace with its neighbors. As in Uruguay,
despite its diplomatic equilibrium with the U.S.,
anti-Yankee literature of Argentina was notably
violent. Two of the most prominent anti-U.S.
writers emerged from this atmosphere: Ruben Darío
and Manuel Ugarte. The major Argentinian-U.S. conflict emerged in the 1930s when Argentina could not
decide which of its allies to support on the eve of
World War II, and for a time was sympathetic towards
the Nazi powers.[24]

While the majority of Argentina's population is
white, Paraguay's people are almost all non-white.
The histories of these two nations during this period
show a wide divergence in many areas. Paraguay had
many problems in the early years of the century with
border disputes and terrible poverty. The long Chaco
War with Bolivia cost many lives and much territory

in the 1930s. The United States aided in the settlement of the conflict and Paraguay emerged as the
definite loser. The major American involvement came
in 1940 when the U.S. gave loans to Paraguay in order
to insure the nation's sovereignty because Argentina
threatened to take over the shaky government. Once
again, as in Guatemala, the U.S. stayed away because
there was so little to gain economically in the
area.[25]

Peru's history in the twentieth century combines
the features of many other nations. As in Paraguay,
border wars hurt the nation and the United States
helped with loans. As in Venezuela, a corrupt strongman, President Augusto Bernardino Leguia, ruled and
was closely associated with U.S. interests. And, as
in Chile, the U.S. was most involved in mining corporations. In brief, Peru was relatively stable
despite many problems, and anti-Yankee feelings diminished significantly after the regime of Leguia
ended in 1930. U.S. financial aid helped the country
in the next decade and U.S. intervention also helped
maintain Peru's borders in a serious dispute with
Ecuador.[26]

Ecuador was, likewise, aided by the U.S. and
this nation represents one of the most pro-American
Latin countries. Although poor, Ecuador was helped
by U.S. aid in the areas of public health and finance.

For a time, the distinguished economist,
Edwin W. Kemmerer, of Princeton, reorganized the
economy in Ecuador. As in Peru, by 1940, the "good
neighbor policy" and healthy U.S. relations led to a
high level of cooperation between the two countries.[27]

Bolivia's tin and oil welath attracted the
United States in the early years of the century and
by the 1920s there was much U.S. investment in the
nation. As the U.S. became more involved in Bolivia,
the ills of the society were attributed by the populace to these American influences and anti-U.S.
sentiment became widespread. This movement grew in
the 1930s until finally in 1937 most U.S. interests
in Bolivia were taken over by the Bolivian government. The leader of this anti-U.S. movement was
German Busch, who became president in 1937. He was
an extremist ruler, aided by European fascists, who
instituted economic reform similar to that of
Adolf Hitler. Busch may not have been a true Nazi,

77

but he was violently anti-American. He was mysteri-
ously shot in 1939 and was replaced by Enrique
Penaranda de Castillo who was sympathetic toward the
United States. It would be easy to attribute the
death of Busch to the U.S., but a view of the evidence suggests that a cabinet member's personal grudge
was the motive for the murder. In any case, Bolivia
became a close ally of the U.S. after 1940, although
it never regained the position it held prior to
1937.[28]

    In the first forty years of the twentieth century
the United States was most deeply involved in Mexico,
Central America and the Caribbean. This involvement
continued from the administration of Teddy Roosevelt
to Franklin Roosevelt. The policies of the two men
were totally dissimilar, yet there was definite
involvement throughout the period. In Mexico, it
was under the guidance of a liberal Democrat that the
United States invaded. Even under the "good neighbor
policy", U.S. marines could be found on the islands
of the Caribbean. There is much evidence in word and
deed that the peoples of these areas strongly opposed
U.S. actions. Curiously, in all of the nations occupied and invaded openly by the U.S., and even in
all of the surrounding nations, only in Venezuela was
there any real anti-Yankee literary protest - in the
writings of Romulo Gallegos. The deep-seated anti-
U.S. feelings must have been felt strongly by those
people whose nations were occupied by Americans, but
the most stirring works emerged from Chile, Uruguay
and Argentina.

    In most of South America, the United States
maintained a rather benevolent "big brother" attitude. The economics of "Dollar Diplomacy" involved
the U.S. in most nations of the South through investments and loans, but the U.S. was hated no more than
the local strongman. Anti-Yankee feelings appear to
be based more on the perception of the situation
rather than on the reality. In almost all nations
of the South, the economic infiltration of the national economy by the United States was a positive,
rather than a negative, influence. Nevertheless, the
Latin peoples perceived the U.S. as the aggressor.
Writers and intellectuals sought to encourage the end
of U.S. influence because in their view this influence
was delaying the birth of a Latin American consciousness. Because the most vocal cries came from the
more stable, educated, and intellectual segments of

the population, they were often philosophically inspired.[29]

As the twentieth century began, Latin American culture was dominated by the Modernist movement in literature. The major figure in Modernism, Rubén Darío, broke with Spanish tradition in literature and with mid-nineteenth century Romanticism. Both his style and language were new and Darío led the parade as other Latin writers abandoned the "Ivory Tower" of Parnassianism.

This abandonment led writers from this period to a new concept in realism to deal with the questions of the future of Latin America. Dario carried the bloom of Modernism with him to the grave in 1916. While there were other modernist writers, for the most part after 1900, few Latin writers can accuately be placed in any category, and must be viewed as distinctive individuals.

A variety of styles and forms typified the literature of the early twentieth century. Some of the more famous authors were Amado Nervo (1870-1919), a modernist poet; Mariano Azuela (1873-1952), one of the greatest Latin American novelists; and José Vasconcelos (1882-1959) an influential educator and intellectual leader. From Colombia the writer, José Eustacio Rivera (1889-1920); from Venezuela, Gonzalo Picon Febres (1860-1919), a renowned novelist; and the aforementioned Romulo Gallegos (1884-1966). These authors shared a common feeling of the growing excellence of Latin American culture, and some of them carried this orientation to a position which led them to oppose the United States for hindering the full birth of Southern culture and civilization. They all gained world-wide recognition, as did a number of writers from farther South.[30]

Among the foremost literary figures south of the Equator were Jose Enrique Rodo (1871-1917) and Juan Zorrilla de San Martin (1857-1931) of Uruguay. Both were poets, and Rodo gained fame both as a writer and as a philosopher of anti-Yankeeism. Rodo's style was more Classical than Modernist, and in many ways he represented an earlier age.

From Chile, a superb poet, Gabriela Mistral (1899-1957) reached international status as a literary figure. Mistral was known for her poetic works

and has never been labelled "anti-Yankee", but in one
brief, eloquent prose passage written in 1922, she
brilliantly summed up the feelings of the Latin intellectual community.[31] In the same year, Mistral
wrote Desolación, her most famous book of poems. As
noted, she was in Mexico, working with Vasconcelos in
1922. In 1945 she received the Nobel Prize for Literature, the first ever awarded to a Latin American
author. She was, throughout her career, concerned
with the influence of the United States on Latin
America and with the cultural unity of the nations
of the South. Her lectures, more than her writings,
reflect her position as a socio-political leader.

Writer and social commentator, Baldomero Lillo
was very influential in Chilean social and political
thought. His masterful short stories, poignantly
and realistically reveal the sufferings of the exploited.

Cesar Vallejo (1892-1938) of Peru wrote the
novel El Tungsteno (1931) containing many anti-U.S.
elements, but he was best known as a poet. As such
his strong voice echoed a plea for the people of
Latin America to rise up against Yankee imperialism.
His orientation in El Tungsteno, like Lillo in
Sub Terra, was economic and generally concerned with
the plight of the lowest working classes such as
those involved in mining. The following is an excerpt
from El Tungsteno:

> Ah, gentlemen! The U.S. is the strongest
> country in the world! What a fantastic
> progress! What a wealth! What great men
> are the Yankees. Can't you imagine that
> all South America is in the hands of the
> North American financiers! The best mining
> companies, the railroads, the exploitation
> of rubber and sugar, everything is being
> made with the dollars of New York! Ha!
> This is formidable! You will see that the
> war in Europe will not finish until the U.S.
> participates! Remember what I say to you!
> Of course, it's clear! This Wilson is
> ballsy! What a talent! What speeches he
> gives. The other day, I read one. Christ,
> there are no doubts about it!

Vallejo was a radical thinker and was to have widespread influence in Latin America. This work, in

particular, with its anti-imperialistic stance, mercilessly dissects the exploitation of Indians by a U.S.-owned mining company.

From the peaceful giant of the South came the Argentinians Leopoldo Lugones (1869-1938), a poet and prose writer; Jose Ingenieros (1877-1925), one of the most important intellectual leaders of the South; and Manuel Ugarte (1878-1951), a writer who was violently anti-American and who was quite influential among the youth of Latin America. Convinced, as early as 1901, that Latin America was in extreme danger from the United States, he wrote, propagandized, and lectured in Europe, Mexico, and South America for the next two decades and became an heroic figure to those who resisted Yankee imperialism.

In other areas, also, the first half of the twentieth century was a time of tremendous cultural growth. Artists such as Diego Rivera, David Sigueiros and Miguel Cavarrubias, and composers such as Carlos Chavez, Daniel Alomia Robles, and Hector Villa-Lobos gained world-wide recognition. But it was in the literary world that Latin culture excelled and gained international acclaim.

Foremost among the early twentieth-century writers was Jose Enrique Rodo of Uruguay. He spearheaded the widening assault by Latin authors who attacked the United States for its imperialist policies in Cuba and Panama. His Ariel (1900) became one of the most popular works in the history of anti-Yankee literature. Rodo admired much in the U.S., but he felt that the United States lacked the spiritual values and concern for the future necessary for a truly dynamic society. His works point out his unqualified admiration for the vigor and pace of North American life, but his classical and intellectual philosophy made him acutely aware of the inherent dangers of these qualities, especially the peril of mediocrity.[32]

Another very influential author of this period was Baldomero Lillo of Chile. Lillo's works show a keen concern for social problems, and his writing was both naturalistic and realistic. His books, such as Sub Terra, written in 1904, contain a great deal of information regarding conditions in Chile's mining industries. These conditions, along with a hatred of American and governmental subjugation of

the working classes, led to revolts in 1907.  Lillo
was an astute observer of conditions in Chile and
foresaw some of the social problems and conflicts
which were to become more evident later in the
century.[33]

The one major figure in this century who was
both politician and writer was Romulo Gallegos of
Venezuela.  His Dona Barbara (1929) was one of the
most popular works ever produced in Latin America.
This novel is considered one of the best and most
original ever produced in Spanish.  Gallegos spent
much time in the U.S. and Europe, at times as a
political exile, for he espoused liberal causes in
his native Venezuela, and was even president for a
time.  Dona Barbara is one of the few works that is
at once entertaining, important from a literary stand-
point, and also, astute in its overview of society.[34]

The last of the authors which we shall view in
this chapter is representative of the conditions in
the Latin American community in the first four decades of this century.  He was Manuel Ugarte of
Argentina.  Ugarte was educated at the Colegio
Nacional in Buenos Aires and travelled to Paris in
1898 where he became the darling of the Parisian
literary community.  In travels to Mexico and the U.S.,
he became violently opposed to U.S. imperialism, and
this position was further solidified by time spent in
Spain after the Spanish-American War.  Ugarte became
a radical propagandist, but maintained his literary
and intellectual prominence through his excellent
prose style and also through poetry.  Two of Ugarte's
works stand out as examples of anti-U.S. theory.  They
are The Future of Latin America (1910) and The Destiny
of the Continent (1923).  These works became the hand-
books for the radical youth of the South.  As writer,
lecturer, and radical theorist, Ugarte was the most
eloquent, consistent voice of Latin America, and he
gained world-wide fame during his lifetime.[35]

# José Vasconcelos

## *Mexico*

## (1882-1959)

Jose Vasconcelos was born in Oaxaca the 28th of February 1882. His first experience with education was not very pleasant; his father's position as a customs agent caused him to be continuously transferred from one place to another. In 1897, while in Mexico City, he finally finished his college preparatory studies and there he enrolled in the University to study Jurisprudence. In 1905 Vasconcelos finished his doctoral studies with a dissertation entitled "Dynamic Theory of the Laws".

On October 28, 1909, Vasconcelos formed an association of young intellectuals called Ateneo de la Juventud (Athenaeum of the Youth). It was a center for innovating the political, artistic, and philosophical life of the country. Some of the most important members were philosopher Antonio Caso, writers Alfonso Reyes, Pedro Enrique Urena, Julio Torri, Carlos Pena, and Martin Guzman, and the artist Diego Rivera.

Jose Vasconcelos was soon to emerge as one of the more prolific writers of his time. His biographical works gave a unique account of the problems he encountered when he was fighting for the revolution. His poems went beyond a simple description of Mexico and its internal political problems. He criticized the role of the United States in the prevailing revolutionary unrest. It was another voice condemning Yankee imperialism.

Under the Carranza Administration, Vasconcelos was named Minister of Public Education. He took this assignment as a mission to save children and youth

from ignorance and to redeem the Indian. He lost
his job under Huerta and got it back under Obregon
in 1921, during which time he sought to replace
Catholicism with Revolutionary Nationalism. This
was a threat to the Catholic Church, especially
since the Third Article of the Queretaro Constitution
planned the eventual end of all Catholic primary
schools. His efforts in education were recognized
not only by many Central and South American adminis-
trators, but also by the students themselves; they
gave him the honorary title of "Teacher of the
American Youth".

The complete works of Vasconcelos cover more than
thirty volumes, ranging from drama, short stories,
and poems, to several essays in the field of politics,
sociology, and philosophy. However, his best known
works in Latin America are primarily his sociological
essays such as "The Cosmic Race" (1925), and
"Indology" (1926). One particular book in which the
author shows serious concern over the North American
policy of aggression was Bolivarismo y Monroismo
(1934); this book revealed to the world Mexico's
fear of its belligerent northern neighbor.

# Hispano-Americanism and Pan-Americanism

We shall call Bolivarism the Hispanic-American ideal of creating a federation with all the nations of Spanish culture. We shall call Monroeism the Anglo-Saxon ideal of incorporating the twenty Hispanic nations to the Northern empire by means of the politics of Pan-Americanism.

Bolivar took the initiative to create an inter-Hispanic American organism and for that purpose he called together the Congress of Panama. Nevertheless, his ideas were not very clear since the presence of North American delegates in the congress was accepted and there was even talk of a vague union "between all the nations of the world of republican regime", to serve as a counterpoise of the Holy Alliance, refuge of all monarchies. The idea of race did not have weight in an epoch in which the insertion of English had replaced the influence of the mother tongue, Spanish. A common language did not spark enthusiasm, perhaps because the threat was unseen; English was not yet a world language of conquest. And, finally, the problem of religion had not yet surfaced because all the constitutions of the new nations had guaranteed their privileges to Catholicism. No one foresaw the ambush of the Protestant missionaries, sowers of discord between Christians since they invaded our countries, when there are in Asia and Africa so many nations that would benefit from any of the aspects of Christianity.

No man of the era could see clearly the problems that an emancipation created, which, in reality, was not our doing exclusively, but the result of a European crisis; a consequence of the defeat of Spain, in the peninsula, not only in America, and an act associated with the patriot armies and the English ships and the largest states of the Empire itself, the eve of which would be our bitter enemy.

On the Hispanic side, the confusion could not have been greater. On the other hand, on the English and North American side, the plan was clear and perfect. First of all, Canning had excluded Spain from the New World, with which, we, not having a merchant marine, all trade went, _ipso facto_, to the English commercial fleet. Later on, Adams, grabbing the booty from Canning, formulated the theme. "America for Americans", but with the understanding that these

would be divided in one group of younger brothers
under the exclusive care of an older brother who
would play the part of regent.

I don't know what opinion Bolivar had concerning
Canning's Doctrine. From what I know, I have not
found condemnation nor even an inkling of the risk of
leaving it without an expressed rejection. Nobody had
the vision to sense the partial destiny of all these
nations as he did. What seems proven to me, but little
known, is that the first attempt to deal a blow to the
Monroe Doctrine is due to Lucas Alaman, the Mexican...
What is that? Ninety percent of my readers will exclaim, and they are right. I, a Mexican of the
learned class, came to really know who Alaman was
only in the maturity of my independent reflection.
Previously, Alaman was, for me, as for the majority
of my fellow countrymen, a reactionary, almost a
traitor, and an enemy of the nation. Not in vain
has the Juarista School, a Pan-American school,
poisoned the conscience of the multitude throughout
this long period, with obscurity and treason manifested or implied.

But let us not get ahead of ourselves; let us
not judge; let's record the facts openly, in brutal,
shameful nakedness.

II

Lucas Alaman was the name of the Minister of
Relations of the first cabinet of a man who gave himself the extravagant name of "Guadalupe Victoria" -
Guadalupe in honor of the Patroness of Mexico, the
virgin by the same name, and Victoria for the victory
of independence. In Mexico, the independence movement had been defeated, the rebels executed; it was
accomplished by a strange coup d'etat, one that, if
it had not created a nation, we would all call pure
treason and an ugly one at that. Actually, what
happened was that one fine day the last Viceroy,
O'Donoju, obeying instructions from (God knows what)
lodge, called in Iturbide. He commanded royalist
forces and had distinguished himself for his hatred
for the insurgents. Between the two of them they
proclaimed the independence of Mexico, created a flag,
and to give the conspiracy national appearance, they
incorporated the old guerrilla fighter, Don Vicente
Guerrero. O'Donoju left right away and Iturbide
proclaimed himself Emperor. Not long afterward, the

insurrection that had created him, overthrew him and a series of political bosses and military leadership began. Nevertheless, around the year 1833, in the midst of one of these confused bosses, there appeared a man with a clear conscience. His name was Alaman. The first thing he did, to place Mexico in front of the exterior was to begin again the broken effort in Panama. To that end he called together the "Congress of Tacubaya". This Congress is not mentioned in the elementary history in the schools of Hispanic America. Even though it was honored by the presence of representatives of each nation of Ibero-America and came to conclusions, no longer simply romantic as the postulant candidacy of Panama, but highly novel and transcedental. This, no doubt, was lost, since already Monroeism took pleasure with our oratory, but took apart, without pity, our actions.

The most important thing for the future of Ibero-America was defined in the Congress of Tacubaya, but it was there also that it was condemned. The most important thing ever made by a statesman of the continent was the formation of an Ibero-American Customs House League, which Alaman made the Congress of Tacubaya approve. It was signed unanimously by the delegates, in spite of the opposition of the North American delegate and the United States Department of State. At the head of this was the famed Adams, a worthy opponent for a man of the stature of Alaman. Adams was represented by the famous Poinsett. Previously, Poinsett had travelled over the continent, informing himself of our miseries and local problems; he knew that the political bosses favored disintegration in order to better dominate land control. In spite of it all, Alaman succeeded in using for the good, the influence which Mexico exerted then as a nation, the quality of which was the most powerful and cultured of the Hispanic family. It was necessary to destroy Alaman. Adams' delegate prepared the coup by opposing the resolutions of the Congress. It wasn't fair, he argued, to leave the United States out of that economic consortium created by the League for the Advancement of Spanish-America. The United States "was also a Republic". This Bolivarian argument had no more weight in the spirit of Alaman. Monroeism, insisted Adams, excluded the Europeans from the profits of America, but it had helped the nations of America, therefore the United States should join the League. But Alaman had no obligation to Monroeism. He was not from the same generation which

formed an alliance with England to defeat Spain.
Alaman believed in race, language, and the religious
community.  In short, Alaman gave Bolivarism the content which it lacked.  And without hesitation, he was
dismissing Monroeism.

With Alaman, Hispanic-Americanism was born in a
clear and defined position confronting the Pan-
Americanist hybridism.

Alaman convinced the delegates of Spanish-America,
which, without exception, voted for his plan.  Alaman
triumphed in the Congress in the light of enlightened
discussion.  But, Adams, defeated, was not satisfied.
Under Adams' command was Poinsett, who began to
organize in Mexico the Lodge of the Anglo-Saxon Rite,
a society contrary perhaps, to the society which had
made the independence?

The truth is that Poinsett's lodge (the Yorkinos)
overthrew the government that Alaman served.  The
first "liberal" revolution was triumphant and Alaman
was excluded, not only from the government, but also
from the opinion of the nation, from the heart of its
citizens.  He was persecuted by the new government;
he was slandered by the Monroe propaganda.

And Pan-Americanism scored its first Mexican victory.

Hispanic-Americanism fell with Alaman, never to
rise again all century long, notwithstanding an occasional attempt, more or less falsified.  That is
why, my readers, until a few years ago, not even I,
who now speak of him, knew who Alaman was.

It is known that each victorious ideal fabricates
its own sainthood at the same time that it creates a
martyrdom from the defeated ideal.  Hispanic-Americanism has been creating "Baptists" and martyrs in
the generations of the present.  And we begin to
give ear to Manuel Ugarte and Rodo and Sandino, but
only a few remember the names of the victims of the
first era of Hispanic-Americanism.  Nobody in the
South knows who Alaman was, the same way no one in
Mexico knows who Monteagudo was.  And, if in Mexico,
Alaman, because of his extraordinary personality, has
been an object of a systematic campaign of approba-
tion, Monteagudo is forgotten in his own country.  His
doctrine lacks the contacts with the wheat export, the

promotion of the English investments or the expansion of the refrigerated Yankees.

On the other hand, daily, in publications, speeches, and books, it is proclaimed to us the fame of the bilingual heroes, or at least ambidextrous in patriotism. We need not mention their names; for there is no high mercenary speaker, no journalism of great following that does not repeat their names throughout the whole continent.

We shall detain ourselves, nevertheless, with one personage who, perhaps, without knowing it, was the embodiment of Pan-Americanism even before it determined precisely its objectives in congresses and institutions. He is, for many, the highest figure of Mexican history and also "The Worthy One" of not few "Latin Americas" of the continent. His bust occupies a place of honor in the Pan-American temple in Washington and his statues were multiple in his native land, by law, which ordered one to be placed in each public square. I speak of Benito Juarez. No Mexican has ever achieved more extended notoriety. No Mexican did more harm to Mexico nor created greater confusion in America. In his hands reappears the Aztec hatchets consummating the useless sacrifice of Maximilian - nevertheless, a chorus of praises persist in proclaiming him great.

We find Juarez in the center of an anguished epic in which the soul of Mexico is shipwrecked, in spite of the tinsel of victory in which it has been clothed. The official history tells us that France, the imperialist, and Austria, with its noble lineage, with the Pope behind the scenes in collusion with Mexican traitors sought to snatch away from the people of Mexico their liberty and goods. Then, Benito Juarez, an Indian, humble, but with iron-like persistence, heads his nation and directs it towards an apothesis of justice and righteousness. Such is still the Pan-American version. And in this sole creed four or five generations of Mexicans have been brought up. And without the disaster of the present Mexican situation, perhaps the light in the conscience of a few Mexicans would have never been made. Let us raise that light high, which was so painfully ignited.

Let us dedicate a few words to the myth of Juarez.

89

It doesn't matter that perhaps not many are
ready to hear the truth to its completion being
blinded by anger, without being overcome by prej-
udice.

As liberals, we have been bred and as liberals
we write, but without a compromise of sect or opinion,
with no more compromise than the truth, and the interest of our people, in danger from one border to
the other of Hispanic America.

Let us go deeper into the double leit motif of
life of the New World. Since the time we emancipated
ourselves from Spain, the conflict masked with words
of treason or deceit or candor, prolonged itself,
brutal in its effects. Hispanic-Americanism and
Pan-Americanism; Bolivarism and Monroeism. Around
the rude conflict, the nations of the New World tear
and exhaust themselves.

Even before Juarez and not long after the fall
of Mexico embodied by Alaman, we would have had to
suffer one of those auxiliaries which the forces of
evil furnishes for the muddled causes predestined to
triumph. I'm referring to the scoundrel named Santa
Ana who with his outrageous tyranny, his blood-
thirsty megalomania and his bad habit of illegal
cockfighter (literally or poss., cocky, bully), exas-
perated the people of a nation not yet consolidated.
To such a degree that, entire provinces such as Texas,
blessed the new conqueror which liberated them from
an administration of outlaws. Remember the case of
Zabala, the first Pan-American associated with Houston
for the Independence of Texas, in bilingual unholy al-
liance/cohabitation with the Monroeism of the conquest of Texas. Its result, the eradication of the
Mexican-Spanish culture in Texas and the proletarisa-
tion of the inhabitants who were not Saxons. Without
Pan-Americanizing itself, New Mexico was absorved but
its more united and patriotic population made a pact
with the invader and imposed conditions: respect for
their language; respect for their Catholic religion;
no Methodist missionaries imposed by force on the
New Mexicans. Nothing of Pan-Americanism; fundamental Hispanicism, even in defeat. The result is
that the Mexicans of New Mexico not only kept their
property but also elect representatives and officials
of their own race and obtain that the laws and decrees
be published, for them in Spanish, and for the other
residents, English.

Let's leave these islets of the continental tide
and turn our eyes back to the case of Mexico which is
the mold and anticipation of the task of Monroeism of
the continent.   In Mexico, Santa Ana had crushed nationality.   He represents among us what Rosas does in
Argentina, what France does in Paraguay.   A pseudo-
nationalism of pure arrogance without spiritaual content to liven it.   For us, Santa Ana cost us half of
the territory and what is worse, the Reform.   For
Argentina, Rosas cost them not only a long delay in
their progress, but also the foreign, Pan-Americanist,
Monroeist current which, without noticing the risks
involved men of high capacity such as Sarmiento de-
veloped.   The black legend justifying the de-
Hispanicisation finds in effect in Sarmiento a stand-
ard-bearer which it doesn't deserve.   The black legend
prepares for the meddling of Monroeism which, in the
case of Argentina still is the Canning Doctrine.   In
other words, the meddling of England in the life of
Argentina, by way of the capitalist investments and
anti-Hispanicism, since it could not do it with
weapons, defeated by the patriots headed by Liniers.

Without the moral penetration of the English,
Liniers today would figure at the same level as
San Martin.   A patriotism of Liniers style instead
of the incomplete and unconscious patriotism of the
caudillos would have avoided the breakaway of Uruguay
from Argentina.   And La Plata River would have been a
Latin river.   The way it is, it is not known whether
it is English or not.   At least, without Uruguay there
would not be the dangerous wedge between Brazil and
Argentina; Pan-Americanism would have had no place in
the South.   A dangerous race that for example, during
the great war compromised the autonomous position of
Argentina, opening the Uruguayan ports to Pan-
Americanism.

With a patriotism inclined a bit more to Liniers'
style the question of the limits of Tierra del Fuego
would not have been submitted to England and that
error, a typical expression of ill faith which traces
an absurd boundary according to geography, but studies
in a way that multiplies the neighborly conflicts.   In
a way that the strait would not remain altogether under the power of either Argentinian nor Chilean sovereignty, but free for the ships of the British fleet.
And, perhaps, converted into an expansion of dominance
of the Malvinas Islands.   And, the proof is that along
with the error, there came to Tierra del Fuego the

missionary invasion; the same as in Texas before the war of conquest and the same as in Mexico of today resembling a Methodist pickled fish for the slow consumption of the Colossus.

Therefore, let no one fall in the trap of saying that the South is free of snares. In many respects South has been and is more susceptible than the Mexicans. And, at least, there the struggle has been unceasing. Our better made personality compels us to a higher conscience. Anyway, this concerns a continental situation; proven by the penetration of protestant missionaries and North American capitalists in the interior of Argentina and Bolivia, in Chile and Peru and Ecuador and Colombia. Let us conclude that in spite of everything, it is perhaps Colombia that has better defended herself and let us resume the thread of our exposition by returning to the case of Mexico which shows us the process in the wholeness of its elements.

For the details of Pan-Americanism history, we refer the reader to the masterly work of the Mexican, Carlos Pereyra, who without being thanked, has done more for the recovery of all that which is Spanish in America than all the institutes with official assistance. And to awaken the Hispanic-American conscience, more than quite a few statesmen. We especially recommend his "Brief History of Hispanic-America". Monroeism is revealed to us in it as a serpent which constricts the lethargic body of Hispanic-America. We, without a single pretension of historic erudition, limit ourselves to extract from the events known and elemental conclusions which seem to us alarming and that for the same reason, perhaps stimulate a feat of salvation.

# GABRIELA MISTRAL

*Chile*

## (1889-1953)

Gabriela Mistral, born Lucila Godoy Alcayaga, on the 7th of April, 1889, in Vicuna, Chile, would become her nation's most famous poet and writer. The daughter of Jeronimo Godoy Villanueva and Petronila Alcayaga, she was a teacher at the age of fifteen at "La Compania" School. She held this post until 1909. During that year the man she loved, Romelio Ureta, committed suicide. This tragedy in her life would inspire her first famous work, "Desolacion", and would so disillusion her that she would never again be able to love and marry.

In 1911, she became a professor and inspector of the Lyceum of Traiquen. Three years later, in a national poetry competition, she received its highest distinction, "the natural flower, gold medal and crown of laurel". Following this, she adopted Gabriela Mistral as her pen-name. In 1921, she helped to found a new lyceum in Santiago de Chile and was its director. A year later, she was invited by Jose Vasconselos, the Secretary of Education of Mexico, to collaborate with him in developing educational reforms and in the establishment of public libraries in Mexico. During the same time, "Desolacion" was published in New York by the Instituto de Las Espanas, which brought her international acclaim. Also, while she was in Mexico, that nation dedicated the Home School to her, naming it the Gabriela Mistral School, and a statue of her was erected publicly.

She toured the United States and Europe before returning to teach in Chile in 1925. Her career in diplomacy began in 1926 when she represented Chile in the League of Nations. For the next six years she served as a diplomat in various countries in Europe.

In 1945, while she was in Petropolis, Brazil, she was informed that she had won the Nobel Prize in Literature, the first Latin American woman to do so. Other awards included the National Prize in Literature in 1951 from Chile. On January 10, 1957, while visiting the United States, she died at the General Hospital of Hampstead, N.Y. The Chilean government declared a three-day period of national mourning. In her last will and testament she bequeathed the royalties of her work to "all the poor children of Montegrande, Chile".

The earlier works of Mistral are personal and are concerned with her love for Romelio Ureta. Beginning in 1924 with "Ternura", the characteristic themes of her writing are more universal, encompassing love for mankind (especially children), and justice for the hopeless and abandoned. Her other major works include "Tala" published in 1938 and "La Gar" published in 1954.

With the exception of "The Scream", published after her contact with Vasconcelos, none of her work could be considered political. Her anti-Yankee sentiment, even in this work, is tempered with hope and a call for understanding.

## "THE SCREAM"

## from

## Paginas en Prosa

America, America! Everything for her because
everything comes from her, good and bad. We are
still from Mexico, Venezuela, Chile, the Spanish
Aztec, Spanish Quechua, Spanish Araucano, but tomorrow will be when misfortune will make us clench between his hard jaws one sorrow and just one longing.

Teacher: Teach your class the dream of the
believer, the first seer. Nail it in the soul of
your pupils with the sharp hook of understanding.
Spread your America with her Bellow, her Sarmiento,
her Lastarria, her Marti. Don't be drunk with
Europe and inebriated with far away lands, with the
far away alien that is, furthermore, perishable, a
fatal, perishable beauty. Describe your America.
Love your bright Mexican plateau, the green steppes
of Venezuela, the southern black forest. Say everything of your America; of how people sing in the
Argentine Pampas, of how pearls are taken in the
Caribbean and how it is populated by whites in
Patagonia.

Journalists: Make justice for your entire
America. Do not disparage Nicaragua to praise Cuba,
nor Cuba to praise Argentina. Think that one day
the time will come when we will be one. And then
your seed of hatred and sarcasm will bite your own
flesh.

Artists: Show in your work your finesse, your
quality, your exquisiteness, and the depth that we
have. Express to your Lugones, to your Valencia,
and your Dario and your Nervo. Believe in our sensi-
bility that can vibrate like the other, distill like
the other the crystalline drop of the perfect work.

Industrialists: Help us to win, or even to
detain the invasion that we call inoffensive and that,
in reality, is fatal, the invasion of the blond
America that wants to sell us everything, to populate
our lands and cities with her machinery, to use our
resources that we don't know how to exploit. Instruct
your worker, instruct your chemists and your engineers.

95

Industrialists: You should be the chief leaders of
this crusade that lacks idealists.

Do I hate the Yankee? No! He is winning, he
is lulling because of our fault - for our torrid
weakness and for our Indian fatalism. He is crumb-
ling us by virtue of some of his qualities and because of all our racial vices. Why do we hate them?
Let us hate what is in us that makes us vulnerable
to his steel and gold nail, to his will and to his
opulence.

Let's point all our activity toward this in-
evitable future: The Spanish America unified by two
beautiful things; the language given by God and the
sorrow that comes from the North. We make the North
proud with our inertia; we are creating with our
laziness his opulence; we are making him look serene
and even just with our petty hatred.

We talk tirelessly while he does it, executes;
we tear ourselves to pieces while he firms, like
young flesh; he makes himself hard and formidable,
welding his states from sea to sea. We talk, we
allegate, meanwhile, he seeds, he founds, he saws,
works, multiplies, forges, creates with fire, land,
air, water; creates every minute, believes in his
own faith and because of his faith, he is divine and
invincible.

America! and only America! What inebriation for
such a future, what a beauty, what a great kingdom
for freedom, for great accomplishments.

# BALDOMERO LILLO

## *Chile*

## (1867-1923)

Baldomero Lillo was born in Lota, a small mining
town in the province of Concepcion. His father worked
as a foreman in a mine where young Baldomero had his
first contact and first-hand experience with the cruel
world of the miners. He did several types of jobs
until the year 1898 in which he moved to Santiago to
reveal his true nature by joining a group called
"generation of 900", an active movement protecting
and fighting for the interest of the miners and
against the exploitation of workers that had just
then started to organize.

A few years later, he assumed a position with
the University of Chile, where he worked until his
bad health forced him to retire in 1917. Six years
later he died of tuberculosis, after writing his
last book, Inamible. Lillo was a great reader, he
knew the European novelists such as Dostoyevsky and
particularly the French, Zola. He is considered one
of the great "cuentistas" (story tellers) of the
continent that showed a deep concern for the social
problems of his country by painting with crude colors
a reality that was totally unknown outside of the
experience of the miners of Chile. He was, in fact,
one of the first writers to deal with sociological
realism. A master of the short story, Lillo relates
the struggles of many classes of the Chilean population; miners, farmers, fishermen, and the Indian.
With vigorous realism he cries in protest but his
protest does not remain an outcry; it becomes literature. Today, we have only three books left:
Sub Terra (1904), Sub Sole (1907) and his last, a
masterpiece of Chilean humor, Inamible.

In the stories of Sub Terra, the prose advances

effectively with measured steps. From the same recesses of his soul where the protest echoed, came his understanding. It was this understanding, more than the protest, that made Lillo one of the most effective writers of his time. His compassion and understanding led to the denunciation of those responsible for the inequities, and they served to rank him highly among the Modernistic writers of the period.

## "FIREDAMP"

from

### Sub Terra

In the shaft, all movement had come to a stand-
still.  The unloaders sat smoking silently between
the rows of empty cars.  The overseer, a thin little
man, whose shaven face with its high cheekbones revealed firmness and slyness, stood waiting motionless, with his lantern lit, next to the stopped
elevator.  Above them, the sun shone in a cloudless
sky and a light breeze from the coast brought with
it, in invisible waves, the salty tang of the ocean.

Suddenly, at the door of the shaft house appeared the chief engineer.  As he came forward his
footsteps rang out on the iron platform.  He wore a
raincoat and carried a lantern in his left hand.
Without even bothering to answer the timid greeting
of the overseer, he entered the cage, followed by
his subordinate.  A second later they disappeared
silently into the darkness of the mine.

Two minutes later, when the elevator stopped at
the main entry, the bursts of laughter, the voices
and the shouts which usually echoed through that
part of the mine, ceased, as if by magic.  A fearful
whispering rose from the shadows and extended quickly
under the black vaults.

Mister Davis, the chief engineer, was somewhat
fat, but very tall and strong with a red face on
which whiskey had stamped its characteristic mark.
He inspired the miners with an almost superstitious
fear and respect.  Hard and inflexible, he knew no
pity in his treatment of the miners.  In the pride
of his race, he considered the lives of these beings
unworthy of the attention of a gentleman.  But that
same gentleman would roar with fury if his horse or
his dog were the victims of the slightest neglect in
the care that their precious lives demanded.

The most timid protest on the part of these
poor devils infuriated him as though it were a
rebellion.  He believed that their animal-like
passivity was right and that any deviation from it
deserved severe punishment.

99

The inspection, which his job as chief engineer required of him from time to time was the bane of his refined and sybaritic existence. A devilish humor possessed him during those wearisome visits. His irritability spent itself on punishments and fines fell indiscriminately on great and small. His presence in the mine - announced by the light of his lantern - was more feared than cave-ins or explosions.

That day, as always, the news of his coming had produced a certain nervous excitement in all parts of the mine. The miners cast suspicious eyes on every little light that shone in the shadows, expecting to see at any minute that dreaded white ray. Everywhere the work proceeded at a feverish pace; the diggers, their bodies bent over in impossible positions, hacked out the brittle mineral, piece by piece, and the loaders pushed their creaking cars down the haulageways.

The chief engineer, with his companion, stopped for a few moments in the foreman's office where he informed himself of the details and needs which had made his presence indispensable. After giving a few orders, still accompanied by the chief overseer, he headed for the interior of the mine through winding levels and narrow passageways filled with mud.

Seated on the bottom of a car from which the sides had been removed, he made some observation to the overseer from time to time, who, with great difficulty, followed behind. Two boys, clad only in cloth trousers, moved this unusual vehicle. One pushed from behind, and the other, hitched like a horse, pulled in front. The latter showed serious signs of fatigue: his body, bathed in perspiration, and the anguished expression on his face, revealed the exhaustion of excessive muscular effort. A kind of leather harness pressed against his bare chest and from the belt around his waist ran two ropes which were tied to the front of the car.

At the entrance to a level which led to the new workings, the chief engineer, whose attention was fixed on the roof timbers, called a halt. Directing the beam of his lantern upward, he began to examine the seepage through the rock, poking with a thin iron rod the timbers which held up the roof. Some of these had menacing curves and the rod went through them as though they were some soft, spongy thing.

100

The overseer anxiously looked on in silent foreboding. He already felt one of those storms that so often crashed about his head, in his position as a humble and servile subordinate.

"Come over here. How long ago was this collar timbered?"

"About a month ago, sir", answered the troubled overseer.

"A month - and the timbers are already rotted. You're stupid! You let yourself be fooled by the timberers who put white wood in saturated places like this. You'll see to it right now that this is remedied before your negligence catches up with you!"

The terrified overseer withdrew hastily and disappeared into the darkness.

Mister Davis prodded with his rod the bare back of the boy who was in front and the car moved, but slowly, because the slope made the pulling painful on that slippery, soft floor. The one in back helped his younger companion with all his strength, but suddenly, the wheels refused to turn and the car stopped. The young lead boy lay face down in the mud, both hands still on the rails in pulling position. In spite of his courage, exhaustion had taken its toll.

The angry voice of the chief engineer rang out through the tunnel. He was beside himself at the prospect of having to drag himself, doubled in two, over those dirty wet puddles.

"You blithering idiot! Lazy scoundrel!", he shrieked, infuriated.

The boy dragged himself up on his knees and, making a supreme effort, stood up. There was in his eyes, a look of rage, pain and despair. With a nervous movement, he threw off those beast-of-burden trappings and leaned against the wall, where he remained motionless.

Mister Davis, who observed him carefully, got off the car and approached him with his rod held high, saying: "Oh, so you resist, eh? Just wait..."

101

But seeing that the victim's only defense were the arms that he held crossed above his head, he stopped, hesitated a moment, and then, in a thundering voice, shouted:

"Get going! Get out of here!"

Turning to the other boy, who was trembling like a leaf, he ordered, imperiously:

"You - follow me!"

And all doubled over, he headed down the dark tunnel.

After having dispatched a group of repairmen to reinforce the timbers, the overseer had gone to wait for his chief in an open space that adjoined the new working areas. To his astonishment, after a long while, the chief engineer appeared with a very red face, breathing heavily and spattered with mud from head to toe. So great was the overseer's surprise, that he didn't even move toward the chief engineer, who, letting himself down heavily on some timbers, began to shake his clothes and to wipe away with his fine handkerchief the flow of perspiration that flooded down his face.

The boy who came up pushing the small car told the overseer briefly what had happened. He listened to the news with trepidation; then, assuming the most alarmed and tragic expression he could muster, he solicitously approached the chief engineer.

The latter, realizing that the whole incident would hurt his pride, had recovered his usual haughty and supremely disdainful attitude. Fixing on the servile face of his subordinate the cold, implacable stare of his gray eyes, he asked with a voice that hid a certain controlled irritation:

"Does that boy have any relatives?"

"He only has a mother and three small brothers. His father died, crushed in a cave-in, when they began the new workings. He was a good miner", added the overseer, trying to minimize the faults of the son with the good qualities of the father.

"Well, you will order immediately that that woman

102

and her children vacate their house.  I won't have
slackers here", he ended with increasing severity.

His tone admitted no reply.  The overseer, with
one knee on the wet ground, wrote a few lines in his
notebook by the light of his lamp.  While he wrote,
his imagination carried him to the home of that poor
widow and her orphans.  Accustomed as he was to these
evictions, in his role of executor of the owner's
inflexible injustice, even he could not help feeling
a certain distaste for this measure that would bring
ruin to that miserable hovel.

His scribbling finished, he tore out the sheet
and calling the boy to him he said:

"Take this outside to the housing manager."

The chief engineer and the overseer were now
alone.  In this space, which served as a materials
depot, by the light of the lantern could be seen re-
inforcement timbers, heaps of rails and pick handles
scattered about along the walls where here and there
blacker spots marked the openings to sinister manways.

From these holes, in short and intermittent
vibrations, came the sound as of faraway breaking
waves.  The squeaking of wheels, the babble of human
voices, dry crackling noises and a slow drumming,
impossible to localize, filled the massive vault of
that deep cavern.  Here, the black shadows limited
the circle of light to the smallest radius; against
it their compact masses lay in constant ambush, ready
always to advance or recede.

Suddenly, in the distance, there appeared a
light, followed by another, then another, until they
made several dozen.  They seemed like small balloons
floating on a sea of ink that rose and fell following the undulating curve of an invisible tide.

The overseer took out his watch and interrupted
the embarrassing silence:

"These are the diggers from Media Hoja.  They
are coming to talk about the special allowances.
Yesterday they were summoned to this place."  And,
he went on elaborating the minute details of the
matter, to which his superior listened with obvious
displeasure.  He frowned; everything about him

103

revealed a growing impatience and when the overseer began to repeat his arguments:

"It is therefore impossible to raise the allowance because then the price of coal...", a dry and harsh, "I already know that", cut him off abruptly.

The overseer cast a furtive glance at his interrupter and, in the darkness, a scarcely perceptible, skeptical smile played over his lips as he noticed the long line of approaching lights. It was easy to see that the business of these poor devils ran the grave risk of turning into a disaster. He was more than ever convinced of this when he saw the chief engineer's frown and the state to which the journey through the mine had reduced his person and his clothes.

The knees of his trousers showed great splotches of mud. His hands, usually so white and well-cared for, were those of a miner. He had doubtlessly tripped and fallen more than once. Besides, the stains on his crushed hat, from the soot that the lamps deposit on the tunnel roofs, indicated that his head had really tested how hard and solid were those timbers that he had before found so fragile! As the overseer continued his observations, a malignant joy lit up his astute face. He felt, at least in part, avenged for the daily humiliations he had to suffer.

The lights gradually drew near and there could be heard, distinctly now, the sound of voices and the splashing of feet in the liquid mud. The head of the column reached the storage area. The men lined up silently, facing their superiors. The lampsmoke and the acrid odor of sweating bodies soon impregnated the air with a nauseating and asphyxiating stench.

In spite of the considerable increase in light, the shadows still persisted. In them were sketched the blurred silhouettes of the miners, like confused masses of indeterminate and vague outlines.

Mr. Davis sat impassively on his stone bench, hands crossed on his fat paunch, the strong contours of his powerful muscles barely visible in the gloomy light.

The sepulchral silence was suddenly broken by the hollow, hacking cough of an old man. The chief engineer raised his lantern head high and projected its luminous rays on the miners. Cap in hand, a man detached himself from the group and stopped three paces away.

He was short, sunken-chested, with angular shoulders. His bald head, blackened as was his face over which hung long wisps of gray hair, gave him a ludicrous and grotesque appearance. A knowing glance from the overseer gave him courage. In a trembling voice, he stated the problem that had brought them there. It was quite simple:

As the new vein was only sixty centimetres thick, they had to excavate four decimetres more of hard clay in order to make room for the cars. This was the hardest work of all because the clay was very solid. The presence of firedamp a combustible mine gas that consists chiefly of methane prohibited the use of explosives. They had to deepen the cut with their picks, all of which took considerable time and effort. The small raise in price per car, fixed at thirty centavos, was not sufficient since, although they began at dawn and didn't leave the mine until nighttime, they could scarcely fill three cars. Those who could raise that number to four were so few that they could be counted on the fingers of one hand. After painting a serious picture of the misery of their homes and the hunger of their wives and children, he ended up saying that only the hope of the allowance, promised when they took on the job in the new vein, had kept him and his companions going during the last two weeks.

There followed a lugubrious silence broken only by the light hissing of the lamps and an occasional chronic cough. Suddenly, the whole group stirred, heads were raised and everyone listened. The chief engineer's questioning voice sounded out:

"How much allowance do you want per metre?"

That concrete and final question received no answer. A murmur from the lines and some isolated voices could be heard, but they were silenced immediately when the imperious voice bitterly rang out:

"What's the matter? No answer?"

105

The old man, shifting his hat indecisively from one hand to the other, questioned thus directly, took a step forward. Trying to see in the hidden face of his interrogator the effect of his words, in a slow, insecure voice he answered:

"Sir, the just thing would be that we be paid the price of four cars for each meter, because..."

He didn't finish. The chief engineer had risen and his obese figure stood out with menacing proportions in the shadowy darkness.

"You're a bunch of insolent imbeciles", he screamed, his voice boiling over with anger, "to think that I am going to throw away the company's money to foster the laziness of a bunch of slackers who, instead of working, go to sleep like pigs in the corners of the mine!"

There was a pause as he took a deep breath, then he added, as if to himself:

"But I know all your tricks and take the hypocritical complaints of such trash for what they are worth."

Then, emphasizing each word, he turned to the overseer and ordered:

"You will pay an allowance of thirty centavos per meter of clay to those who mine a minimum of four cars of coal a day. Those that do not reach that number will receive only the price of the coal."

He was furious because, in spite of all attempted economics, the coal from that vein was costing more than that of the other sections. The demands of the miners, which made the failure of the whole project more obvious, only served to increase his anger.

Under their black masks the miners' faces turned livid. Those words vibrated in their ears, echoing in the depths of their souls like the apocalyptic trumpeting of Judgment Day. Their eyes reflected a stupid, almost idiotic expression; their knees weakened as though suddenly the whole shadowy mine vault had come down upon them.

But so great was the fear that this irritated

and imposing figure inspired in them and so powerful the domination that this almighty authority exercised over these poor spirits - weakened by so many years of enslavement - that no one made a gesture nor let escape a single protest.

But later the reaction set in. The deprivation was so enormous, the punishment so severe, that for an instant their brains had been stunned by the blow, but they soon recovered. The first to come to his senses was the old man with the blackened bald head. Seeing that the chief engineer was about to leave, he stood resolutely in his way, pleading:

"Sir, be merciful! Have pity on us! Make them keep their promise, we beg you on our knees!"

But the chief engineer didn't even hear him. He was too busy discussing with the overseer the new tunnel which was to join the old diggings to the new.

A menacing murmur arose behind him as he started off. When the old man saw that he was leaving, he grabbed him by the sleeve. In the obscurity, a formidable arm rose and with a furious blow landed the daring miner three paces away. A muted thud, a moan - then all was silent. A moment later the chief engineer and the overseer disappeared around a corner of the corridor.

Then there ensued a scene worthy of the souls condemned to Hell. In the blackness of the shadows the lamplights moved to and fro in all directions. Terrible curses and atrocious blasphemies resounded in the darkness and echoed sadly down the walls of rock which were as insensible as human egoism to their immense desolation.

Some had thrown themselves down on the floor where, like mute, inert masses, they lay, completely oblivious, neither seeing nor hearing what went on about them. One old man wept silently and the tears ran down the deep furrows of the coppery, wrinkled skin of his blackened face. In other groups, heated discussion, with must gesticulation, were going on while curses and roars of anger and disappointment interrupted the noise of the dispute. One tall, skinny boy, his fists tightly clenched, paced from one group to another, listening to the different opinions. Finally, convinced that there was no

107

remedy, that the sentence imposed was without appeal, in a fit of fury he hurled his lamp against the wall where it shattered into a thousand pieces.

Little by little they quieted down. One big, strong young man exclaimed:

"I'll not dig one more piece of coal - to hell with it!"

"That's easy to say when you haven't got a wife and children", was someone's prompt reply.

"If we could only use powder - that damned fire-damp!", complained the old baldhead.

"Oh, that wouldn't make any difference. As soon as they saw we were making a little more, they'd lower the pay."

"And you young ones are to blame", piped up one old man.

"Come now, gramps, hold your horses", spoke up the strong young miner.

"Oh, yes!", insisted the old man, "you and no one but you are to blame. You work so hard the rest of us can't keep up with you. If only you'd ease up, check your strength, prices wouldn't go down and this dog's life wouldn't be so hard to take."

"It's just that we don't like to loaf."

"Well, I've never loafed and you can see how well I've done!"

They all lapsed once more into silence. An old man who had been moaning in a corner rose and slowly left. Very soon the rest followed his example and in the depths of the gangway the vacillating lights were again submerged in those tenebrous waves that engulfed in an instant their fugitive dying radiance.

In the new tunnel the excavation work had been interrupted momentarily and only the repairmen were there, three men and a boy. Two were busy sawing the timbers and the other two were putting them into place. They were finishing up now and only a few meters separated them from the rock wall which was

being opened up.  A workman and the boy were trying
to set up a vertical timber.  The man held it while
the boy, with a sledge hammer, hit heavy blows high
on the timber.  But since they were getting nowhere,
they decided to take it out and shorten it.  But the
timber was stuck so solidly that, in spite of all
their efforts, they could not move it.  Then they
began to blame each other bitterly for the faulty
measurement.  After a sharp exchange, they separated
and each sat down to rest on the rock-strewn floor.

One of the workmen who had been sawing came over,
examined the upright, and seeing the hammer marks so
high on the timber near the ceiling, he said to the
boy:

"You watch out.  Don't hit it so high.  One spark,
just one, and we'll all be blown to bits in this hell.
Come over here, come see", he added, squatting at the
foot of the wall.

"Put your hand here.  What do you feel?"

"Something like a little breeze blowing."

"Breeze - nothing, my friend.  That's firedamp.
Yesterday we covered several cracks with clay but this
one must have escaped us.  The entire airway must be
filled with the damned gas."

And to make sure, he lifted the safety lamp high
over his head.  The flame reached out, growing con-
siderably longer.  His arm came down swiftly.

"The devil", he said, "there's enough firedamp
here to blow up the whole mine!"

The boy, about eighteen or nineteen years old,
was known by the unusual nickname of Black Wind.  He
was very dark, with strong, sinewy muscles and his
pockmarked face showed a firmness and resolution that
contrasted sharply with the timid and expressionless
faces of his companions.

The boy and the miner continued their conversation, seated on a timber.

"You see", said the latter, "we are, worse luck,
right inside the barrel of a shotgun in the place
where the charge is put", and pointing out before him

the high passageway, he continued:

"At the slightest carelessness, should a spark fly or a lamp break - The Devil pulls the trigger and out comes the shot. As for those of us who are here, we simply would be the dead partridges."

Black Wind did not answer. Down the airway he saw the chief engineer's lantern. The other workman had also seen it and both hastily leaped to their interrupted task. The boy began to hammer again, but his companion stopped him.

"Don't you see, stupid, that it's useless?"

"But there they come and we have to do something."

"I'll do nothing and when they get here I'll tell them to give me another assistant, because you just won't listen to me."

So the argument started all over again. They would have come to blows had not the arrival of their superiors interrupted them.

The chief engineer and the overseer examined the reinforcements carefully. Immediately, the keen eye of the overseer lit upon the timber that had caused the fight.

"What's this, Juan?", he asked.

"It's his fault", answered the workman, pointing to the boy. "He does what he wants and won't obey orders."

The overseer's penetrating eyes fixed themselves on Black Wind and suddenly he exclaimed with a threatening tone:

"Why, you're the one who cut the signal wire in the foreman's office yesterday. That will cost you a five-peso fine for your little trick."

"I didn't do it!", roared the boy, pale with anger.

The overseer shrugged indifferently. Then, noticing the boy's furious look, he screamed

110

imperiously:

"What are you doing, you damned loafer?  Get that upright out right now!"

The boy didn't move.  The unjust fine lashed his wild and rebellious soul and drove his fiery, strong character to its limit.

The overseer, infuriated by this defiance of his authority, grabbed him by the collar, pushed him forward, and added insult to injury with a violent kick.  He had gone too far!  Black Wind turned on him like a tiger, charged head first, hit him full force on the solar plexus and stretched him out cold on the floor.

At the sound of the thud, the chief engineer, who had been taking down notes, turned to interfere.  As he did, he saw a dark shadow slipping along the wall. With a leap, he stood in its path.  The fugitive tried to slip by, but an iron fist grabbed his arm and dragged him back.

Having regained consciousness, the overseer, breathing heavily, sat on a stone, surrounded by the workmen.  When he saw his aggressor, he wanted to go for him, but a sign from the chief engineer stopped him.

"He butted him", explained the workmen.

Without letting go his prisoner, the chief engineer dragged him to the upright.  His tone was quiet, almost friendly:

"Before you do anything else, you're going to put that timber in place."

"I've said, I don't want to work", answered Black Wind, with a voice deathly and opaque.

"I say you shall work and if the hammer isn't enough, try your head, you're so good at using that."

At the burst of laughter that followed this sally, the boy's disfigured face turned livid with rage.  He looked around like a caged beast and in his eyes was the dark flame of an unswerving resolve.

111

Suddenly, contracting his muscles, he jumped, trying
to escape between the chief engineer and the wall. A
terrible punch that caught him head on knocked him
flat on his back. He got up on his hands and knees,
but a furious kick in the kidneys sent him rolling on
the debris. The men watched avidly with bated breath.

Black Wind, horrible looking, full of mud and
all bloody got to his feet. A stream of blood spout-
ed from his right eye and ran down to the corners of
his mouth, but with a firm step he went forward.
Grabbing the sledge hammer, he hit the leaning timber
with furious blows.

A smirk of satisfied pride lighted up the chief
engineer's fat face. He had tamed the wild beast.
At each blow, he repeated:

"Fine, boy, fine - bravo!"

Only the overseer saw the peril, but he just
managed to get to his feet. One after another in
the blackness overhead shone great sparks. Black
Wind had let the handle slip down through his hands
to the very end and the steel as it struck full force
against the sharp edges of the rock, like a great
flint, produced the flaring sparks.

A blue flame shot down the curved collar of the
tunnel and the mass of air within its walls ignited
in a tremendous blaze. Just one brief second of that
vision - then a powerful explosion tore at the bowels
of the earth. Enveloped in a whirlwind of flames,
stones and cracked beams, the six men were blown down
the whole length of the tunnel.

At the sound of the formidable explosion, the
inhabitants above rushed to their windows and doors
where before their amazed eyes the mine structure
erupted like a veritable volcano.

Beneath the serene blue sky, where not a trace
of smoke nor flame was visible, the beams of the
tripple, yanked as though by some prodigious force,
suddenly flew skyward in all directions. One of the
steel cages, travelling upward in the shaft, like a
ball out of a cannon, shot straight up into the air
to a tremendous height. There was a mad rush of
women and children to the mine. Chaos everywhere.
Workmen ran about aimlessly, terrified, not knowing

what to do. But the presence of mind of the overseer on duty calmed them down somewhat. Under his direction, they set to work with feverish activity.

The cages had disappeared, and with them, one of the cables, but the other cable was still intact, wound up on its drum. A pulley was hurriedly set over the shaft, a wooden bucket tied to the end of the cable, and all was set to go down. Just as the overseer and two workmen were about to get started, a great puff of thick smoke stopped them. They would have to wait for the ventilators to clear the air.

Meanwhile, the crazed wives of the trapped miners had invaded the platform, greatly impeding rescue operations. In order to clear their working space, the men had to fight them off, and their screaming made it difficult to hear the orders of the foremen and engineers.

Finally, the smoke cleared away and the workers got into the wooden bucket. The down signal was given and they disappeared in the midst of profound silence.

At the entrance to the haulageway they left the improvised cage and went inside. It was deathly quiet and as black as night. The whole place was swept clean of obstacles. Not a sign of timbers nor cars. Pulleys, cables, signal cords, beams - all had been swept away in the explosion. Only one thought was uppermost in the rescuers' minds: were all their comrades dead?

Soon a great number of lights appeared and they found themselves surrounded by a compact group of workers. On hearing the commotion they had headed for the exit as fast as their feet would carry them, but out in the central haulageway they were brought to a halt by the smoke and poisonous air. They could only guess about what had happened to the workers at the entrance: ninety-nine chances out of a hundred, they were buried under the rubble at the bottom of the shaft.

The consensus of opinion was that the explosion must have taken place in the new tunnel and that the workmen's team, the chief engineer and the head overseer must have perished.

A unanimous shout - "Let's go!" - rang out and
they all started to move, but the energetic voice of
the overseer stopped them:

"Nobody moves", he said with authority, "this
place is reeking with black wind.  The first thing
is to activate the ventilators.  Shut the gates of
the second airways so that the air can work directly
into the haulageway.  Then, we'll see what we can do."

While everyone ran to carry out the orders, Tomas,
a tall, strong lad, came over and said, resolutely:

"I'll go if there is someone who will come with
me.  It's cowardly to abandon them like this.  There
might be someone still alive."

"Yes, yes, let's go", shouted twenty or more
voices.

The overseer tried to dissuade them, saying they
were going to an almost certain death.  The explosion
had occurred more than two hours before, so there was
no chance at all that any of them might have survived.
But, seeing that the men would not listen to him, he
finally gave in.  They all wanted to be in the rescue
party, and after a violent argument, Tomas selected
three and set off at once.

At the entrance to the tunnel, the four men
kneeled and made the sign of the cross.  Then, holding their lamps high, they entered in a single file.
Soon their heads throbbed and their ears were buzzing.
A hundred meters up ahead, the leader felt a thud on
his back:  the man behind him had fallen.  They picked him up at once and carried him to safety, then
found a replacement, and again, entered the passage.

About a hundred meters from the new workings,
they found the first body.  It was blown to pieces.
They tripped over a second, then a third, a fourth
and a fifth.  The last was that of the overseer,
whom they recognized by his nail-studded boots.  The
chief engineer was missing.  They hurried on.

Suddenly, an enormous block fell thundering
right in front of them, raising a cloud of dust.  It
had to be cleared away.  Soon after, they reached
the spot of the explosion.  For the most part, the

114

wooden head-frames had been torn from the ceiling and twisted into a thousand crazy shapes. The men listened cautiously for sounds of an avalanche, but hearing none, they proceeded onward. Suddenly, there was a sound of cracking and Tomas, at the head of the line, was struck on the shoulder. He nearly keeled over. He writhed in unbearable pain and was blinded by the dust, but managed to keep going on. Now his teeth were chattering. He leapt upon a heap of stones over a meter high that blocked off the tunnel and began to remove the rubbish from that horrible tomb at a furious pace. His companions joined him, but after a great deal of work, they found only three bodies.

Some of the rescuers gathered up the corpses while the others searched for the chief engineer, whose strange disappearance awakened in their superstitious souls the idea that the Devil had taken him away, body and spirit.

"Suddenly, someone shouted, "Here he is!"

They all ran over with their lamps. At one end of the tunnel, far back, a great bulk hung from the ceiling. It gave off the peculiar stench of burnt flesh. It was the body of the chief engineer. The point of a tremendous iron rod had pierced right through his stomach and stuck out more than a meter from his shoulders. The impact of the explosion had bent the rod and made it almost impossible to remove the body. Finally, they managed to get it down.

Since the clothes he wore turned to ashes at the slightest touch, the men took off their shirts and respectfully covered him with them. In their simple souls there was not a vestige of hate or rancor. Marching forward, with the stretcher on their shoulders, they panted under the crushing weight of the dead man whose oppressive force still bore down upon them like a burdensome mountain on which Humanity and Time had piled pride, egoism and ferocity.

# José Enrique Rodó

## *Uruguay*

## (1872-1917)

Jose Enrique Rodo was born in Montevideo,
Uruguay in 1897.  He distinguished himself as a
journalist, scholar, political writer, essayist,
and humanist.  Although Rodo was shy and seemingly
aloof from most of the world around him, he was not
untouched by the realities of society.  He was a
thinker, a philosopher, a literary being; but he was
also a social and political theorist.  Despite his
intellectualism, he became a hero to university students while he was little more than a student himself.
In 1895 he helped to found a magazine of literature
and social science, "Revista Nacional de Literatura
y Ciencias Sociales" which helped bring his name and
work to the attention of many young people in turbulent Uruguay.  Three years later, at the age of 26,
although he never had an academic degree, he was appointed professor of literature at the National
University.

By 1900 he was also appointed director of the
National Library.  This period of time was also his
most productive in writing.  In 1897 he published
El que vendra, and in 1900, his most famous book
Ariel was published.  The latter was timely because
its publication occurred shortly after the disastrous Spanish-American War and was accepted as a
sort of ethical breviary by Latin American youth.

His humanism transcended the turmoil of his
times and offered a voice of serenity in the midst
of a stormy political climate.

The optimism of his work was wholeheartedly accepted by his people who were frustrated by the fail-
ures of their fledgling democracy.  It should be

noted that while Rodo supported liberalism and the
concept of democracy he was personally skeptical of
the mediocrity the latter could produce.  His
intellectual resistance to democracy was balanced,
however, by his unwavering belief in the nobility and
goodness of man.

# ARIEL AND CALIBAN

The UTILITARIAN CONCEPT as the idea of human
destiny, and equality in mediocrity as the norm of
social proportion, intimately related, make up the
formula of what has been called in Europe the spirit
of Americanism. It is impossible to meditate on both
of these as inspirations for human conduct or society,
while contrasting them with those which are opposed
to them, without at once conjuring up by association
a vision of that formidable and fruitful democracy
there in the North, showing off its manifestations of
prosperity and power, as a dazzling example in favor
of the efficiency of institutions and the direction
of its ideas. If one could say of utilitarianism
that it is the word of the English spirit, the United
States may be considered the incarnation of that word.
Its gospel is spread on every side to teach the material miracles of its triumph. And Hispanic America
does not completely qualify with relation to the
Yankees, as a nation of Gentiles. The powerful confederation is realizing over us a sort of moral conquest. Admiration moves forward with great steps in
the spirit of our leading men, and even more among
the masses, fascinated by the impression of victory.
And from admiring, it is easy to pass to imitating.
Admiration and belief are already for the psychologist
but the passive mood of imitation. "The imitative
tendency of our moral nature", says Bagehot, "has its
seat in that part of the soul where lives belief."
Common sense and experience would suffice of themselves to show this natural relation. (We imitate
the one in whose superiority we believe.) So it
happens that the vision of a voluntarily delatinized
America, without compulsion or conquest, and regen-
erate in the manner of the archetype of the North,
floats already through the dreams of many who are
sincerely interested in our future, satisfies them
with suggestive parallels which they find at every
step, and appears in constant movement for reform or
innovation. We are Yankeephiles. It is necessary
to limit this condition by the indicators of sentiment and reason.

Not that I would make of those limits an absolute
negation. I well understand that enlightenment,
inspiration, great lessons lie in the example of the
strong; nor do I fail to realize that intelligent attention to the claims of the material and the study

119

of the useful, directed abroad, is of especially useful result in the case of people in the formative
stage, whose nationality is still in the mold.  I well
understand how one must aspire by persevering education to rectify such traits of a society as need to
be made to fit in with new demands of civilization and
new opportunities in life, thus by wise innovation so
balancing the force of heredity or custom.  But I see
no good in denaturalizing the character of a people -
its personal genius - to impose on its identity with
a foreign model to which they will sacrifice the
originality of their genius, that, once lost, can
never be replaced; nor in the ingenuous fancy that
this result may ever be obtained artificially or by
process of imitation.  That thoughtless attempt to
transplant what is natural and spontaneous in one
society into the bosom of another where it has no
roots, historically or naturally, seemed to Michelet
like the attempt to incorporate by simple aggregation
a dead object to a live organ.

     In societies, as in art or literature, uncon-
trolled imitation gives but an inferior copy of the
model and in the vain attempt there is also something
ignoble; a kind of political snobbery, carefully to
copy the ways and acts of the great; as, in
Thackeray's satire, those without rank or fortune
ineffectually imitate only the foibles of the mighty.
Care for one's own independence, personality, judgment, is a primary form of self-respect.  Usually, in
the books of ethics the comments of the moral pre-
cepts of Cicero that it is part of our human duty
that each of us should take care in maintaining
jealously the originality of his personal character,
what is in him that makes him different, respecting
in everything not being inadequate for the good,
the primal impulse of nature as founded in the
various distribution of its gifts, the order in the
harmony of the world.  A much-commented passage of
Cicero teaches how it is our duty sedulously to
preserve our original character; that which differ-
entiates and determines, so far as may wisely be, the
primal natural impulses, as they derive from a
various distribution of natural gifts and so make up
the concert and the order of the world.  And even
more would this seem to be true as applied to collective humanity.  But perhaps you will hear said
that there is no seal, no peculiar and definite
thing to mark the quality for whose permanence and
integrity we should fight the actual organization of

our people.  Perhaps there lacks in our South
American character the definite contour of a
personality.  But even so, we Latin-Americans
have an inheritance of Race, a great ethnic tradition to maintain, a sacred link which unites us
to immortal pages of history and confiding in our
honor its continuity in the future.  That cosmopol-
itanism which we have to respect as the irresistible
necessity of our development need not exclude that
sentiment of loyalty to the past, nor that molding
and directing force of which the genious of our race
must avail itself in the fusing of the elements that
shall constitute the American of the future.

It has been observed more than one time that
the great evolution of history, its great epochs and
most bright and fertile periods, are always the result of distinct but coexisting forces which by
their very agreement to oppose maintain the interest
and stimulus of life, which in the quietism of a
universal accord will disappear.  So the two extremes
of Athens and Lacedaemon revolve on an axle around
which circles the race of the greatest genius man
has known.  America needs to keep its original duality,
which has converted from classic myth to actual
history the story of two eagles, loosed at the same
moment from either pole, to arrive at the same moment
at each one's limit of dominion.  This genial difference does not exclude honorable emulation, nor
discourage in very many relations agreement or even
solidarity.  And if one can dimly forsee even a
concord in the future, that will be due not to a
unilateral imitation, as Tarde would say, of one
race by the other, but to an exchange of influences
and a skillful harmonizing of those attributes which
make the peculiar glory of either race.

On the other hand, the dispassionate study of
that civilization which some would offer to us as a
model, affords a reason no less potent than those
which are based only on the indignity and unworthi-
ness of mere imitation to temper the enthusiasm of
those who propose it as our idolatric consecration.
And now I come to the very theme of my discourse,
and the relation to it of this spirit of imitation.
Any severe judgment formed upon our neighbors of
the North should begin, with gentlemanly formality,
saluting one another.  This is easy for me to comply
with.  Failure to recognize their faults does not

seem to me so insensate as to deny their qualities.
Born - to employ Baudelaire's paradox - with the in-
nate experience of liberty, they have kept themselves
faithful to the law of their origins; and have devel-
oped, with the precision and certainty of a mathemat-
ical progression, the fundamental principles of their
organization.  This gives to their history a unity
which, even if it has excluded the acquirements of different aptitudes or merits, has at least the intellectual beauty of being logical.  The traces of its
progress will never be expunged from the annals of
human right, because they have been the first to
evoke our modern ideal of liberty and to convert it
from the uncertainty of experiment and the imaginings
of Utopia into imperishable bronze and living reality.
For they have shown by their example the possibility
of extending the immovable authority of a republic
over an immense national commonwealth, and with
their federal organization, have revealed - as de
Tocqueville happily puts it - the manner in which the
brilliancy and power of great states may be combined
with the happiness and peace of little ones.

Theirs are many of the most daring deeds for
which the perspective of time shall distinguish this
century; theirs is the glory of having revealed completely the greatness and dignity of labor, thereby
accentuating the firmest note of moral beauty in all
our civilization; that blest force which antiquity
abandoned to the abjection of slavery, and which
today we identify with the highest expression of
human dignity, based on the consciousness and the
activity of its own merit.  Strong, tenacious of
purpose, holding inaction as opprobrious, they have
placed in the hands of the mechanic of their shops
and the farmer of their fields the mystic key of
Hercules, and have given to human genius a new and
unexpected beauty, girding it with the leathern
apron of the smith.  Each one of these presses on
to conquer life as his Puritan ancestors did the
wilderness.  Persistent followers of that creed of
individual energy which makes of every man the maker
of his own destiny, they have modelled their commonwealth on a kind of imaginary population of Robinson
Crusoes, who, as soon as they have roughly attended
to their training in the art of taking care of themselves, will turn to the making of themselves into a
stable State.  And, never sacrificing to this their
conception of the sovereign individual, they yet have

known how at the same time to make of their association the most admirable instrument of their greatness
and empire; to research, industry, philanthropy, results that are the more marvellous in that they were
secured with the most absolute integrity of their
personal autonomy.

They have a sleepless and insatiable instinct
for curiosity, an impatient eagerness for the light;
and, carrying a fondness of public education almost
to the point of monomania, have made the common school
the surest prop of their prosperity, believing that
the mind of the child should be the most cherished of
their precious things. Their culture, while far from
being spiritual, or refined, has an admirable efficiency so far as it is directed to practical ends and
their immediate realization. And, while they have
not added to the acquisitions of science a single
general law, one new principle, they have done wonders
in its application to new inventions and made giant
strides in its service to utilities; in the steam
boiler, the electric dynamo, are now billions of
invisible slaves who multiply for their Aladdin the
power of the magic lamp. The growth of their greatness and power will astonish future generations. By
their marvelous gift for improvisation they have
found a spur to time, so that in a few years they
conjure, as it were from a desert, the fruit hitherto
the work of centuries.

And that Puritan liberty which gave them light
in the past unites with that light a piety which
still endures. Together with the factory and the
school their strong hands have also raised temples
from which rise the prayers of many millions of free
consciences. They have been able to save from the
shipwreck of all the idealities that which is the
highest of all and kept alive the tradition of a
religious sentiment which, if it does not uplift on
wings of the highest idealism, spirituality, at least
maintains over the utilitarian stampede some rein of
the moral sense. Also, they have known how to maintain a certain primitive robustness even amidst the
refinements of a highly civilized life; they hold to
the pagan cult of health, sanity and strength; they
preserve in strong muscles the instrument of a strong
will; obliged by their insatiable ambition to employ
all human energies, they fit the torso of the
athlete over the heart of the free man. And from
all this springs a dominant note of optimism,

confidence, faith, which makes them face the future
with a proud and stubborn assurance; the note of
"Excelsior" and the "Psalm of Live", which their
poets have opposed as a balsam to melancholy and
against all bitterness in the philosophy of stress
and action.

Thus it is that their Titanic greatness impres-
ses even those made most distrustful by their exag-
gerations of character and the recent violences of
their history; and I, who do not love them, as you
see, admire them still.  I admire them, first, for
their formidable power of desire; I bow before that
"school of will and work" - which Philarete-Chasles
tells us they have inherited from their forebears.

In the beginnings was Action.  With these famous
words of Faust, the future historian of the great
Republic may begin; the Genesis, not yet concluded,
of, of their national existence.  Their genius may
be defined as the universe of the Dynamists; force in
movement.  Above all, it has the capacity, the
enthusiasm, the fortunate vocation, for doing things;
volition is the chisel which has sculptured this
people from hard rock.  Their characteristic points
are manifestations of the will power, originality,
and audacity.  Their history is above all a very
paroxysm of virile activity.  Their typical figure
should be entitled, not the Superman of Nietzche, but
He who wants.  And if anything saves them collectively
from vulgarity, it is that extraordinary verve of
energy which they always show and which lends a
certain epic character to even the struggles of self-
interest and the material life.  So Paul Bourget could
say, of the speculators of Minneapolis and Chicago
that they are of the mould of fighters, that their
fighting power of attack or of defense is as of
Napoleon's soldiers of the Guard.  Yet that supreme
energy with which the North American seems to cast,
as if by hypnotizing, a spell and suggestion over
the Fates, is found only in just those things which
are presented to us as exceptional, divergent, in their
civilization.  No one will deny that Edgar Allen Poe
was not an abnormal individual, rebellious to the
influences around him; his chosen spirit represented
a particle inassimilable by the national soul, which
vainly struggled to express itself to others as from
an infinite solitude; yet the fundamental note -
Baudelaire has deeply pointed out - in the character
of Poe's heroes is still the inner temple, the

124

unconquerable resistance of the will. When he imaged
Ligeia, most mysterious and adorable of his creatures,
Poe symbolized in the inextinguishable light of her
eyes the hymn of the triumph of the will over death.

If now by a sincere recognition of what is great
and brilliant in the genius of that mighty country I
have acquired the right to complete the picture by
meeting even-handed justice, one question, full of
interest, still presents itself: Does that society
realize, or at least tend to realize, the ideal of
such rational conduct as satisfies, to the heart's
desire, the intellectual and moral dignity of our
civilization? Is it there that we shall find the
most approximate image of our perfect State? That
feverish unrest which seems to multiply in its bosom
the movement, the intensity of life - has it an end
that is worth while a motive sufficient for its justification?

Herbert Spencer formulates with a noble sincerity
his greeting to the democracy of America at a New York
banquet, pointed out as the chief feature of North
American life that same overflowing unrest which shows
itself both in the infinite passion for work and in
vainglory in all forms of material expansion. Later
he said that so exclusive a preoccupation with those
activities which make for immediate utility revealed
a notion of life, tolerable indeed in a young country
as a provisional stage of civilization, but which
already needed rectifying as it tended to make "useful"
labor the end an object of all living; whereas in no
case can it mean more than the accumulation of those
things which are only the necessary elements to a full
and harmonious development of our being. Spencer
added that it was necessary to preach to the North
Americans the gospel of rest and recreation; and we,
identifying these words with the idleness of the
ancient moralists, will include in this gospel to be
taught those restless toilers any ideal concern, any
disinterested employment of one's time, any object of
meditation or study divorced from all relation to immediate utilitarian interest.

North American life, indeed, describes that
vicious circle which Pascal remarked in the ceaseless
for well-being when it has no object outside of one-
self. Its prosperity is as great as its incapability
of satisfying even a mediocre view of human destiny.
Titanic in its enormous concentration of human will

power, in its unprecedented triumph in all spheres of
material aggrandizement, its civilization yet produces
as a whole a singular impression of insufficiency, of
a vacuum. And if man's spirit demands, with all the
reason that thirty centuries of growth under classic
and under Christian influence have conferred upon it,
what are in this new world the directing principles -
which is the ideal substratum, the ulterior end of
all this preoccupation with the positive interest that
so informs that mighty multitude - he will only be met,
as a definite formula, by that same exclusive interest
in material triumphs. Orphaned of the profound tradition that attended his birth, the North American has
not yet replaced the inspiring ideals of his past
with any high unselfish conception of the future. He
lives for the immediate reality of the present, and
for this subordinates all his activities in the egoism of material well-being, albeit both individual and
collective. Of all his amassing of the elements of
wealth and power, one might say what Bourget, the
author of Mesonges, said of the intelligence of the
Marquis Norbert, who appears in one of his books, "a
mountain of wood to which they have not yet known how
to set fire". The vital spark is missing to throw up
that flame of the ideal, restless, life giving, from
that mountain of dead wood. Not even the natural selfishness, for want of higher impulses, nor the pride of
race, both of which transfigured and exalted in ancient days even the prosaic hardness of the life of
Rome, can light a glimmer of ideals or beauty in a
people where a cosmopolite confusion and the atomism
of a badly understood democracy impede the formation
of a veritable national conscience.

126

# RÓMULO GALLEGOS

*Venezuela*

(1884-1966)


Romulo Gallegos was born in Caracas, Venezuela in 1884. At the age of 44, he wrote and published what soon became his best and most famous literary work, Dona Barbara (1929). This book, in a very short time, was translated into sixteen different languages and has been printed sixty times. Dona Barbara is in chronological order, the third of nine novels and considered by most critics, one of the "famous six". These six, of the most known novels in Latin America, were considered free from European limitations and inspirations and totally the product of American work.

After the disastrous defeat by Spain, in the Cuban War of 1898 by the intervention of the U.S.A., Spain remained prostrated and humiliated by the Colossus of the North; but as paradoxical as it might seem, the shock waves of this war were heavily felt not only in the Iberian peninsula, but all over Latin America. Latin America might have been expected to see the U.S.A. as a liberator and the dawn of a new era of progress and freedom; instead , all countries felt very deeply the humiliation forced upon the motherland and strongly and openly diagreed with such offensive intrusion. What was left now was to face the reality of the situation and try to make the best of it. The new rulers had problems with creating legislation and regulating immigration. Education was left as a last measure to help the future of the country, and so it became the focus of the attention of many thinkers such as Domingo Faustino Sarmiento (1811-1888) who made the first attempt to study the educational problems of Latin America. And it was to Sarmiento that Romulo Gallegos turned in 1901 for help. The answer was at this point more education as advocated by Sarmiento and to this Romulo Gallegos added a better and different kind of education. Most of Gallegos' life was spent serving his dream as a teacher; he intended to style his educational system to the Anglo-Saxon model in which character and knowledge were part of the curriculum.

Upon returning from a short period of solitary exile to the U.S.A. and Spain, Romulo Gallegos returned home to be nominated the following year (1936) Minister of Education, by the president, Lopez Contreras. Later, in 1941, he was elected president of Venezuela by a great majority, and removed in 1948 by a coup-d'etat from the military. Romulo Gallegos was very prolific, having written several novels, short stories, and essays. He reached his great reputation with his trilogy: Dona Barbara (1929), Cantaclaro (1931), and Canaima (1935).

Dona Barbara is primarily a novel of the land in which the conflict between the barbarism of the country and the civilization of the city is the central theme. Many other ideas are conveyed in the form of symbolism; Dona Barbara represents the violence and barbarism of the plains, and Luzardo is the light brought from the city, and finally Mr. Danger represents the exploitation by foreigners. In this specific case, Mr. Danger is tall, blonde, and with blue eyes - who knows how to win and how to conquer these simple people, who are so unsophisticated and naive. The novel is full of authentic characters from the plains of Venezuela, and a true description of the landscape and tropical scenes is also an integral part of the work.

# "THE RIGHTS OF MR. DANGER"

### from

### Dona Barbara

He was a great mass of muscles under a ruddy skin, with a pair of very blue eyes and flaxen hair.

He had arrived some years before with a rifle on his shoulder as a hunter of tigers and alligators. The country pleased him because it was as savage as his own soul, a good land to conquer, inhabited by people he considered inferior because they did not have light hair and blue eyes. Despite the rifle, it was generally believed that he had come to establish a ranch and bring in new ideas; so many hopes were placed in him and he was cordially received. But he had contented himself with placing four corner posts in land belonging to someone else, without asking permission to do so, and throwing over them a palm-thatch roof; and once this cabin was built, he hung up his hammock and rifle, lay down, lighted his pipe, stretched his arms, swelling the powerful muscles, and exclaimed:

"All right! Now I'm at home."

He said his name was William Danger and that he was a North American, a native of Alaska, son of a Danish woman and an Irish prospector; but that this was his real name was doubted, for he always added immediately: "Senor Peligro" - and as he was a humorist in his own particular fashion, that of a naive child, it was suspected that he called himself Danger merely to be disconcerting.

For the rest there was a certain mystery about him. It was said that in the first period of his settling in the country he had several times displayed clippings from New York newspapers, always headed, "The Man Without a Country", and who was unnamed - himself, according to Mr. Danger. And although he had never satisfactorily or clearly explained what the injustice had been, or why his name was concealed in such a description, all doors had opened to him in expectation of the flood of dollars about to overrun the Plain.

Meanwhile, Mr. Danger displayed skill only in shooting alligators, whose hides he exported every year in large quantities, and, for sport's sake, tigers, moutain lions or whatever wild animals came within range of his rifle. One day, after he had killed a female jaguar which had recently borne cubs, he took the little ones and succeeded in rearing one, exercising the humor of the great brutal boy that he was. The cub had given him many a scratch already, but he enjoyed showing the scars, and these added to his prestige as much as the clippings.

Within a short space of time, the hunter's cabin changed into a house, sufficiently furnished for comfort and surrounded by extensive corrals. The history of this transformation, which seemed to indicate that "The Man Without a Country" had put down roots, touches at certain points on Dona Barbara's story.

It was in the time of Colonel Apolinar, when they were founding the recently baptized El Miedo, Mr. Danger, having learned about the legend of the Familiar, wished to witness the barbarous rite which the superstitious Amazon could not forebear. With this purpose, he went to pay a visit, owning it to her anyway, since the bit of land on which he had built his cabin was her property.

To see the stranger, hear him express his desire, fall in love with him, and form her plans was all the work of an instant for Dona Barbara. She had Apolinar ask him to dinner, took upon herself the service of the drinks they both enjoyed so much, and as the native was a weakling and senselessly drunk, he took no notice of the glances with which his wife and the guest, during the meal, concerted their plan for his betrayal.

The peons had, in the meantime, rapidly dug the trench where they were going to bury an old lame horse, the only thing at hand to serve as Familiar.

"We'll bury him at midnight, which is the right time", said Dona Barbara.

"And just as three, because the peons ought not to see the business. That's the way it ought to be, according to the legend."

"Fine!" the foreigner exclaimed. "The stars

130

overhead and we beneath them throwing earth over a
live horse. How pretty! How picturesque!"

As for Apolinar, he was neither familiar with
the custom, nor in any state to make an objection,
and it was necessary for Danger to pick him up and
set him on his horse when it came time to go to the
new foundations, some distance from the present ranch-
houses.

The trench was all ready, and the lame old horse,
victim of the barbarous sacrifice, was tied to one of
the posts of the corral that was being constructed.
Three shovels for the gravedigger lay beside the
trench. The starry night enveloped the lonely scene
in a thick darkness.

Mr. Danger untied the old horse and led him to
the side of the pit, speaking compassionate words to
him between noisy guffaws which roused Apolinar to
idiotic hilarity; then, with a fearful push, he flung
the beast into the pit.

"Now pray to your devilish friends, Dona Barbara,
not to let the horse's spirit escape, and you shake
yourself, Colonel. We're buryers now and the thing
must be done right."

Apolinar had seized one of the shovels and was
struggling with the laws of gravity in his attempt
to lean over and fill it with the earth heaped beside
the trench, meanwhile muttering obscenities which
seemed to give him huge delight, for he nearly split
himself laughing over every atrocious remark he
brought forth. At last, he succeeded in filling the
shovel and swung it stupidly, stumbling after it with
each sway.

"What a load you've got on, Colonel!" Mr. Danger
had just said. He was absorbed in his role of buryer
and was throwing in shovelful after shovelful with
remarkable dexterity when he saw Apolinar, staggering,
his face hideously distorted, clapping his hands to
his sides, and giving a mortal cry, pitch into the
trench with his own lance-head in his back.

"Oh!" the American exclaimed, interrupting his
task. "This wasn't on the program. Poor old Colonel!"

"Don't waste any pity on him, Don Guillermo. He

had me marked out for death, too.  What I've done was
to get there first", said Dona Barbara, and she added,
taking the shovel which had fallen from the Colonel's
hands:  "Help me with this!  You're certainly not the
man to shed tears over such things.  You must have
done worse in your own country."

"Damn it!  How you talk!  Mr. Danger doesn't
shed any tears, but Mr. Danger doesn't do anything
that isn't on the program.  I came here to bury the
Familiar, and nothing else."

But he kept the secret, first to keep from being
involved in any difficulties which might be complicated by his own mystery, and secondly, because for
him, the scornful stranger, there was little difference between Apolinar and the horse buried beside him.
He allowed the rumor to prevail that Colonel Apolinar
had been drowned in Bramador Channel trying to swim
across it; the only proof of this story being the
discovery, in the stomach of an alligator he had
killed in the same channel, of a ring Dona Barbara
identified as the Colonel's.

As remuneration for secrecy he converted the
cabin into a house and built corrals on land belonging
to La Barquerena, changing himself from alligator-
hunter into rancher, or more properly speaking,
rustler, for those cattle that he branded as his own
were either from Altamire or El Miedo.  Some time
passed thus without his being molested by Dona
Barbara or bothering himself with her, until one day
he presented himself at El Miedo with this declaration:

"I have learned that you are thinking of taking
from Lorenzo Barquero the bit of land next to the
palm grove, which you have allowed him to keep, and
I've come to tell you that you can't commit this
injustice, because I'm protecting his rights.  I'm
going to take charge of that strip of land for him,
the only land he owns, and you can't send your people
in there to take out cattle, either."

But Lorenzo Barquero's rights did no more than
pass from the hands of one usurper to another.  The
only earnings he saw from his land were the bottles
of whiskey that Mr. Danger sent him on his return
from San Fernando or Caracas, with a good supply of
his chosen beverage, or the flagons of the Aguardiente

132

Mr. Danger had sent from the El Miedo Commissary, and that without paying a cent to Dona Barbara for them.

In return for this, the foreigner enriched himself by stealing cattle at pleasure. The remains of the old La Barquerena were scarcely more than a plot of savannah crossed by a creek, dry in winter, called the Lick, whose salty banks attracted the cattle belonging to neighboring ranches. Numerous herds were always seen there licking the creek bed, and thanks to this it was very easy to capture unbranded heads wandering over the prairie. Mr. Danger, however, found it easy to vault over legal obstacles and seize his neighbor's cattle, because the Luzardo overseers were always corruptible and the owner of El Miedo did not dare to protest.

When he had reaped his little harvest in this manner, he departed to sell it as soon as winter came; and since the creek was full during the rainy season and the cattle ceased to come to it, he stayed in San Fernando or Caracas until the water ran out again, throwing his money away on extravagant drinking bouts, for he was not very much attracted to it, and his hands were never quite equal to squandering all of it.

# Manuel Ugarte

*Argentina*

(1878-1951)


Manuel Ugarte was born in Buenos Aires of well-to-do parents and received an excellent education, which included several years of the Colegio Nacional of Argentina. As a poet and writer, he received recognition and departed his homeland for the literary capital of the world, Paris. By 1899, Ugarte had become the favorite of the Parisian literary elite, and was able to travel throughout Europe and the U.S. and Mexico as well. It was between 1900 and 1910 that Ugarte solidified his views of the danger which the U.S. represented to the Latin nations. Although still producing non-political literary works, Ugarte turned more and more to political writing, and in 1910 produced The Future of Latin America. After this period, he turned exclusively to political matters. As lecturer and writer, Ugarte travelled extensively and became a popular and influential figure in the history of Latin American thought.

By the age of 40, Ugarte was the foremost intellectual leader of the South, as he appealed especially to the youth of Latin America. In his The Destiny of a Continent, he presented the most eloquent account of the continuing U.S. threat to the South. After 1924, Ugarte continued his lecturing and became a renowned intellectual leader as he spoke and taught in many nations including France, Spain, and most Latin American countries. His views were also prophetic, for in his long life, he saw many things which he had predicted come to pass.

From

## THE DESTINY OF A CONTINENT

A similar procedure was later employed in Mexico.
ABC took charge of lessening the harshness, facilitat-
ing actions and covering up the maneuver before the
world, without obtaining, on the other hand, more than
the natural resentment of the sacrificed.  Because
what distinguishes these politics - is that imperialism, widening the radius of action, attempts to prosper
now in Spain.  In order to shield the reputation of the
ancestor a general movement in America - it is, rather
than the floating loyalty of attitudes, the painful
nullity of the outcome!  Neither Mexico in Central
America, nor ABC in Mexico, nor Spain, tomorrow in
America, will obtain any advantage in the commercial,
political, or spiritual order.  If any calculation was
made in that order of ideas, it will always turn out
to be ridiculed; and it will only serve to confirm the
destiny of the nations or races which instead of scar-
ing in their solidarity will dissolve in selfishness.

As if wanting to know how far the complacency and
general disorder would go after the tour of Mr.
Roosevelt, the advance upon the South was unchained.

On the 22nd of April, 1913, the fleet of Rear
Admiral Frank Friday Fletcher appeared in Veracruz and
took over the city, defeating an improvised resistance,
during which more than four hundred men, students of
the naval school, soldiers of the regular army, patriotic civilians, paid with their lives for the carelessness and incapacity of politics.  The nation, surprised
in the midst of its internal agitations, weakened by
its long struggles, anarchized by the legendary declaration that the landing was aimed at the government and
not at itself, found, nevertheless, the necessary
strength to prepare in its interior the uprising that
modified the plans of the invader.

The impression made in Buenos Aires by these
events was contradictory.  The official organs remained
impassive.  Public opinion, on the other hand, rose
instinctively in a movement of reprobation.  From the
unanimous impulse was born that same day the committee
pro-Mexico with the support of the university federation and close to ten thousand members.  Those who attended the first reunion have not forgotten, surely,

its significance. Many of those who formed part of
the commission, have later occupied political office,
like Dr. Diego Luis Molinari, undersecretary of foreign
relations, in the government of Mr. Irigoyen; Obdulio
Siri, minister of the provincial government, etc.

The generous impetus of the new generations, gave
rise in all the districts of Buenos Aires and in all
the cities of Argentina to the commotion which put the
government in great difficulties. As president of the
commission, I was in contact with the authorities. The
journals of those days give account of the interviews
and conferences which took place* and of the official
resolution, prohibiting all sorts of demonstrations.
El Diario Espanol, among others, after recalling the
ease with which were tolerated in Argentina the manifestations in favor of Free Cuba, thus wounding the
feelings of Spain, confronted the problem in its
general aspect.

--------------

*"In the morning, Manuel Ugarte summoned by the Chief
of Police, met with the Central Department where he
had a small conference with Mr. Udabe. This official
mentioned to Mr. Ugarte in the name of the Minister of
the Interior the convenience of suspending the manifestation. That afternoon, Mr. Ugarte was asked by
the Minister of Foreign Relations to come to the
Chancellory where a meeting took place with Dr. Murature.
The minister asked him to give up the idea of a protest
because it would be inappropriate at the present time
while mediations are in progress."
                    La Prensa de Buenos Aires,
                    April 29, 1914

\* \* \*

The tragic episodes of the European war exerted
a fascination so exclusive, that almost everyone had
forgotten the presence of an invading army in Mexican
territory. They followed with tiny flags on the maps
the slightest wavering in the stockades that separated
the European belligerents; but nobody knew in Buenos
Aires where the state of Chihuahua was located, much
less El Carrizal, where on the 21st of June, 1916,
the Mexican patriots and the North American troops of
occupation clashed. * When these initiated the retreat,
our Association celebrated a new popular assembly and
from Mexico arrived new telegrams of congratulations.

---------------

*"The North American troops had arrived up to the
vicinity of Naquimipa and as they tried to continue
the advance, General Trevino, Chief of Operations in
Chihuahua checked with President Carranza. The order
was clear. If they try to proceed, they must be
stopped. On the morning of the 21st of June, General
Felix Gomez had news that a strong detachment under
the order of Capt. J. Moore was trying to take over
the central railroad. He left to meet with the
invaders, prepared his defense, and in order to avoid
blooshed, moved forward, followed only by his aide and
a Texan interpreter, H. L. Spilliburg. He proposed to
the Americans to stop their advance. Moore announced
that he would continue his march regardless. General
Gomez and his aide were the first casualties. But
Colonel Rivas, second in command, gave the order to
attack and defeated the North American troops, causing
several deaths, taking 17 prisoners, 15 of them blacks.
He took possession of all the horses and ammunition.
General Obregon, today President, then Minister of
War, responded in this way to the action of General
Trevino: 'I congratulate you for the compliance of the
order that you have been able to give by not permitting
the North American armies to make new incursions in
the south, east or west of the place where they are.
With sorrow and perhaps with envy, I am informed of
the death of General Felix Gomez who had the glory of
forming the vanguard of those who are willing to
sacrifice themselves to defend our national dignity.
The prisoners should be sent to Chihuahua. I have
informed the Commander in Chief of your message.'"
                    Obregon

But the significance of El Carrizal goes further than the small martial skirmish. The encounter, which lasted two hours and placed on the line of battle only a few hundred men, did not have from the point of view of war, more than a relative importance. Considered from the political point of view, it marked, since 1848, the first time that our America rose in insurrection effectively against the gradual invasion which was subduing all resistance. It was the first shot aimed at the uniform which seemed to have the privilege of circulating in the neighboring nations as if limits and autonomies were abolished. What fell in El Carrizal was not a group of soldiers, but the superstitious respect that surrounded the agents of imperialism. What the presidents of all Latin America had never dared to attempt within peaceful diplomacy, was accomplished, with rifle in hand, but a mere colonel, and the tragic sanctions, which our governments evoke before the least dissidence, were not felt in any form. The invading army gathered its dead and withdrew from the country. But does this mean that the bloody attack is enough to change conclusion, that a military effort could save us?

Nothing would be more childish than to assume that imperialism, fearful, renounced the struggle. It would have been easy for the United States to overturn 200,000 men over the border and arrive in fifteen days on the capital. Why didn't they do it? To the conception of the Latin Americans, the gesture was far from being brilliant. We would have been obstinate invoking military honor and all principles. The psychology of the great nation of the North is different. Before the resistance that was announced, with its parade of surprises and endless guerrillas in the mountain, a calculation was made of the advantages and inconveniences, the problem was stated in practical terms, taking under consideration the moment, the sacrifices, the enterprise demanded, the benefits it could bring and the possibility of achieving the same end by other means. As far as the opportunity was concerned, the events that were revolutionizing Europe forced the United States to reserve all its power for the decisive intervention, which had already appeared in the minds of its shrewd rulers. Concerning the expenses of the enterprise and the effort that would be necessary to develop, a knowledgeable general on this subject, gave in figures the summary of the story. Concerning the possible benefits, they seemed insufficient compared to the risks. The mental equilibrium, the sense of reality, the clearer characteristics of that nation, prevented the venture. The greatest wish of Germany was to immobilize the United States through the intervention of Mexico. A reflection of Europe snaked across the border. And was such a thrust necessary within the mentality of the century? Was it useful? From the economic point of view, didn't the United States have in its hands the entire future of the nation?

Because the same formidable conflagration which devastated the world was proving axiomatic that coal, oil, food supplies, capital, the organization of the forces of peace, were even in full struggle stronger than cannons. The same final result of the war has come to reveal to us later that military victory is a formula made obsolete by the evolution of humanity. What was once a conclusive fact, today is only relative, subject to posterior phenomena of industrial and commercial activity, to diplomatic subtleties, to forces not derived from strategies or gun powder. A new imperialism, based on secure premises, could not let itself be mocked because of counterproductive impetuousness. Thus came the retreat from which, in reality, the Mexicans could not extract, no matter how noble and plausible the gesture was, any ulterior advantage. Only by universalizing the effort and extending it equally to all the orders; only by mobilizing, on an equal basis the impetus of war, the thought and productive potential of the nation; only by extending that spirit of resistance to the commercial and ideological field, could the fleeting advantage give fruit. Summarizing it all in one phrase, we can say that El Carrizal was an attempt, but not an accomplishment, with which we rest no merit, naturally, neither on the personal heroism of those who fought it, nor on the moral heroism, even greater yet, of those that assumed the responsibility of the attitude.

# ❦ 4 ❧

# Hope and Disillusionment

*To Luis Spota*

The period from 1940 to 1960 began with a time of close cooperation between the United States and Latin America. Before the two decades ended however, there occurred years of broken relationships and disillusionment in the area of inter-American relationships. This was a period during which Americans united to fight Nazi totalitarianism and during which totalitarianism of another breed infiltrated the Hemisphere. As we shall see, the situation between North and South was good in the mid-1940s, but by 1959 it had deteriorated enormously.

From 1940 to 1949, North and South were closely allied. World War II drew most of the South to the side of the Allies versus the Axis Powers. The only long-term holdout to the general cooperation between North and South was Argentina, but even this nation sided with the Allies in 1944. Even Mexico and Panama which were openly unfriendly towards the U.S. in the 1930s became strongly allied with their Northern neighbor. In general, in 1946 and 1947, the Latin nations and people hoped for a continuing cooperation between North and South. U.S. aid was expected, for it became obvious that the U.S. expected Latin America to join in the battle against the spread of worldwide Communism. But most U.S. aid was channeled to Europe, and by the early 1950s many Latin leaders felt abandoned by the U.S. This situation was further worsened by continuing U.S. economic involvement in the South. The

143

lower classes, especially, perceived that the U.S. was giving little, but taking a lot from the Latin peoples.[1]

The post-war U.S. policy could be called "Conference Diplomacy" for the period was one of many inter-American conferences to deal with all sorts of matters. The first such meeting was the Inter-American Conference on the Maintenance of Peace and Security which met in 1947 in Rio de Janeiro, and from this conference came the Inter-American Mutual Assistance Treaty or the "Rio Pact". This document created a defense zone within the Hemisphere to combat any aggression. In 1948, at Bogota, Colombia, the Ninth Pan-American Conference created the Organization of American States (OAS). In 1954, the 10th Conference at Caracas attacked totalitarianism, especially Communism and during the period up to 1961 many economic meetings were held and agencies were established. These were largely to give aid in the form of loans and economic funds to Latin America.[2]

It was into this general situation that the left-wing political philosophies came in the years following World War II. In this chapter and the next, we shall see that anti-U.S. sentiment in the South has become closely linked to Socialist or Communist politics. As such, many anti-U.S. writers attacked the very roots of the United States, the democratic political system, and the economics of free enterprise. We shall view, in the following pages, the growth of these left-wing ideas in the South in a brief historical survey of the Latin nations.

The course of U.S.-Mexican relations was far different during World War II than during World War I. There occurred close cooperation between the nations in the 1940s and for good reason, since Mexico was threatened by fascist and leftist forces from the outside. Also, the currency was highly unstable during this period. Inflation and economic problems swept the nation. In all these things the neighbor to the North helped, and the aid was accepted with popular appreciation. The Fascist-Communist conflict in Spain during the 1930s was viewed with great apprehension in Mexico, and during World War II the Mexican government depended upon the U.S. to help maintain internal stability and avoid Civil War.

As we ended our discussion of Mexico in the last

chapter, relations with the United States were strained, most severely in the area of oil company expropriations. The problems were not totally solved even though some solutions were agreed upon in 1947 and 1948, but the era of improved relations turned the oil questions into minor matters. Mexico pursued a policy of close cooperation with the U.S. to aid in financial matters and ensure political stability. In both areas, Mexico was successful. Manufacturing increased 43% between 1937 and 1947. U.S. loans and outright grants and aids increased greatly, and in the mid-1940s, a movement to lessen illiteracy was begun.

The events in Mexico parallel in many ways, the course of Latin history during and after the war. In 1946, there was great promise that U.S. aid would increase and that Pan-Americanism would perhaps become a reality, but this was not to occur. The U.S. turned away from the South and towards Europe in an attempt to check Communism and send aid there. Very little anti-U.S. feeling was manifested during the War, but by 1947, an anti-Yankee, pro-fascist, pro-Spanish movement was gaining in popularity. This was the Union Nacional de Sinarquistas, which at its peak had as many as 1,000,000 members. The government of Mexico, however, remained strongly in support of a friendly policy towards the United States, and in 1948, the Union was outlawed. The government also feared the threat of Communism, and as such was drawn closer to the U.S. During the 1950s, numerous leftist groups were attacked and suppressed mostly for causing workers' riots, and in 1959, the Russian diplomats were expelled for the same reason. As the 1960s began, Mexico was firmly allied with the U.S. as both government and citizen favored stability and freedom to the possibility of revolution and chaos.[3]

The situation in Central America and the Caribbean was generally much different than that of Mexico. U.S.-backed dictators and counter-revolutions were commonplace and the forces of the left and right met on a bloody tropical battlefield. Through treaty, revolution, and violence, the U.S. strength in this area was lessened between 1940 and 1960. And the most important anti-Yankee writings emerged from this area. The following section will analyze the specific areas of concern.

The problems between the U.S. and Panama continued into the period of World War II. President Arias sided

with anti-U.S. forces within Panama and threatened to
"find other allies" in 1940, but internal forces and
pressure from the U.S. pushed Arias out of office, and
the new administration allowed the U.S. to set up bases
in Panama. Panama allied strongly with the U.S. It is
interesting that even the populace of Panama supported
a close alliance with the U.S. during the war. In
fact, President Arias was reelected in 1948 on a pro-
U.S. platform. The fear of post-war Communism led
Panama to outlaw the Communist Party in 1950, and
Panama enjoyed friendly relations with the U.S. until
1955. In that year, a public outcry arose over a
revised treaty with the U.S. The Panamanians working
in the Canal Zone demanded the same pay as American
workers in the Zone. The question of sovereignty also
emerged as Panama demanded that the U.S. recognize
Panamanian sovereignty in the Canal Zone. A new agreement in 1959 tacitly dealt with both problems, as
Panamanian workers were paid more and a Panamanian
flag was flown at the same height as the American flag
at one location. Even after 1959, however, Panama remained a trouble for the U.S. as popular opinion in
Panama opposed U.S. involvement in Panama.[4]

In Costa Rica, the U.S. and the O.A.S. averted
total chaos by intervening in 1949 and again in 1955.
In the latter incident U.S. troops were called in to
restore order. Despite these actions, Costa Rican
stability was not strong. And the people continued to
fear the U.S. In the 1950s, the populace supported
politicians who promised to keep U.S. dollars out of
the nation, and a "Carib Legion" was formed to fight
the U.S.-supported regime in Nicaragua. A similar
course of history occurred in El Salvador, except that
the instability was not corrected by intervention and
the government became increasingly leftist in an attempt
to placate the majority of the pupulace. By 1960, there
was more stability but no prosperity and little growth.

Nicaragua and Honduras followed a similar course
of instability, as chaos was averted in the former only
with U.S. aid. A strongman, Somoza, was backed by the
U.S. and maintained a degree of stability. There was
also some economic and social gains under Somoza, who
was assassinated in 1956 and replaced by his son, Luis.
As ever, Honduras was a poor nation, and was controlled
by a series of strongmen until 1952. In that year a
new constitution and a new president appeared. But
rather than social, political, or economic improvement,
the new government did little other than become involved

in a small scale war with Somoza.

The course of history in Guatemala from 1940 to
1960 is like a microcosm of Latin America.  The nation
was unstable in 1940 but aided and allied with the
allies during the war.  Anti-fascist emotions led to
the election of a number of liberal presidents after
the war, including Aravelo, the anti-Yankee writer and
reformer.  Stability could not be maintained as the
poor demanded more wealth and saw their dreams in
leftist political philosophy.  Whereas in most of the
South, the leftists were banned, in Guatemala they
were elected to run the country in 1951.  President
Jacobo Arbenz Guzman was a socialist and land reformer
who gained the support of most of the populace by
promising prosperity and property for all.  Whatever
this intentions, his regime was infiltrated by Russian
Communists who supplied arms and terrorist plans to
overthrow the upper classes and the Church.  The U.S.
took action.  Honduras and Nicaragua were armed, and
a force of Guatemalan exiles was supplemented by U.S.
forces in order to overthrow the government of Arbenz.
To give further support to these moves, the U.S.-led
Pan-American Conference in 1954 specifically delineated
the actions to be taken to fight Communism.  Guatemala
was invaded, Arbenz resigned, and the U.S.-supported
Colonel Carlos Castillo Armas became president.  The
Communists were purged, but not effectively, for by
1957, another uprising led to the death of Armas and
bloody fighting between Left and Right.  Only with
President Ydigoras and with U.S. support were the
Communists suppressed.  This occurred in 1960 after
the Communists of Guatemala were inspired by Castro's
policies.  This represents a new hard-line stance taken
by the U.S.  It would be difficult for another Cuba to
occur after 1960.[5]

Cuba is the area in which U.S. policies have been
least successful, and has become the leader of anti-
Yankeeism in Latin America.  During the 1940s, Fulgencio
Batista ruled Cuba as a dictator, and with the support
of the United States.  Cuba was prosperous in the 1940s,
especially when compared to the conditions in the 1920s
and 1930s, and trade with the U.S. was largely responsible.  Tourists from the North were common in Cuba,
and the island became almost like a U.S. territory.  A
strong but small cadre of Cubans, however, opposed what
they perceived as U.S. subjugation.  It is true that
the lot of the poor did not improve all that much in
the 1940s, despite general economic booms.  Thus,

Batista had trouble maintaining control, and his problems were compounded by inept and corrupt officials at all levels. He was in and out of power several times between 1940 and 1952 when he was finally victorious in overthrowing the constitutional president Carlos Prio Socarras. During these same years, a new personality appeared on the scene. He was a lawyer, leftist politician, and former violent student activist, Fidel Castro. Castro led a band of rebels against the Batista fortress in Santiago de Cuba on July 26, 1953, and his revolutionary movement thus took the name "July 26 Movement". These actions, however, failed, with Castro being sentenced to fifteen years in prison. Batista released him in 1955, and Castro went into exile in Mexico where he prepared for an invasion of Cuba. This occurred the next year in Oriente Province and led to three years of guerilla warfare during which Castro operated out of the Sierra Maestra region. Castro was victorious in 1959 largely because his attacks on Batista had forced the president into taking extreme measures. The suppression of liberties led to widespread opposition and general strikes, and on January 1, 1959, Batista fled.

The new regime began as Castro entered Havana and reorganized the government. He was aided by his brother Raul and Ernesto "Che" Guevara, an Argentinian communist who had returned from Mexico with Castro. Guevara was the Communist influence in the new government, but throughout 1959, Castro maintained that he was not a "Communist" and that he did not intend to confiscate the considerable U.S. property in Cuba. Business, political, and military leaders quickly sided with Castro and his seemingly moderate policy. In early 1960, however, Castro grew closer to Russia and began to take U.S. property.

The U.S. banned Cuban sugar exports, and Castro expropriated all U.S. property in Cuba. He also savagely attacked the U.S. and scheduled anti-U.S. demonstrations throughout Cuba. The final break came in the Fall when Castro and Nikita Kruschev, the Russian premier, savagely attacked the United States at the United Nations. President Eisenhower broke diplomatic relations and the 1960s saw a hostile, Communist nation just south of the U.S.[6]

Puerto Rico has been a real problem area in the twentieth century for the island's status has long been in question. The natives have openly opposed

U.S. ownership and subjugation, but real progress was made in the period after 1940. The progressive Popular Democratic Party won the election in 1940, and they brought economic and electoral reform. The two areas where a problem still existed were in the area of the constitutional status of Puerto Ricans and in the seeming gap between rich and poor people on the island. The most vocal and active opposition to the status quo was the group that favored independence, but the U.S. dealt with the problem effectively. In 1946, the U.S. appointed the first native governor, Jesus T. Pinero. In 1947, the U.S. allowed the local election of the governor. The majority Popular Democratic Party remained in power into the 1960s, but continued to have problems with the Nationalist movement. Rioting swept the island in 1948; and in 1950, the Nationalists attempted to assassinate President Harry Truman in Washington. The U.S. agreed to submit the autonomy question to the populace, which occurred in special elections in 1951 and 1952. The outcome? Puerto Ricans voted to remain under U.S. control by a four-to-one margin, and the Commonwealth of Puerto Rico was established.

Progress was made after 1952 in both social and economic areas. The Popular Democratic Party and its Governor, Luis Munoz Marin, stayed in power until 1964, and were popular favorites. In fact, a plebescite in the early 1960s showed that those in favor of independence were outnumbered over 170 to one. The second problem, that of poverty, was not so easily overcome, for the island's economy depended almost totally upon the U.S.-controlled sugar industry. Although the per capita income increased greatly between 1940 and 1960, the lower classes still felt subjugated by the sugar companies. Land reform also allotted land to poor families and formed large land holdings into cooperatives. Mechanization on the farms and the influx of other industries further alleviated the problem, but popular opinion in Puerto Rico in 1960 was still quite anti-U.S. due to the control of the economy by U.S. companies.[7]

The island of Hispaniola contains two nations which have followed a rocky course in the twentieth century. Both Santo Domingo and Haiti had severe problems between 1940 and 1960. The former was totally controlled from 1940 to 1961 by the dictator Rafael Leonidas Trujillo Molina and several family members. He supported U.S. interests and represented the most

149

horrendous style of absolute ruler. Civil rights were non-existent in Santo Domingo, and on a number of occasions, the nation was invaded by "freedom fighters" from Cuba, Venezuela, and Puerto Rico. But Trujillo stayed in power and ruled with an iron hand. He did improve the economy up to 1955, but then the nations of the OAS began to place sanctions on Trujillo's regime, and the economy suffered. In 1960, Santo Domingo was implicated in the attempted assassination of President Romulo Betancourt of Venezuela. This led to further sanctions, even by the U.S., and the end of Trujillo was not far off. In 1960 Rafael Leonidas Trujillo Molina was assassinated and few people were sorry.

Haiti's problems were equally difficult. The U.S. came to Haiti's aid in the early 1940s for much trade had been conducted with Europe, and World War II ended that. The political system was chaotic, the economy was the worst in Latin America, and illiteracy was the highest. None of these problems were really alleviated even with U.S. intervention. Some stability was regained by the election of Dr. Francois Duvalier in 1957, but his regime was even more repressive than that on the other half of the island. U.S. aid was sent for social and economic improvement, but most lined the pockets of corrupt officials.

We thus see in Central America and the Caribbean a very troublesome area in many ways. Dictatorship emerged nearly everywhere, and reaction to the possibility of Communist takeover occurred in many nations. The U.S. supported many of these regimes, and in general continued to be hated and feared by the populace of these areas. The nations of this region were disappointed as the U.S. sent aid to Europe, and more disillusioned as it appeared that the U.S. was interested in Latin America only to fight Communism. Many peoples felt abandoned by the U.S. policies of the 1950s. And allied with the philosophies of the Left, a number of eloquent writers voiced this feeling of abandonment and subjugation.[8]

The events in Colombia followed a typical course between 1940 and 1960. There was support for the Allies in the War, and there was general political instability. After 1946, there occurred Communist riots and infiltration. This led to censorship and the removal of civil liberties. In 1958, the new president, Lleras Camergo appealed to the U.S. with a realistic plea. He pointed out that if the U.S. would aid the poor nations of the South, they would best combat Communism. Helping the poor, according to Camergo, would be a better policy than arming dictators![9]

In Venezuela, Communist influences were very strong, for the nation has a large proportion of industrial workers, mostly in the oil fields. Romulo Gallegos was elected president after the war, but his fame as a liberal and anti-Yankee attracted Communists from outside. He was thus forced out of office. Chaos followed into the 1960s. President Chalband was killed in 1950, and much bloodshed occurred during the next decade. Leftist forces continued to infiltrate Venezuela and to stir up trouble, especially among the oil workers. A somewhat more liberal leader, President Betancourt, was elected at the end of the decade, and some stability came as the petroleum workers were given better pay and conditions. But in general, into the 1960s, "chaotic" describes the conditions in Venezuela[10]

Ecuador and Peru are two poor nations of the South, and as such the U.S. was never greatly involved in either. But between 1940 and 1960, both enjoyed generally friendly relations with the U.S., the only opposition coming from Communists. Many loans and grants were given by the U.S., and some genuine progress was made, especially in Ecuador, which was more stable than Peru. Both nations had both liberal and reactionary governments, but by 1961, both were in the control of anti-Communist forces. An example of the political situation is the case of Velasco Ibarra of Ecuador. He was a popular leader who allied with Castro in 1959 and 1960. As such, internal forces and the U.S. exerted pressures which forced him out of office in 1961. In Ecuador, as elsewhere, the majority of the populace seemed anxious to keep Communists, especially Russian Communists, out of the nation.[11]

Bolivia did not follow the general pattern in this period, and a more careful analysis of this nation is required. The U.S. had been involved in Bolivia due to the wealth of tin which was present, and much U.S. aid had found its way to Bolivia prior to 1940. But during the War, a large segment of the population questioned these relations with the U.S. A candidate who was anti-U.S. and in favor of nationalizing the mines was elected president in 1943. This man, President Villarreal, was recognized by the U.S. in 1944, and the tin industry was not nationalized. Villarreal was overthrown and killed in 1946, and violence and chaos followed. In 1951, an election was held, and the candidate who favored nationalization won. He was Dr. Victor Paz Estenssoro, and it was months before the violence abated and he could take office. Once president, Paz initiated actions to nationalize the tin industry, which was done in late 1952. Anti-U.S. forces, however, were disappointed, for the nation was swept by severe economic problems, and Paz and his successor turned to the U.S. for aid. Paz and his party did make progress, however, as the lot of the Indians was improved, and a more stable government was created.

President Hernan Siles Zuazo ruled from 1956 to 1960 and once again stability was maintained, but in 1959 problems occurred. First, a U.S. magazine quoted a U.S. diplomat as stating some extremely derogatory remarks about the Bolivians. Rioting ensued and much damage was done to U.S. property. The rioting spread and numerous attempts were made to overthrow Siles, and in 1960, he was indeed replaced by Paz. The new president began a policy of friendship with Russia and arranged for extensive Soviet investments, but by 1961, Russian and Cuban supported rebels had mounted numerous attacks on the administration. Paz broke off negotiations with the Russians, declared martial law, and aligned himself closer to the U.S. as a result. Fear of world Communism had once again driven a potential ally into the camp of the U.S.[12]

As in Bolivia, leftist leaders were in control of the government in Chile after the War, but Russia's overaggressive policies led the Chileans to pass laws in the late 1940s to curb Communist activities. In 1948 Chile broke diplomatic relations with Russia and Czechoslovakia. Economic and social problems were evident in the 1950s, but stability was maintained, progress was made, and women gained the vote. U.S. influence in Chile grew, with much U.S. investment, mostly for the good of Chile. In fact, only natural disasters marred the relative stability in Chile. In May, 1960, earthquakes, volcanoes, and tidal waves killed 10,000, and damaged half of the cultivated land. U.S. and international agencies aided Chile and a surprising recovery followed.[13]

Argentina is a special case in the period 1940 to 1960. A group of army officers pushed for neutrality in the War and appear to have been Nazi sympathizers.

The country was unstable in this period and finally relations with the Axis Powers were broken in 1945. The Vice President and Minister of Labor and Social Welfare, Juan Domingo Peron, was a leader of the pro-Axis group. He was removed from office in 1945 and imprisoned, but by 1946 he was a nationalist labor candidate for president. Peron won, over U.S. opposition, and undertook a vigorous policy of reform and social welfare. Perhaps too vigorous, for Argentina was suffering from tremendous inflation. Peron also proved a vicious enemy, for through reforms and repressive measures he managed to eliminate most opposition and to promulgate a new constitution. In 1951, the great daily newspaper, La Prensa, was taken over by Peron. This was a shock to the world, for La Prensa was renowned for its democratic and honest spirit. A series of riots in 1951 were suppressed by Peron, and he accused the U.S. of backing them. Peron was re-elected in 1951, but troubles spread. Relations were strained with Uruguay, and inflation exceeded 600% in the decade ending in 1953. Perons' downfall began with his attacks on the Catholic Church, and in 1955 the enemies of Peron united to overthrow his regime. But the course which Peron had followed was a destructive one in the economic realm. His successors were unable to check inflation or to control the strength of the Labor Organization. The country was saved from serious disaster by the U.S. Export-Import Bank which extended credits of $100,000,000 to Argentina in 1956. By 1960, stability had been restored and Peron's longtime enemy, Arturo Frondizi was president.[14]

Paraguay and Uruguay have been totally dissimilar in their course of history both before and after 1940. Paraguay suffered from poverty and instability, and Argentina took advantage of this to gain much control in the nation. The U.S. combatted this with aid and loans, but instability continued into the 1950s. A strong Communist Party was a further deterrent to peace. "Coups" and "Juntas" were the order of the day. In 1954, a strongman and astute leader, General Alfredo Stroessner was "elected" president with the support of the army. He worked hard at bringing stability to Paraguay and had, by 1959, achieved some success, so that constitutional rights were reinstated. In Uruguay, on the other hand, one sees a prosperous and stable nation. Strongly democratic, Uruguay supported the U.S. in World War II, and maintained a stable government with little trouble from totalitarian forces. To further ensure stability, Uruguay instituted a multiple

153

executive branch of government. Nine men made up the
National Council of Government: six majority leaders
and three minority. Each council sits for six years
with each majority member serving as chairman for one
year. This system works well and until the early 1960s
few problems plagued Uruguay. At that time, however,
Cuban and Russian Communists were active in Uruguay,
and violence and bloodshed resulted.[15]

The year 1961 is the last discussed in this
chapter. It is interesting that in 1960 and 1961 very
important events changed the shape of future U.S.-Latin
American relations. A tour of Latin America by
President Eisenhower in February and March 1960 was
very successful, and he was also successful in reaffirm-
ing the Monroe Doctrine in response to Russian infiltration. On March 13, 1961, President John F. Kennedy
instituted his "Alliance for Progress" which was a
sweeping developmental program affecting all areas of
Latin American life. This was carried out at the Punta
del Este Conference in Uruguay in August. At this
conference, every Latin nation except Cuba signed the
Alliance for Progress agreement and U.S. monies began
to pour to the South.[16]

The literature which emerged from this twenty-year
period was widely varied. For the most part, the world
knows Latin American literature from 1940 to 1960
through a large number of excellent novelists, and
through the words of a few renowned poets. Most novelists in this period were surrealists. Briefly, the
surrealist movement in literature was a reaction
against reason and form in favor of a higher form of
thinking - something beyond form and reason. As such,
surrealism hardly lends itself to political or social
commentary. As a movement, surrealism emerged in
Europe around 1925. In literature, its leaders were
Andre Breton and Philippe Slupault, but in art was
found surrealism's true expression with artists such
as Salvador Dali and Joan Miro. The Latin American
surrealist novel emerged a bit later, especially after
1940, with Carlos Fuentes of Mexico, one of the foremost novelists. His Death of Artemio Cruz has become
one of the most popular novels in the world. Also from
Mexico, Juan Rulfo's novels, especially Pedro Paramo
have gained worldwide fame. A large number of
Argentinian novelists are excellent examples of
popular surrealist writers; among these are Julio
Cortazar, Jorge Luis Borges, Leopoldo Marechal, and
Ernesto Sabato.[17]

The second group of writers who also require little discussion in this section are those authors who we have already discussed in the last chapter but whose careers continued into the forties and fifties. Among these are Mistral, Gallegos, and Vasconcelos.

The last group of writers are those whose words were indeed anti-Yankee, and whose careers spanned those years when social and political upheaval threatened to demolish the stability of the Hemisphere. The foremost representatives of this group are Pablo Neruda (1904-1973), Miguel Angel Asturias (1899-1974), Carlos Luis Fallas (1909-1966), Juan Jose Arevalo (1904-1956), and Luis Spota (1925-    ).

Aravelo was a Guatemalan of liberal persuasion who supported the Labor Union movement in the period prior to 1940. He was a university professor and not a politician, but in 1945, a union of workers and students supported Arevalo for President, and he was victorious. His administration was plagued by problems, and he served but one term. His importance for our purposes is as an eloquent voice of anti-Yankeeism. As political scientist, Arevalo put together the single most documented work denouncing U.S. involvement in the South. His book, The Shark and the Sardines, was written in the 1950s and published in 1961. The following sections, taken from Chapter 2, clearly express the purpose and intent of Arevalo in The Shark and the Sardines:

> In criminology it is known that the criminal commits a new crime to cover up the first. The Panama Canal was already under construction when the State Department map makers and the Wall Street bookkeepers took notice of a danger. Was Nicaragua not still there, exposed for some transatlantic Shark to open another canal, resulting in economic and military pressure on the one that the Yankees were constructing? After all, between 1887 and 1893, private enterprise had once attempted to build a canal in Nicaragua.

> The fantastic sums of money being invested in the building of the Panama Canal constituted sufficient pretext for prohibiting the building of any rival canal. Besides, the Shark is not accustomed to recognizing the rights of competition. As soon as the Panama Canal was

constructed, a Nicaraguan Canal would no
longer be a real need, but it began to
pose a threat in the ocean struggle between one Shark and the others. The
elementary logic of the Sharks - psychology and morals arm in arm - indicated
that Nicaragua should be occupied
militarily so that nobody would be able
to build the feared rival canal.[18]

Pablo Neruda was a Chilean, and showed a great
promise as a poet from an early age. He was sent
abroad as a diplomat and travelled the world from 1924
to 1937. While in Spain, he was greatly impressed by
the Communist cause in the Civil War. He was next sent
to Mexico where he continued to publish and gain fame
as a poet. On his return to Chile in 1946, he was
elected to the Senate as a Communist Party candidate,
but was expelled to Mexico in 1949. He continued to
travel especially in Russia and China, and he received
the Stalin Prize in the early 1950s for his contributions to the Communist cause. His writings were
strongly anti-Yankee, especially in his attacks on the
United Fruit Company. He views Latin American history
as a series of struggles in which the lower classes
will eventually be victorious. In 1971, Neruda received
the Nobel Prize for poetry, and in 1973 he died leaving
the most well-known body of anti-U.S. poetry in the
world.[19]

Like Arevalo, Asturias was born in Guatemala. He
grew up in hard times, with political oppression and
natural disasters. He became interested in the Indian
heritage of his native land, and in 1923 wrote "The
Social Problem of the Indian". He became a student of
Central American Indians and studies in London and
Paris. He found in the sixteenth century Indian work
the Chilam Balam the basis for his protest writing.
For this work attacked the Spanish conquest of Central
America. Asturias became a well-known novelist, and
between 1946 and 1960, he published half a dozen excellent works which attacked U.S. involvements in Latin
America. Of special importance are The Green Pope
(1954), The Strong Wind (1950), and Weekend in Guatemala (1956). For his writing and social consciousness,
he was awarded many prizes including the Lenin Prize in
1966, and the Nobel Prize for Literature in 1967. He
was the first Latin American novelist to be so honored.[20]

Carlos Luis Fallas was born in Costa Rica,

June 21, 1909. He was raised in a poor environment and was influenced early in life by leftist philosophies. He lived in an area dominated by the United Fruit Company, and Fallas became involved in the workers' movement. He helped organize workers and led violent attacks on capitalist forces. He also became involved in politics and began a career as a serious writer. Mamita Yunai was published in 1940, and was little known until Neruda began to promote it heavily. By the 1950s, this work which accurately and bitterly recounts the activities of the United Fruit Company, was known and read throughout Latin America. It also was translated into most European languages. Fallas thus gained renown through his words and through his position as a "proletarial" writer attacking capitalism and the United States. His other works are also popular and have been often translated, but Mamita Yunai remains his major effort.[21]

Luis Spota is a Mexican who was born into a wealthy family in 1925. At age nine, his family lost its status and he grew up under severe conditions. He began his literary career during World War II as a journalist but he turned away from journalism by 1947. As an adventurer, many of his works are based on personal experience. His They Died in the Middle of the River was published in 1948 and was based upon his experiences while posing as a "wetback" in Texas for almost a year. His social concern and his leftist, anti-American leanings were established during this period. And Spota was, by 1950, recognized as an award-winning literary figure. Spota was also recognized as a leader of Latin and Mexican youth and a spokesman for anti-Yankeeism, especially in the treatment of Mexicans within the United States.[22]

In Neruda, Asturias, Fallas, and Spota we see the last of a generation, four angry men, and four leftist political thinkers. They also represent the end of an era, for after the 1950s there are few anti-Yankee writers who are truly literary figures. In these four, one sees respected literary talent, social consciousness, and leftist leanings. By 1960, the literary giants are no longer politically conscious, and the anti-Yankee writers are no longer literary in their talent or intent.

# PABLO NERUDA

*Chile*

(1904-1973)


Pablo Neruda was born in Parral, Chile, on July 12, 1904. His real name was Naftali Ricardo Reyes y Bascalto. His father, Jose del Carmen Reyes, was a railroad man. His mother, Rosa Basoalto, died when Pablo was only three years old. Soon the family left the native Parral to go to Temucho, a place very damp and densely forested that left an everlasting image in the mind of the poet. This untamed nature was an obsessive source of inspiration and it was there where the young Pablo wrote his first verses and won his first prizes.

At the age of 20, Pablo Neruda was one of the most promising young poets and his government, complying with a long tradition, sent him abroad on a consular mission as a reward for his poetic work. In 1927 he went to Europe, then he travelled in the Orient (1927-1932) visiting several important cities such as Rnagoon, Colombo, Singapore, etc., with few excursions to Asia and Oceania. When he finally returned home in 1933 from the Orient he was assigned to Buenos Aires and then to Spain where he was acclaimed by other poets such as Federico Garcia Lorca, Rafael Albert, and many others, and it was there in Madrid where he published his first and second Residencia (1935) with great success. When in 1936 the Civil War started in Spain, Pablo Neruda clearly expressed his anti-fascist feeling. That caused his quick recall by his government in 1937, but a new president sent him back to Spain to facilitate the emigration to America of Republican Spanish refugees.

After a period of work (1935-1945) in Mexico in which his political convictions became stronger, he published his third Residencia in 1947. When he

159

returned to Santiago he participated actively in
politics; he was elected to the Senate and enrolled
in the Communist Party. However, in 1949, the government by an act of Congress declared illegal the Communist Party, and Neruda was thus expelled from his
senatorial post. While in exile in Mexico he published his General Song (1950), but he also travelled
in Europe, Russia, and Red China and it was somewhere
between the years of 1950-1953 while back home in
Chile he received the Stalin Prize. Since then,
Pablo Neruda has confined himself to Isla Negra from
where he has written one volume after another. And
finally a great poetic reward was given to him in
1971 by the King of Norway in the form of the Nobel
Prize.

Pablo Neruda's poetry is closer to political
reportage than simply poetry for the sake of poetry.
In his work he summarizes the history of the evolution of modern surrealistic thinking and follows hand-
in-hand the "nouvelle vague" already so popular in
painting. One of his poems finds its equivalent in
the works of Dali, Picasso, etc. In General Song, the
obsession with the political thinking that permeates
the whole of Latin American life surpasses the topical
for the message and his work creates a strong link with
the Mexican proletariat painting of Rivera and Orozco,
in which the struggle between the Indians and the
ruling class is the obsessive theme of the artists.
In the same way Pablo Neruda views Latin America as a
continuous battleground where opposite forces clash
to protect and to rape the country. Some with good
ideas such as San Marti, Bartolome de las Casas,
Jose Marti; and some with bad ones such as Cortez,
Somoza, and the leaders of the United Fruit Company
and Anaconda Copper and others.

Toward 1945 the poet faces a great change in his
life that will influence his entire world, as a man
and as a writer. His total dedication to the Communist ideology becomes a search for a faith and
political conscience. He finds in the political
struggle an answer to the dramatic circumstances of
life; and it is during these moments that the poet is
most creative.

To better understand the poetic trek of Pablo
Neruda, it is necessary to follow his work since his
earliest writing, and out of this study, six major
cycles will emerge. The first one is his very early

writing which started his reputation as a poet. In this period no traces of Modernism are to be found and some of his poems still have traces of his adolescent character. In the second cycle, love and eroticism is the constant and obsessive theme. His age is about 20 and he is starting his first experiments with surrealism. In cycle three, surrealism is paramount. This is the period in which Residencias are created and give to the reader a feeling of nightmare with the running of the time, E.S.P., anxiety, the omnipresent death. Most of his production in this cycle is hermetic and it is not always possible to fully understand the real meaning of the work. This period is the longest and the most complex. In cycle four, Neruda lets the world know his political feelings and his work assumes a political and social tone. He has discovered that the oppressive forces of humanity are to be found in the social condition and thus in the political fight he finds the answer to the many social problems of man. Some of his poems of this period are very suggestive such as: Song to Stalingrad and Song to the Red Army at His Arrival to the Doors of Prussia. In the fifth cycle the artist turns his attention to America and focuses his mind on his people. A Song for Bolivar can be considered a new starting point in the poems of Neruda and like those of the New Worldism (Mundonovismo) he is a man among men and puts aside his materialistic instincts and searches for the sensual erotic to defend his land.

In 1950 his General Song is born. Formed by 15 long chapters which were increased every time a new addition was ready. His sixth cycle covers modern times. Some elements from his first cycle are present which would make everything in his life seem like it has come a complete loop. Here the poet turns to the very simple theme of nature and drops the much more fiery ideas of previous cycles.

# THE UNITED FRUIT COMPANY

When the trumpets had sounded and all
was in readiness on the face of the earth,
Jehovah divided his universe:
Anaconda, Ford Motors,
Coca-Cola Inc., and similar entities:
the most succulent item of all,
The United Fruit Company Incorporated
reserved for itself: the heartland
and coasts of my country,
the delectable waist of America.
They rechristened their properties:
the "Banana Republics" -
and over the languishing dead,
the uneasy repose of the heroes
who harried that greatness,
their flags and their freedoms,
they established an opera bouffe:
they ravished all enterprise,
awarded the laurels like Caesars,
unleashed all the covetous, and contrived
the tyrannical Reign of the Flies -
Trujillo the fly, and Tacho the fly,
the flies called Carias, Martinez,
Ubico - all of them flies, flies
dank with the blood of their marmalade
vassalage, flies buzzing drunkenly
on the populace middens:
the fly-circus fly and the scholarly
kind, case-hardened in tyranny.
Then in the bloody domain of the flies
The United Fruit Company Incorporated
sailed off with a booty of coffee and fruits
brimming its cargo boats, gliding
like trays with the spoils
of our drowning dominions.

And all the while, somewhere, in the sugary
hells of our seaports,
smothered by gases, an Indian
fell in the morning:
a body spun off, an anonymous
chattel, some numeral tumbling
a branch with its death running out of it
in the vat of the carrion, fruit laden and foul.

# THE STANDARD OIL COMPANY

When the barreno opened a passage
towards the rocky chasms
and submerged its relentless intestine
in the subterranean property,
and the dead years, the eyes
of the ages, the roots
of the imprisoned plants
and the scaly systems
made layers of the water,
lowered through the tubes the fire
converted into cold liquid,
in the customhouse of the heights
at the departure from its world
of gloomy profoundness,
a pale engineer and
a title of property met.

Although the roadways are entangled
from the petroleum, although the napas
change their quiet site
and move their sovereignty
between the bowels of the land,
when the jets shakes
its paraffin branch
before Standard Oil arrived
with its learned and its stupid,
with its checks and its rifles
with its governments and its prisoners.

Its obese emperors
live in New York, they are suave
and smiling assassins,
that buy silk, nylon, cigars,
small tyrants and dictators.

They buy countries, towns, seas,
police, disputes,
foreign commerces where
the poor guard their corn
as the greedy their gold:
Standard Oil wakes them,
standardizes them, designates
who is the brother enemy,
and the Paraguayan makes his war
and the Bolivian undoes it
with their machine gun in the forest.

165

A president assassinated for a
drop of petroleum,
a mortgage of millions
of hectareas, a rapid execution
in a fatal morning
of light, petrified,
a new camp of subversive
prisoners, in Patagonia,
a treason, a shooting,
under the petrolated moon,
a subtle change of ministers
in the capital, a noise
like a high tide of oil,
and then the big blow, and you will see
how they shine, above the clouds,
above the seas, in your house,
the letters of Standard Oil
illuminating its dominions.

# THE LAWYERS OF THE DOLLAR

American hell, our bread
soaked in poison, there is another
language in your treacherous blaze:
it is the creole lawyer
of the foreign company.

It is he that clinched the sprout
of slavery in his country,
and he walks disdainfully
with the caste of managers
watching with a supreme air
our ragged banners.

When they arrived from New York
the imperial advance
engineers, calculators,
surveyors and experts,
and they measured conquered land,
tin, petroleum, bananas,
nitrate, copper, manganese,
sugar, iron, rubber, land,
an obscure dwarf moves forward
with a yellow smile,
and advises, with suaveness
to the recent invaders:

It is not necessary to pay so much
to these natives, it would
be stupid, gentlemen, to raise
these salaries. It is not convenient.
These beggars, these half-breeds
would know nothing but to get drunk
with so much monies. No, by God.
They are primitive, little more
than beasts, I know them well.
You are not to pay them so much.

He is adopted. They put him
in a tuxedo. He dresses as a Yankee,
he spits as a Yankee, he dances
as a Yankee, and he climbs.

He has a car, whiskey, a press,
they elect him judge and
they decorate him, he is a senator
and he is heard in government.
He knows who is bribable.

167

He knows who is bribed.
He laps, bribes, decorates,
coaxes, smiles, threatens.
And thus, the bloody republics
spill through the door.

Where does he live, you will ask,
this virus, this lawyer,
this rotten ferment,
this bloody louse,
engorged with our blood?
He lives in the lower equatorial
regions, in Brazil,
but also it is his residence,
the central belt of America.

You will find him in the steep
heights of Chuchicamata,
where smelling wealth he climbs
the mountains, he crosses the abysses,
with the recipte of his codes of laws
to rob our land.
You will find him in Puerto Limon,
in Ciudad Trijillo, in Iquique,
in Caracas, in Maracaibo,
in Antofagasta, in Honduras,
jailing our brother,
accusing his fellow countrymen,
plundering peons, opening
doors of judges and landholders,
buying press, directing
the police, the stick, the rifle
against his forgotten family.

He struts, dressed
in tuxedo, in the receptions,
inaugurating monuments
with this phrase: Gentlemen,
the fatherland before life,
it is our mother, it is our soil,
we defend the order, we make
new prisons, other jails.

And he dies gloriously, "the patriot"
senator, eminent patrician
decorated by the Pope,
distinguished, prosperous, feared,
while the tragic race
of our dead, those that submerged
the hand in copper, scratched

168

the profound and severe land,
die beaten and forgotten,
hastily placed
in their funeral boxes:
a name, a number on the cross,
that the wind shakes, killing
even the number of the heroes.

# PUERTO RICO

Mr. Truman arrives to the island
of Puerto Rico,
he comes to the blue
water of our pure seas
to wash his bloody fingers.
He just ordered the death
of two hundred young greeks,
their machine guns will function
strictly,
every day
by his orders the doric
heads - grape and olive -
eyes of the ancient sea, petals
of the corinthian corola,
fall to the greek white dust.
The assassins
raise the goblet
of sweet Chipre with
the expert North Americans
between great bursts of laughter, with
the mustaches dripping
of fried oil and greek blood.

Truman arrives to our waters
to wash the hands red
from distant blood. Meanwhile,
he decrees, preaches and smiles
at the University, in his language,
he closes the Castilian mouth,
he covers the clarity of the words
that circulated there like a
river of crystalline lineage
and he orders: "Death to your language,
Puerto Rico."

# AGAIN THE TYRANTS

## XL

Again today the hunt
spreads through Brazil,
searched by the cold greed
of the slave traders:
On Wall Street they decreed
to their filthy satellites
that buried their eye teeth
in the wounds of the town,
and the hunt began
in Chile, in Brazil, in all
our Americas leveled
by traders and executioners.

My town hid my course,
covered my verses with its hands,
preserved me from death,
and in Brazil the infinite door
of the town closes the roadways
where Prestes once more
again rejects the wicked.

Brazil, may your sorrowful captain
be saved.
Brazil, that does not have tomorrow
to collect from its memory
bit by bit its image
to elevate itself in a serious position
without having it left in the middle
of your heart to take advantage of
the liverty that yet, yet
is able to conquer you, Brazil.

# THE ANACONDA COPPER MINING COMPANY

Name coiled like a snake,
faces insatiable, green monster,
in the bunched up heights,
in the thin mount,
of my town, under the moon
of harshness, excavator,
you open the blemishing craters
of mineral, they imagine the galleries
of copper packed
in its arenas of granite.

I have seen burning in the eternal night
of Chuchicamata, in the heights,
the fire of the sacrifices,
the overflowing crackling
of the cyclope that devours
the hand, the weight, the waist
of the Chileans, wrapping them
under their vertebra of copper,
draining them of lukewarm blood,
grinding the skeletons
and spitting them in the mountains
of the desolate deserts.

The air dreams in the heights
of starry Chuquicamata.
They destroy the tunnels
with little hands of man
the resistance of the planet,
the sulfidious fowl vibrates
from the ravines, the cold ferrous
mutinies from the metal
with its diffident scars,
and when they deafen the horns
the land swallows a parade
of small men that go down
to the jaws of the crater.

They are very small captains,
my cousins, my sons,
and when they empty the lingots
towards the seas, and cleans
the front and return trembling
in the last chill,
the large snake eats them,
diminishes them, grinds them,
covers them with malignant slobber,

175

casts them out into the roads,
kills them with the police,
makes them rot in Pisagua,
jails them, spits on them,
buys a traitor president,
that insults and harrasses them,
kills them with hunger in the plains
of sandy immensity.
And there is another twisted cross
in the infernal slopes
as the sole breath disperses
from the mast of the mining.

# Miguel Ángel Asturias

*Guatemala*

(1899-1974)


Miguel Angel Asturias was born on October 19,
1899 in Guatemala. He was the son of Ernesto Asturias,
a magistrate, and Maria Rosales, a school teacher. Because of a political disagreement with President
Estrada Cabrera, his father had to retire to the
country in the house of his parents in Solama (Baja
Verapaz) in 1905.

From 1914 to 1918, the great earthquakes caused
major change in the life of Asturias and people in
general. At first they were distrustful of each other
because of the oppressive regime of the president; now,
forced by the destructive power of nature to live in a
communal atmosphere, they gained respect for each other.
It was from this closeness that a new spirit of solidarity emerged, and in 1920, the president was overthrown.
In 1922, the Popular University of Guatemala was founded, and Asturias and other students had a major role in
its establishment. Capable people were encouraged to
contribute to the general welfare by teaching free
courses to the underprivileged. In 1923, Asturias wrote
a dissertation for his law degree entitled "The Social
Problem of the Indian", for which he was awarded the
Galvez Prize. Miguel Angel Asturias never stopped being a student of life. While in London he spent a
great deal of time in the British Museum's Maya Indian
Collection. In Paris, he enrolled at the Sorbonne to
study Central American Anthropology and Mythology under
Professor Georges Raynaud, a scholar who supposedly
gave forty years of his life to translate the Popol
Vuh considered the bible of the Mayas-Quiches. With
some help, Asturias translated this work into Spanish
in 1927 and the year after he did the same with the
French version of Raynaud's Annals of the Cakchiguels.
In 1946, he privately published his first novel,

177

El Senor Presidente. In 1954 a new dictatorship de-
prived him of his passport and citizenship and compelled him to go into exile. In 1955 he was in Chile
with the poet Pablo Neruda and then travelled to
Genoa. In 1939 the new president of Guatemala returned his citizenship and appointed him Ambassador
to France. In 1966 he received the Lenin Prize for
Literature. The following year he was the first
Latin American novelist to be awarded the Nobel Prize.

Asturias' writings are mainly a literature of
protest, committed to correcting injustices and com-
plaining against the excesses of exploitation. Such
literature of social protest finds its roots in the
Maya writing of Chilam Balam the Indian writing ex-
presses his resentment against the evil and the
Barbarity of the Spanish Conquest. Now, in our generation, a new enemy is exploiting the riches of Latin
America's natural resources; corporations from abroad
have been taking the oil wells, plantations and mines,
by employing cheap local workers and thus making a
huge profit. From this form of capitalistic taking
over of land and people gave birth to a spontaneous
type of literature which was a dispassionate testimony
of reality, true and documentary most of the time.
From this type of situation in which the native had no
power to defend himself, again the Thinker recorded for
posterity his grievance. Novelists such as Ciro
Alegria, and Romulo Gallegos, obtained from this
situation their strength and materials.

For a complete reading on Asturias' writings
with an anti-imperialistic theme, the following books
should be consulted: Strong Wind (1950), The Green
Pope (1954), The Eyes of the Burried (1960), and
Weekend in Guatemala (1956).

From

## THE GREEN POPE

Chipo Chipo came looking for them.  They were
crossing the beach that was cottony with shadows,
dampness, and foam, a moony silence, the rustle of
palm trees.

"A brand-new locomotive arrived", Chipo explained
to her, "and they say it gets up good speed and can
be bridled down.  They can drive it like any animal.
It brung a lot of cars with people and fruit.  Your
mama came."

"Where did you take her, Chipo?"

"To my house..."

It's funny she didn't go to my godparents."

"She came with the commander and they were talking to Mr. Kind.  They alsmost caught him without his
arm.  He didn't have it on.  I had to get it for him.
It bothers him.  It bothers him and it's a nuisance.
Why doesn't he leave his sleeve empty?  That's what
I'd do. Less weight.  If a person could take off an
arm, a leg, and the bones that weigh the most, he
could go lighter, and be comfortable.  It's a lot of
skeleton we carry around, and one gets tires."

"You're going to meet my dear mama...She's a lot
younger than I...You don't believe me?...What a man!...
He doesn't dream and he doesn't believe...I'm going to
go home and change my clothes...God save me if my mother
should see me dripping with water!..."

Dona Flora - she preferred to be called Florona
and would not answer to Florita, pretending to be deaf,
and if someone close to her used the diminutive she
would answer: "I've got your florita, your little
flower, hidden here!"  Pointing at her navel - Dona
Flora, after being introduced to George Maker Thompson,
embraced her daughter trembling.  Every time she saw
her she would embrace her, overcome with an inexplicable
feeling.  When, during her school years, the girl would
come back from boarding school after seven long months
in the capital, or when, as now, she returned after
fifteen or twenty days of vacation in the port where

her old friends the Aceitunos were, Dona Flora would tremble, because her daughter was so different from her, a practical person, that she seemed to be embracing an absent person, an inhabitant of the moon.

Thompson wanted to flatter Dona Flora, confessing that he found her as springlike as her daughter, but the young lady, autumn and springtime, paid no attention to the flattery, which was out of place in the business world, and continued speaking.

"As the Commander was saying, Mr. Kind..."

"Yes, yes; I say that the private owners will sell blindfolded if they get a good price. It's land that isn't worth very much: swamps, woods, lots of snakes, sickness, fever; but it will be necessary to make them a nice offer, more than what it's worth, because for them it's a matter of the land where they were born, that they inherited from their forefathers, and which they'll refuse to leave unless they're dazzled by the greenbacks you wave in their faces."

"Planting can start on the collectives so there won't be any loss of time", Dona Flora interjected, "and we can begin buying from the ones willing to sell, at their price."

"There's no problem there", Kind said. "The problem is with the ones who don't want to sell. What can be done, what can we do with the ones who refuse to sell their land at any price?"

"There", Dona Flora sighed, "is where our friend the Commander comes in. When Mr. Money can't do it, Mr. Rifle takes over."

"And don't you think I wouldn't shoot them", the head man stroked his coal-colored moustache, "because the country needs progress and if they stand in the way with their negative attitude, logically speaking, it's an act of treason."

"This", emphasized Dona Flora facing the commander and putting down her fan, "is what you have to show to them. Either they sell or they will bear the consequences."

"The bad part", said Kind, after some reflection, "is that according to our information the farmers in

180

that case would go to their town governments and the town governments would complain to high heaven."

"Only two town governments", the military leader was precise, his linen uniform flowed white in the darkness of the shack, as he vainly tried to put his fat man's legs together, leaning back in his chair.

"Well, but there are a lot of people, two municipalities are a lot of people to shoot..."

"Not shoot, Mr. Kind. 'Buy them off'...'Buy them off'...There are lots of ways to kill a person...A lot of people have been shot with gold bullets..."

"Very good, Dona Florona, very good!...Although it wouldn't be so bad to teach them a lesson with some lead bullets too..."

"They're both metals, Commander, but all fo us would rather get gold bullets..."

"But that isn't quite true, you'll see", the commander answered, twirling his moustache with his fingers. "There'll be those who won't be taken off their land at any price. Oh, they exist! And then we'll have to take steps. Progress demands that they leave their land so that these gentlemen can make it produce to the maximum; either they can leave nicely or they can leave their hides nicely behind. Lead bullets or gold bullets, without scruples, an iron hand without qualms; and the one indicated for that, in my opinion, is Mr. Thompson, who believes in force, who expressed it very well the other day in the dining room. His words are still in my head: men are either ruled by force or they should be left alone. They're governed in order to make them develop, the way children are punished for their own good, for their future development."

Mayari raised her ebony eyes, questioning George with those two slivers of precious wood; but the latter, enthusiastic now over the reference, was affirming in a loud voice the necessity of following a policy of vassal and master in the conquest of those lands, lands in their totality, not in fragments, because in that way and only in that way would they serve the progress of the region, the creation of great banana plantations,... thousands of plants, millions of bunches...

Without thinking twice Dona Flora backed the commander in what he proposed. Mr. Kind, the more diplomatic one, would go to the capital and speak to the higher authorities, getting their orders in the matter; and Mr. Thompson the kind of man who comes into life when in full command, as Dona Florona herself said, impressed by the physique and way of thinking of the gigantic boy, would go into the jungle.

"In the capital", the military chief suggested, "Mr. Kind should get the Ministry of the Interior to call in the mayors from the territory in question and make them feel that the government has an interest in the farmers' selling their land, cultivated or not, that it is an indispensable part of the progress of the country. No one will deny that the progress of the country is more important than a few coastal leeches clinging obstinately to land that produces almost nothing."

"And since they're going to be paid, it's not robbery, it's a purchase!" Dona Florona exclaimed.

"And George, young George as Mayari calls him..." What was the commander insinuating? He wanted them to notice that he was not just twiddling his thumbs; glances, sighs, a show of affection from her, because he sat there like a wooden doll. "And young George to the jungle. On your farm, Dona Flora, this gentlemen can set up his headquarters and plant what's possible; there's a lot of land on the river bank just right for bananas; he can buy from those who will sell and see what steps can be taken with the others standing in the way of progress..." And rising now, patting Thompson on the back in a friendly way, "because the Green Pope has guts. The name speaks for itself."

"The commander has it all nicely worked out", the voice of Dona Florona was heard. "No heat and no mosquitoes for Mr. Kind...I'd like to be a diplomat!... The capital - pleasant days...nights that you can't even dream about...Here on the coast I'm a practical woman, but when I'm there I turn dreamy and I wander about for hours on end, as if the dust of a sleeping world had fallen down into my eyes from heaven. This conversation is very nice, but I have a lot of things to do. Let's go, Mayari..."

And when we went out the door into the street, where almost nothing could be seen except the immense hot night - the stars bit one's eyes like golden chili powder - Dona Flora let out a cry as she stumbled into a motionless figure.  Then she said:

"And this Chipo here, listening to what's being said!  Watch out that you don't repeat what you heard, Chipo, because this is a very delicate matter!"

With a bound, the commander confronted the surprised Chipo to punish him.  His defenseless face, fearful, empty like Indian faces, was being threatened with death if he repeated half a word of what he had just heard, and it contracted in pain as if the skin became more alive with the first blow.

"I'll send you to the capital in chains, you damned Indian, and you won't get there alive, if I ever hear that you repeated half a word of what you heard here today!"

Kind went forward to intervene.  He had never seen a man hit in the face in a way which one would not even hit an animal; but George Maker Thompson's strong arm came between.

"You told me that you believed in a non-intervention policy!"

"But he's beating him!"

"And with good reason.  If we're going to intervene, it should always be on the side of the one doing the beating!"

A ship's whistle gathered its sound together in the distance.  The one-armed man did not say anything, but once on the white ship that had come to pick up mail, he told George of his decision to return to New Orleans.  His baggage was already on board, and when he said good-bye, raising his voice over the noise of the chain that was raising the anchor, he shouted in English: .

"We're the rubbish!  the rubbish!..."  He could no longer be heard, only his puppet hand could be seen.  "The rubbish of a country with such noble traditions!"

# CARLOS LUIS FALLAS

*Costa Rica*

## (1909-1966)

Carlos Luis Fallas was born on January 21, 1909, in a humble neighborhood of the Costa Rican city of Alajuela to a mother whose family farmed. When he was five years old his mother married a very poor shoemaker; this marriage produced six daughters. Fallas, in his own biographical notes, considered himself the product of a "proletariat environment".

He had five years of a primary education and two of secondary when he abandoned his studies to become an apprentice in a railway shop. At the age of sixteen he moved to the province of Limon on the Atlantic Coast, which he referred to as "a fiefdom of the United Fruit Company, the powerful North American trust that extends her banana empire in all the countries of the Caribbean."

In Puerto Limon, Fallas worked at many laborer's jobs, first as a stevedore on the docks. Later, he transferred to a plantation where he worked as a common field hand, an apprentice mason, a member of a demolition team, and a truck driver among many occupations.

Of these years, he comments, "There I was outraged by the foremen, attacked by fever, and molested in a hospital."

At 22, he returned to Alajuela to be with his mother when she died. His interest in revolutionary action grew with every negative experience. It was during this time that he enlisted in the newly-created workers' movement in Costa Rica.

He says of this period: "...to be able to live

and fight in the cities, I learned in three months the job of shoemaker (his stepfather's trade) which I kept for many years."

He participated in the organization of the first union in Alajuela and was a leader in the first strikes. His activities placed him in the midst of many bloody clashes with opponents and the police and he was no stranger to the inside of a jail.

"In 1933", he says, "...under the pretext of one of my speeches, the Court condemned me to one year of exile..."

This exile was spent in Limon, the scene of his youthful encounters with the exploitations of the United Fruit Company. It was hardly the place to be seen an activist because he quickly became involved in the Banana Strike of 1934 which mobilized 50,000 workers.

His efforts netted him a year's sentence in prison, where he declared a hunger strike. This rebellion and the subsequent notoriety gained his release. He credits "the people" with his freedom. In 1942, he was elected municipal councilman by his loyal "workers" and in 1944, he became a deputy to the National Congress. Explaining his actions, he says: "I had to improvise, make myself a military leader of the poorly-armed battalions of workers who shed their blood in the Civil War of Costa Rica in 1948. Defeated by imperialistic intrigues and under the brutal and bloody repression that our enemy unleashed, I went to prison."

This time he was very nearly executed by a firing squad and was saved by the influence of local protest and international workers' organizations.

Although he lacked training and his grammar was weak, he published "Mamita Yunai" in 1940. It was little known until other socialist and communist writers, particularly Pablo Neruda, introduced the work to an international audience. Not surprisingly, it was subsequently translated into Italian, Russian, Polish, German, Czechoslovakian, Romanian, Bulgarian, and Hungarian. Additionally, in its original Spanish it was published in 1949 in Chile and again in 1955 in Argentina.

Fallas has also written "Gente y Gentecilla" (1948), some short stories,; in addition, a book of children's adventure tales, "Marcos Ramirez" was published in 1952. The latter is published also in French, German, and Polish. In 1954, he wrote "Mi Madrina", followed by two short novels, published in Poland.

From

MAMITA YUNAI

These Indians almost cried, begging for a piece
of meat or firewater. Weren't they the descendants of
those belligerent ones? Weren't they the ones that,
with their bravery, made famous their region's name in
colonial times? Wasn't this the race that, with their
aggressiveness, held the honor of the Spanish Conqueror?

The greedy prospectors of the mysterious mines of
Tisingal, if they never found the fantastic emeralds
that they longed for, didn't they always stumble on
the sure spears and the deadly arrows of the courageous
Indian warriors? And the old annals of our history,
don't they always speak of the bloody uprisings of the
heroic people, the Talamancas? Wasn't it for this
reason the most prized dream of the strongest Spanish
governors was the conquest and pacification of the
Talamanca?

Threats were flattering but useless in subjugating
them; useless also was the mutilation of ears of hundreds of Indian prisoners in the old colonial metropolis.
They failed. Then, to tame the race, the skilled monks,
with their speeches and prayers and the courageous soldiers of Spain, with their swords, suits of armor and
muskets, also failed.

The taming and the enslaving of the Indian, the
destruction of a courageous race, was left for other
conquerors, one thousand times less courageous, but
infinitely more cruel and greedy and more skilled than
those Spaniards; it was left for the Yankee imperialistic conqueror, aided by servile creoles.

The gringos of the United did not bring muskets
nor armor. They did, instead, bring many checks and
many dollars to corrupt the greedy government and to
hire attacking dogs among the most outstanding children
of the country.

The quiet and placid valley of Talamanca collapsed
to the steps of the pack of hounds turned loose upon
them by the Yankees who did not arrive in pursuit of the
legendary Tisingal. No. They wanted land and slaves to
work it. The poor Indians could not contain the advance
of the "new civilization".

189

Impotent, they cried.  They saw being destroyed the ancient mountain where for many centuries the Heroic Race had sung its song of Freedom.

They burned their cities' walls, their fields were destroyed and the earth was turned over where the bones of the great warriors rested.  (Were they looking for fantastic emeralds?  No.  They were transforming the juice of the land into bananas and cocoa that were later on exchanged for good gold in foreign markets.)

The race was finally overcome and fled past the river and was left to hide its sorrow in the heart of the mountains.  And there, they were kept at bay and the conquerors managed to bring them back by coercion or with the lure of liquor.  The plantation needed slaves for their new fields!

The locomotive arrived and took millions and millions of fruits for the gringos.  Meanwhile, in the capitol of the republic the imbeciles applauded the "civilizing" work of the United.

In the city of Talamanca, firewater ran, and so in the same manner, blood and sweat.

But shortly, the field became too tired to give bananas and the cocoa no longer meant anything to the Yankees.  Therefore, they removed the rails, destroyed the bridges, and after spitting with disdain over the exhausted land, they left in triumph toward other lands to conquer.

They left ruining even the naive creoles, who believing they would be able to survive under the shade of the Yankees' boots, had planted their tents in that region.

Silence fell again in the valley of Talamanca; with the silence that death brings.  The gringos left and their followers, but the Indians did not return.  The humiliated Race, insulted and almost destroyed, remained crying in sorrow in the heart of the mountains.

But, if the Yankees of the plantation finally left, sated with gold and blood, the local authorities, on the other hand, did not withdraw.  There they stay forever, like a curse, ever watching carefully, the mountain, like voracious vultures ready to dine on the

190

carcasses of the defeated Race.

The bosses that paid the leaders against the
Indians with gold left; but the Indians, upon fleeing
to the mountain, had saved parts of their properties.
They still have cows, pigs and chickens and they get
some miserable fruits from working the poor land.
What a juicy boot for the buzzards! It is still possible to make a fortune in Talamanca.

...The Indians sighed for firearms that would
have facilitated the hunt, but there was no money.
He had only a few small animals. An assistant police
officer could dazzle the Indian with a "generous deal".
In exchange for a cow, two pigs and some chickens, the
Indian received a shotgun. A few days later the
police officer dropped in and confiscated the weapon
and took away the rest of the animals as payment for
the fine for "having firearms without a proper license".
Then, another deal with another Indian, and then another
attack, etc., etc.

...The Indians of Yorquin wanted to celebrate a
humble chichada by the light of the stars. (Remember-
ing, perhaps, the primitive rites of the race?) Poorly,
each Indian had put his fistful of coins for the chica
(a strong drink fermented from maize), hoping for the
designated date. But their permission from the authorities was not there. The representative from the police
gave the last word. Twenty-five dollars for the
authorization to celebrate the chichada! (The buzzards, trained by the United, in matters of money, only
accept dollars.)

If they did not have dollars, cattle, pigs, or
chickens would have been accepted in payment. With
resignation and also with sorrow, the Indians sent a
portion of their animals. The rest were taken away by
the Justice of the Peace, sent to keep order at the
party: the Indians had to pay five dollars each for
the bad night.

...The illiterate Indian of Talamanca, like any
dignified citizen of the republic, should have had his
I.D. card; a general order went out to present themselves before the authority, to fill out the proper
forms and to pay two dollars each for the operation.
It doesn't matter if they pay with pigs, or chickens;
the farm of the agent had room for everything.

Severe fines.  Exorbitant taxes.  Shameless attacks.

Little by little, the Indian lost everything until they reached what they are today:  eighty percent have absolutely nothing.  They scrape the mountain to obtain a fistful of coffee, one of corn, and some bananas. And then, breaking their backs under the weight of the load, like animals, they carry this produce to the ranch.

It must not cross the Indian's mind to see a little more for profit.  Women and children, loaded like mules, help in carrying the heavy loads up to the far away valley where the river is.  Then in his canoe, the Indian goes downstream, hour after hour, fighting the current, until he reaches the chasse.  There they take everything for a few pennies.  And what he buys, he pays like gold: sugar is gold-dust for the Indian and so is salt.  That is why he never tastes them.

Tired, oppressed, the poor Indian grabs the paddle and slowly climbs the river, goes to the mountain and returns to his miserable ranch to keep on feeding himself on corn and bananas until dying, destroyed by coughing, diarrhea, swamp fever, or snake bite.

To the only school of the region are sent, with very rare exception, the scum of the magistrates, professional bums, shameless satyrs or filthy perverts. And nothing is given, tools, medicine or medical assistance.

So lived and died the Indians, like filthy carrion, forgotten by God and by the country.  Only in election times do they recover for the government their condition of man and citizen when their votes are needed to elect the officials.  Then, the authorities and the politicians visit the Indian; they make a party.  They make the Indian drunk and they give him tobacco to make him sleepy and to fool him.  And for another thing, also, they leave in payment for his vote the torpor of alcohol in the soul, the bitter flavor of tobacco in the throat and his women pregnant.

# Luis Spota

*Mexico*

(1925-19    )


Luis Spota was born in Mexico City on July 13, 1925.  His early childhood was spent in an atmosphere of wealth and ease as he was the son of a Spanish duchess and a well-to-do Calabrian immigrant.  His family lost their money and position in 1934, a reversal that completely chanted Spota's life.  After considering an adventurous life as a sailor or a bull-fighter, he settled down as a novice journalist, channeling his daring imagination to writing.  By 1947 he had published two books of short stories and won a national literary prize.

Unlike many contemporary Mexican writers, Spota has achieved international acclaim.  His work excites controversy and is the subject of analysis and imita-tion among the young of Mexico and in leftist circles around the world.  His most successful novel, Almost Paradise,  has been considered a ctalyst for the publication of other Mexican literature.

He says of his own life and work, "Politically, I am inclined to the left and act accordingly.  My novels dealt in the beginning with social criticism. In the later ones, the subject of individual loneli-ness - in a society which becomes more dehumanized and alienated all the time - is my favorite."

Despite the negative influence of his journal-istic training, critics view Spota as a master story-teller.  He is a prolific writer, which results in some unevenness, but for the most part, his work is well received in international literary circles.  A number of his books are available in English, French, German, Danish, and Serbi-Croat.  More recent works, La Carcajada del Gato (The Cat's Outburst of Laughter)

193

and <u>Los Suenos del Insomnio</u> (The Dreams of Insomnia) have surrealistic flavor reminiscent of some of the French existentialist writers of post-war Europe and <u>Murieron a Mitad del Rio</u> (Dead in the Middle of the River).

From

## DEAD IN THE MIDDLE OF THE RIVER

"And if they ask, I don't have a passport."

"If you haven't killed anybody, or stolen anything, they won't bother you. Don't you realize it's a game?"

"What game?"

Then, at that moment, Walker started talking with the police officers, inserting his head into the car window.

"Look, we are wetbacks. People without documents. When I arrived, I was also afraid of the troopers. Now, I pretend they don't see me. We are wetbacks; we enter this country illegally across the river. We come here to work and that is what we are doing. They know it and they don't care."

"Then why are they here?"

"To see if we keep on working...Your arms and my arms and those of thousands like us", said Fortis, showing his fists. "produce money for Texas so that Texas can pay them so they can go well-dressed in good cares. If you and I were not here like everybody else, breaking our backs, the valley could not yield a tenth of its harvest. That's why the trooper becomes near-sighted. We are useful, do you understand? We are useful to them."

These words were similar to his thoughts - and also were what he had heard, vaguely, in Mexico, in Matamoros and on the border. And they had to be true because Benito had suffered more than a year and a half there.

He argued:

"Also, the Americans can work."

"Of course, but not like we do. They don't do it for a couple of dollars a day. They don't work for twelve or fifteen hours. They take it easy. They want doctors, medicine, clean housing, and good food."

\* \* \*

Leaving Falfurrias, a group of white men flagged
the bus down. It was about seven o'clock on a Sunday
evening. There were not more than six, but they were
drunk. They sat down. A Mexican passenger in the
company of his wife had his hat on; with a blow to the
head they threw his hat to the floor.

"Pig, uncover your head..."

He was a Mexican who knew better and the best
thing to do with a drunken gringo was to stay quiet.
He didn't say anything and he picked up his hat.

The one who hit him was one of the six who looked
like a rancher. And he was bothered by the non-reac-
tion of the Mexican. He grabbed him by the neck and
spit on his head.

"Greaser, son-of-a..."

Then, one of his friends said, "Hit him for being
a wise guy."

The Mexican let himself be hit because it was
evident that his wish was not to fight with anybody.
The woman at his side looked at everything with fright-
ened eyes. So they arrived at the next town. The bus
stopped near a policeman and the white men forced the
Mexican off the bus, spoke with the officer after turning the Mexican in and went back to the bus to happily
finish their trip. With a bottle that increased their
drunkenness, they commented on the incident. No one
present among the passengers said or did anything in
defense of the poor man or in protest.

\* \* \*

"Then their necks were in a noose", acknowledged
Macario, when Pavan finished telling how and when and
from where he had crossed the river.

The days passed one after the other releasing the
tension between Jose, Lupe, and Luis, and now they were
talking with young Farfan in a small group, drinking
coffee.

196

"Good luck on that side, because there, where it is easier is where they shelter the people!"

He meant that they were sheltered as beasts led to the slaughter are sheltered. He referred to a family of three who were murdered near the fire station in Donna.

A wetback, later identified as Matias Jimenez, returning to Mexico with his wife and a year-old son, born in a camp near Weslaco during the sixty weeks that Jimenez was saving a couple of dollars every Saturday. When he decided to return, he thought he was a rich man. With his one hundred and twenty dollars in his new pants' pocket he took the bus that left him in Donna. He arrived at midday. While he was strolling about, waiting for the night, a character approached him and asked him something. So they started to talk. The Texan found out that Jimenez was planning to cross the river during the night to return to Mexico.

"I fix it", suggested the Texan.

Matias, the sucker, agreed and took from his pocket ten dollars that the other man asked for to help him cross with a _pato_, clandestine canoe.

Jimenez was making the same mistake that most wetbacks do, who return to Mexico with money. That is to leave the U.S. in the same way as they entered, illegally, maybe to avoid the bureaucratic red tape that starts with the Mexican Consul when a worker asks voluntarily to be returned to his country. Although he is safe from theft and maybe from death, it is not as quick as the anxious and nostalgic wetback would like.

Matias Jimenez was not aware of the greed that spread on the face of the Texan when he saw the roll of money. At eleven o'clock that night he was there with his wife and son, waiting behind a bush, for his "friend" to appear. And the "friend" appeared half an hour later, but in the company of four others.

Before Jimenez could defend himself they stabbed him; he was mortally wounded. His wife didn't even try to scream. With her mouth shut, full of terror, everything was quick and silent. They tied up the wounded man and raped his wife in his presence, all four of them, one by one.

197

When the still-nursing child started to cry, the Texan, later apprehended, silenced him, smashing his head with his boot. Then they killed Matias and his wife. The bodies were found the following afternoon, thanks to the buzzards. That same night, in a bar in Donna, one of the murderers fell in a fight. He had dried blood on his shoes.

Macario found, between papers in his wallet, a newspaper clipping that Pavan read aloud:

"The murder of a Mexican family near Donna will be remembered for the excess of cruelty that was committed and as one of the worst crimes of this year. The criminals did it with shocking sadism..."

* * *

The gentleman only likes blondes. Not one Mexican works for him. Those who have their own boats he managed to get rid of. Only very few last. But for how long?

That afternoon they spoke about the dredger.

"There you can be hired", he said, "this boat is a dredger, and if you want, I take you there tomorrow."

The boat was slow and it took almost three hours to arrive. Some gringos, "dandies", as the boatmen called them, made the trip in a bad mood and quietly, away from the stern crowded with about twenty dark-skinned workers.

The foreman, without even looking at them, offered half a dollar daily plus food. They accepted.

"At least we have food and a place to snore", said Luis.

Saturday afternoon the boat arrived to take the gringos ashore and returned to take them back Mondays at daybreak. In one of those trips the boatman called Pavan to tell him that he knew someone who could give them a job.

"Who is he?"

"Chebo Espinoza. He has three fishing boats."

"When will you take us there?"

"Saturday, and if you get it, you wll give me five dollars for a tip."

Lupe and Luis agreed. It was a hard week. They worked as hard as ever, from six o'clock in the morning to seven in the evening with only one half hour to eat. "And what food!" Beans, potatoes, and some tasteless old meat. They didn't tell anybody they were planning to leave. They would have been reported.

Wednesday afternoon Luis Alvarez was trying to undo a know in a chain when the foreman passed by, a huge gringo, accustomed to violent jokes. Luis was bending over, an ideal position to receive a kick. The foreman roared a loud laugh and kicked Luis in the behind with his boot, violently projecting him to the floor. Luis crashed to his nose. Meanwhile, those who saw him roared in laughter like the foreman. Luis, burning with fury, grabbed the heavy monkey wrench that he had been using and threw himself against the meaty wall of the gringo, who was walking away, with his typical tobacco-chewing attitude.

Pavan jumped in front of Luis and managed to stop his armed hand.

"Don't be a fool, let it go!"

At the noise of the struggle, the foreman turned around, looked at them a second, spat his black saliva, and kept on walking, unconcerned.

Luis lowered his arms. He had a bloody nose.

That night, while looking at the still sea, one of the workers sat near them:

"It was good for you not to hit him", he said gently, without looking at Luis.

"Son-of-a-bitch..." said Luis. "He's despicable. He always likes to raise his hand, to anybody", he added, resentfully, pointing with his head toward Pavan.

"If it hadn't been for him I would have beat him up..."

"Or he would have done it to you", whispered Pavan, calmly.

And the other fellow agreed.

"It would have been worse. Not too long ago, a Mexican revenged himself of a kick received and punched him in the stomach. Do you know what happened? Something like this happened. He was drunk and the gringo sunk the tip of his boot in his rear end. But nothing immediately happened. The countryman swallowed his pride until the night when he looked for the foreman and tried to put a screwdriver in his stomach. He missed the first blow, and dropped the iron. Then he managed to hit him with his fist, but the gringo had the better of him. He beat him up, until he left him like a Christ.

"A Rucus ensued. Although the American was almost killing him, no one dared to interfere. 'It is not my problem anyway.' He was on the deck, full of blood, and unconscious. The gringo ordered a bucket of water and threw it on him to make him come back to his senses. He kept on beating him up. The face of the Mexican was bleeding like a raw hamburger. Seven or eight times he fainted, and so many times he regained consciousness with the help of the water. When the foreman got tired, he asked for a rope to tie him up, to the prow. There they undressed him and they tied him up with his shoulders against the boat, naked and still unconscious.

"And what happened then?"

"They kept him all night, all day, until the following day, when the gringo let him go." He paused for a moment, and before spitting in the sea, he sighed and said, "Now, do you see why it was good not to hit him?"

\* \* \*

Texas is a concentration camp...

The fat in the frying pan, now emptied of beans, started to sizzle.

"Isn't that true?"

He blew the fire between the stones. The bitter smoke stings their eyes.

"Two hundred thousand of you or more live here as if you were prisoners of the Nazis. Am I lying?"

They looked at him calmly and they had to recognize that he was saying the truth.

They pushed their hungry eyes to the stew that was almost ready while the man slowly stirred it in silence. Tasting it, he searched in his pockets until he found a small bag of salt.

"This is our democracy. Clean, pure, honest democracy. Texas style, of course."

They had lost, since their skirmish in the thicket, the can with white beans and any interest in talking; they only concentrated on the food.

"Not even enough to scare the appetite of four men."

The hazy smoke came out from the frying pan when he took it away from the fire and set it aside.

Without offering any thing, he started devouring, sticking the morsels into a small hole in his bread.

Pavan untied his shoes. His feet were swollen, enlarged with fatigue.

Sockless, he examined the man who was eating.

# ❧ 5 ❧

# Nemesis.  Dies  Irae

*To Reies López Tijerina*

The sixties opened with a generally positive
prognosis for the entire hemisphere.  With the election of John F. Kennedy to the U.S. presidency, there
was reason for optimism.  Kennedy, as Senator, had
shown a concern for Latin Americans and had promised
to bring an improvement in U.S.-Latin American attitudes.  Along with this policy change from the North,
the Latin nations also experienced a renewed economic
confidence in the years before 1960.  This was due
largely to the renewed interest of a fully-recovered
Europe in Latin American finances.  Japan also was
becoming influential in Latin American economic matters.  The U.S. was not popular in the South in 1960,
but there was hope for the future.

Kennedy coined the phrase "Alliance for Progress"
in his inaugural address.  This program was to contribute U.S. funds to Latin American economic growth
and social justice.  He also promoted more equitable
distribution of land and Latin political reform.  The
"Alliance" was met with overwhelming optimism, as
Kennedy's rousing welcomes in Mexico, Venezuela, and
Colombia showed.  When, in April 1961, Kennedy backed
an abortive Cuban invasion attempt at the Bay of Pigs,
Kennedy's prestige suffered only mildly.  Further, the
U.S.-Soviet confrontation over Cuban missile installations in 1962, saw virtually every Latin nation backing the U.S.

The "honeymoon" was over, however, all too soon.
By the end of 1962, American investments in Latin
America were way below expectations, and little real
progress was realized.  And with Kennedy's assassination, the Alliance as well as Latin attitudes towards
the North suffered a severe blow.  Popular sentiment
in much of Latin America turned away from the U.S.
towards Leftist political promises.  As a result of
more liberal populations, most Latin governments felt
forced into a more conservative stance.  In general,
the dichotomy between ruler and ruled became more
pronounced in the 1960s.  Urban guerillas emerged in
many nations, as terrorism became rampant throughout
Latin America.  The period between 1960 and 1980 also
saw the socialist takeover of several major nations,
and long-term civil wars in a handful of Latin countries.  A number of dictators were expelled or executed, and American prestige suffered greatly as the
U.S. seemed to support most strongly the most reactionary.[1]

The U.S. made strides to reactivate the Alliance
under President Johnson, and some improvements are
evident.  U.S. investment increased and political relations with most Latin nations were at least on an
even keel.  The Alliance for Progress had not brought
the goals that were originally projected, but between
1967 and 1969 there was at least no deterioration in
North-South relations.  In the latter year, President
Nixon sent Governor Nelson Rockefeller on an official
tour of Latin America.  Rockefeller's attitude toward
the area was similar to John Kennedy's, but the people
of the South saw Rockefeller as the representative of
the multi-national corporations.  The trip was met
with chaos in many nations.  The tour had to bypass
several nations due to violence and threats of violence.  Rockefeller's report was, nevertheless,
favorable toward Latin America, advising more investment in the South, additional loans, and social reforms.[2]  In the same year, officials from twenty Latin
nations met at Vina del Mar, Chile, to discuss U.S.
aid and loans, but also added that they wanted fewer
conditions with these monies.  This independent view
was, at least in part, the result of European and
Japanese involvement in Latin America.

In the 1970s, it became obvious that the U.S. was
less interested in Latin America.  Southeast Asia, the
Middle East, and Europe took a dominant position in
U.S. policy.  Under Nixon and his Secretary of State,

Henry Kissinger, a policy defined as the "New Dialogue" was instituted. This basically was a conciliatory policy toward Left and Right alike, and it even included a more friendly attitude toward Cuba. This "New Dialogue" might also be seen as placing Latin American matters on the "back burner", as other geographic areas became more important. Under Nixon and his successor, Gerald Ford, the U.S. even relaxed its grip on the Panama Canal, further evidence of the lessening importance of Latin America in U.S. foreign policy.

During the last four years of the decade, many important things occurred. A new administration headed by Jimmy Carter was resident in Washington, and his policy toward Latin America was "different". Carter claimed that the U.S. was concerned first and foremost with human rights, and that virtually all of the Latin nations had little regard for human rights. Thus, Carter refused military aid to many of these countries. This generally strained U.S.-Latin American relations, as most of the latter pointed out that the U.S. was not above reproach in the area of human rights. Carter's policies were generally inept, and the world diplomatic community held little respect for his administration. American support of dictators such as Somoza of Nicaragua diminished and a number were exiled or executed. Somoza fell victim to both. In a positive vein, the Panama Canal treaties which will totally transfer the canal to Panama by the year 2000 were ratified by both nations. Interestingly, public opinion in the South saw this seemingly benevolent act as a sign of growing U.S. weakness. As the decade ended, violence and Leftist attacks continued in Latin America, and U.S. policies were, at best, indecisive, being at least partially responsible for continuing violence in Central America and economic chaos in Argentina and Chile.

Central America was a key area in the history of U.S.-Latin American relations in the period between 1960 and 1980. The reasons for this significance were the transfer of the Panama Canal to Panama, the rise to power of guerillas in several countries, and the continuing U.S. support of dictators in the area. The sixties began in Panama with a violent wave of anti-Yankeeism. The populace overwhelmingly demanded a new treaty which would give the canal to the Panamanians. The new president, Marco Robles, elected in 1964, spent four years negotiating treaties with the U.S., but the people felt that he had "sold them out", and a liberal president, Dr. Arnulfo Arias, was elected in 1968. He was deposed by a military coup in less than two weeks. This was the beginning of a liberalization and stabilization in Panama, as the National Guard put General Omar Torrijos into power. Torrijos was a fearsome and single-minded opponent of corruption and champion of the canal of Panama "with no strings attached". Torrijos headed the "New Panama Movement", or NPM, which assumed control of all phases of government. From 1968 to 1970, the country faced many crises, and only American aid and invest-ments kept the economy from collapsing, but by 1971 Torrijos was firmly in control. He appointed a civilian president, Demetrio Lakas,[3] but the general was the real ruler. Torrijos wrote a letter to Senator Edward Kennedy, which explained that the real problem with the Alliance for Progress was that it gave aid to corrupt regimes. He turned more anti-American in 1971 as he expelled the Peace Corps, and in the following year, a new constitution contained provisions for keeping the U.S. out of Panamanian politics and finances. Torrijos announced that he would stay in power until the treaty transferring the canal to Panama was signed and he became more anti-American, as relations between Cuba and Panama im-proved, and a possible plot to kill Torrijos was un-covered and linked to the U.S. Many U.S. companies were nationalized, and many businessmen were exiled, but the result was a decline in the Panamanian economy which has been difficult to turn around. Relations became increasingly strained until September, 1977, when the treaties were signed. The treaties called for the U.S. to give up the canal at noon, December 31, 1999. Panama would assume administrative control ten years earlier. In addition, huge payments were to be made to Panama, and the U.S. was allowed to intervene only to ensure the canal's neutrality.[4]

In Panama, one sees a microcosm of the general situation in Latin America. The Panamanians felt subjugated by the "Colossus to the North" throughout this century, U.S. companies were evident in the country, and all of Panama's ills were blamed on the U.S. The hope which the Kennedy ascendence brought to Panama quickly dissipated and by 1968 the country grew violently anti-Yankee. This growth continued even after 1977, as Panama grew closer to the Soviet Union, and by 1980, Leftist groups were powerful and prominent throughout the nation. As we shall see, in the late 1970s, Panama supported revolutionaries in Nicaragua and El Salvador. One might observe that where the United States sought its own self-interest in Panama, that it ultimately had to pay the price, as the Canal was lost, and as an important ally became less than friendly.

Nicaragua seemed much different from Panama in the 1960s. The Somoza family continued to rule, with strong support from the U.S. There was little visible opposition, and general peace and prosperity. Even into the 1970s, there was little change, other than that brought by the terrible earthquake in late 1972. By 1974, opposition to Somoza grew, especially among students, and Somoza was forced to take action against his opponents. Cuba trained Nicaraguan Leftists and supplied them after they returned home, and by 1975 a united revolutionary group, the Sandinist National Liberation Front began to bring violence to the nation.[5] Their terrorist attacks killed many people, and hostages were kidnapped in order to obtain freedom for jailed Leftists. Many political figures were assassinated, and the Sandinistas also stirred up much of the populace against Somoza and the U.S. Also in 1975, the U.S. sent enormous amounts of aid to help rebuild Managua which was largely destroyed by the earthquake. The Sandinistas finally achieved what they wanted as Somoza fled to the U.S. in 1979, and in 1980, he was assassinated. This did nothing to improve conditions, however, as Nicaragua was plagued by economic and political problems. Various coalitions of Leftists and Moderates ruled the country, and tried to effect land reforms, but in reality, the peace and relative prosperity of the previous three decades had been lost by 1979. In one more case, the long-term policy of the U.S. was overturned by internal left-wing forces, and in one more case, the U.S. lost a long-term ally and U.S. business lost a profitable segment of its financial interests.

The United States has attempted, since 1960, to have normal relations with El Salvador, but this too often overlooked nation has caused little but trouble for the U.S. The most stable period of recent Salvadorean history was during the mid-1960s, as a new constitution led to the peaceful election of Julio Adalberto Rivera, and he in turn initiated some moderate reforms in political, social, and economic areas. Left-wing guerillas became an important force by 1968, and in that year they killed the U.S. ambassador to

Guatemala and announced an allegiance to Castro's Marxism. The next year, a soccer game between El Salvador and Honduras was won by the former, and as a result, a violent conflict broke out which led to full-scale war and the death of over 2000. A truce was declared with O.A.S. and American help, but skirmishes continued for some years. By the 1970s urban guerillas were a major problem and President Arturo Armando Molina became extremely reactionary after a Communist plot was uncovered, and as a result of much trouble with the university. Violence continued within the nation, and as Leftists were ignored, their demands grew. During the mid-1970s, the Salvadorean government appeared to grow closer to the U.S. and also more corrupt. As such, anti-American feelings ran high, and even the Church began to turn against the regime. This situation worsened when the Carter administration exposed the new presidency of Carlos Humberto Romero as being incosiderate of human rights. By 1978, strikes and peasant uprisings, organized in part by the Church, swept the country. Virtually, everyone was arming themselves and choosing sides for what promised to be a horrible civil war. Perhaps trying to avoid another Cuba or Nicaragua, the U.S. began to send extensive military aid to the Romero regime. The all-out war came in 1979 as Romero was ousted and Left and Right went on the offensive. Within the next year and a half, 16,000 were killed, and as the year 1980 ended, it appeared that the successors of Romero, the U.S. supported Junta, would be victorious. In early 1981, $35 million in U.S. arms were sent to the government of El Salvador, and U.S. involvement in Central America was obviously continuing into the 1980s.[6]

Due perhaps to the poverty of the nation, Honduras has never been of great concern to the U.S., but in the 1960s, Honduras became an area of turmoil. Agrarian reform was begun in the mid-decade, but problems arose, especially concerning the 300,000 Salvadoreans living on Honduran lands. This was one of the causes of the so-called "Soccer War". By 1970, more U.S. money was flowing into Honduras, as were five F86K fighter planes, which the Hondurans had purchased despite the fact that they had neither pilots nor maintenance personnel. In 1972, a promising joint program with the U.S. was to reform the Honduran educational system, which it needed very badly. But students and teachers in Honduras rioted, and the American advisors were kicked out. By the mid-1970s, President Osvaldo Lopez was growing increasingly liberal, as he nationalized many companies and undertook reform. Lopez was ousted in 1975 after being accused of corruption by the <u>Wall Street Journal</u>. His successor, Colonel Juan Alberto Melgar, returned to a conservative program of government as he reversed land reforms and welcomed foreign corporations. But by 1977, Melgar had moderated and was less than a friend of the U.S., as he supported Panama in the canal dispute, and purchased fighters from Israel over U.S. objections. Melgar was ousted in favor of Policarpo Paz Garcia in 1978, and surprisingly his moderate policies seemed to be bringing excellent advances in the late 1970s.

In Guatemala and Costa Rica, there was relative peace in the 1950s, but in the next decades things changed. Guatemala allowed the CIA-backed Bay of Pigs invaders to train in its country, and even through the 1970s the U.S. businesses were encouraged to expand in Guatemala. Also, regarding internal politics, several presidents were elected peacefully with popular support, and they enacted social reform, but just as in the rest of Central America, left-wing extremists came on the scene in the 1960s and bloodshed and violence ensued. In fact, a state of siege had to be declared on numerous occasions, and a right-wing countermovement grew in the 1970s. Relations between the U.S. and Guatemala remained fairly good throughout this period, and American aid was very helpful in restoration and reconstruction after volcano and earthquake damage which left one million homeless. The Carter administration attacked Guatemala over human rights and even refused to sell fighters for defense purposes. Guatemala was also unique in that it turned to Venezuela for aid when the U.S. refused. Guatemala is poor and the U.S. has been less interested in this area in recent years.

Costa Rica was stable in the 1960s, and relations with the U.S. were good as oil refineries were constructed by an American company; but by the 1970s the new president Jose Figueres Ferrer, was a free spirit who was rumored to be pro-Soviet. Figueres travelled in U.S. and Puerto Rico without permission from the U.S., and began to face internal threats from both Left and Right. U.S. relations also became strained over the fugitive financier Robert Vesco who lived in Costa Rica. Vesco was finally asked to leave in 1977, but the damage was done. The later 1970s saw the outbreak of strikes and leftist violence; unique for Costa Rica. By 1978,

there were relations with Cuba, social reforms were
moving forward, and Japanese and other non-U.S. investment was helping the economy. Costa Rica was not a
strong ally of the U.S., but it was making progress.

In general, Central America was withdrawn from the
U.S. sphere in this period. Although still friendly
with one or two nations, most turned to other allies
and aid. And by 1980, at least three Central American
countries were in the hands of left-wing regimes. Nationalization certainly hurt American business, and
Carter's policies drove several countries from the U.S.
sphere of influence. As stated earlier, by the 1970s,
the U.S. appeared to be most interested in avoiding
severe problems in Latin America. From this view,
both El Salvador and Nicaragua represented a real
thorn in the side of U.S. policy, and Carter's policies
seemed less than efficient.

The Caribbean area had been dominated by concerns
with Cuba since the late 1950s and this period is no
different. Conditions in the Dominican Republic, however, led to U.S. military intervention in 1965, and
so this is certainly significant. In 1961, the
Dominican strongman, Trujillo, was assassinated, and
the president, Balaguer, became the real power. But
trouble followed, as the Trujillo family attempted to
take over. This led to a military coup and to the
flight of the Trujillos. With American aid and support, free elections were held in 1962 and Juan Bosch
was elected, but he was overthrown by the military,
and by 1964 chaos reigned. In 1965, President Lyndon
Johnson sent troops into the Dominican Republic,
ostensibly to protect U.S. citizens, but actually to
prevent a Leftist takeover.[7] The U.S. sought to
legitimize its actions by pressuring the O.A.S. to
send troops also, and they did. A provisional president, Hector Garcia Godoy, was appointed until elections could be held in 1966. Balaguer was re-elected,
stability was reinstituted, and U.S. troops withdrew,
but Left-wing revolutionaries continued to plague the
government, and throughout the 1970s problems continued. Balaguer's regime made progress in many areas,
but it was repressive and hurt by 50% unemployment and
double-digit inflation. By 1975, ten years after the
U.S. invasion, U.S.-Dominican relations were good, but,
in the same year, a guerilla force from Cuba invaded.
Balaguer's regime put down the invasion and became
more repressive. In the 1978 elections, Balaguer was
defeated by Silvestre Antonio Guzman Fernandez, who

promised more liberal reforms.

General repression with tacit U.S. approval was also the situation in Haiti. Duvalier was the dictator, and he appealed to the U.S. for support by claiming that the Communists were trying to take over the country. By 1969, the O.A.S. placed sanctions on Haiti for its human rights violations. In 1971, "Papa Doc" Duvalier died and his son Jean-Claude "Baby Doc" succeeded. He brought some real reforms, and helped the economy by promoting exports and tourism, but by the late 1970s, Haiti was still one of the most backward and repressed areas of Latin America.

Puerto Rico continued to be an enigma during this period. The highly visible and publicized Independence Party (FALN) continued to stir up trouble both on the island and on the mainland. But an honest plebiscite in 1962 showed 425,000 for the commonwealth, 273,000 for statehood, and 4,000 (or one-half of one percent) for independence. Elected governor in 1968 was the pro-statehood candidate Luis A. Ferre, and some advances were made, but by 1970 the economy was still in bad shape. The two most significant matters in U.S.-Puerto Rican relations came to the fore in 1970. First, the government objected to the use of the Puerto Rican island of Bulebra by the U.S. Navy, and the U.S. refused to stop. This led to many demonstrations in Puerto Rico and in Washington and finally the U.S. government agreed to phase out the use of Culebra, which was finally completed in 1975. The second matter was that of independence. Cuba and Russia began to attach the U.S. "subjugation" of Puerto Rico in the United Nations. Castro claimed that Puerto Rico should be classed as a "colony" of the U.S. This measure was emotionally presented every session until 1978 when it finally passed. But by 1978, the government and population of Puerto Rico did not want independence any more than in 1967. The measures of the U.N. were meant to embarrass the U.S. by labelling America a "colonial" power, but this meant little, for even in the election of 1978, Puerto Ricans voted overwhelmingly for the candidates supporting statehood and commonwealth status.

In South America, the course of history followed a course similar to that of the Central American and Caribbean areas. In general, the Leftists became a dominant force, and in most countries this made the existing regimes more repressive. Urban guerillas became a real problem, and inflation swept the continent in the 1970s. We shall briefly survey the Continent, ending with Chile, where Left-wing ideas almost came to their ultimate fruition.

Colombia began the 1960s with a positive outlook, for President Camergo united many opposing parties and brought significant reforms. But his successors were not as successful, for rival parties again fragmented the political system. By 1970, the former dictator Rojas Pinilla was defeated by a small margin by Misael Pastrana Borrero. This election showed that the populace was tired of Leftist threats and that they desired a strong president. As Right-wing forces were strengthened, Leftists also united, often with the help of the Catholic Church. A Church-student-radical union, such as also occurred in El Salvador, led to increased guerilla activity and to strikes. In 1971 alone, seventy-four people were killed by Leftist attacks. President Alfonso Lopez, elected in 1974, was a liberal, and was able to check most guerilla activity, but he was unable to check the inflation which was running over 30% per year. Lopez recognized Leftist governments in Cuba and Chile, and he instituted sweeping reforms, but guerilla activity again flared up in 1976 with the Soviet-backed urban "M-19" guerillas. By 1978 and 1979, the liberals were still in power, but they were still in power, but they were faced with terrible conditions: revolutionaries and guerillas throughout the country, runaway infla-tion, strikes, etc. Added to these problems were the demands from the U.S. that drug traffic from Colombia be controlled and that human rights be preserved. As we shall see, in most of the nations where liberal or socialist parties came to power in this period, the political and economic problems actually multiplied.

In Venezuela, this era was a time of growing prosperity, relative liberalism, and an independent policy regarding the U.S. President Betancourt and his successor Raul Leoni encouraged foreign investment, but also nationalized oil and natural gas industries. In the 1960s guerilla warfare was a problem, and may have been stirred up by Cuba. But by 1974, a liberal coalition was in power, headed by Carlos Andres Perez. He had promised more expropriation of foreign companies and distribution of land and wealth to the poor. This was carried out, and Venezuela became a leader of the "Third World" due to her wealth from oil. There were renewed relations with countries such as Cuba, China,

and Venezuela supported Panama in its conflict with
the U.S. over the Canal.  Despite these liberal acts,
internal guerillas continued to be a problem, and at
one point in 1976 held an entire American company,
Owens-Illinois, ransom by kidnapping the vice president.  The Venezuelan government refused to allow the
company to submit to the rebels, and when they did,
the company was nationalized as punishment.  By 1979,
Venezuela was a champion of liberalism in underdeveloped nations and helped rebels in Nicaragua and elsewhere.  Relations with the U.S. were not the most
friendly, especially over economic matters.  There was,
however, relative peace and prosperity.

Peru and Ecuador were similar in some ways in
this period.  Both were hurt by chaos and finally
ruled by a junta in the 1960s, both turned to Eastern
Europe as a trade partner, and both had difficult relations with the U.S.  Both nations seized American
fishing boats within their claimed territorial waters.
By 1970, both had expropriated U.S. companies and each
country, popular opinion was anti-Yankee.  Peru underwent a "populist" reform and a socialist orientation,
but there was a concerted effort to avoid Castro's
errors.  Russia became a strong ally, and by 1974
Peru had the most Leftist government in South America.
Economic decline and high inflation led to a shift in
1976, especially with the encouragement given to U.S.
investment.  Some industries which had been socialized
were returned to private ownership, and despite Leftist
opposition the shift to the Right continued with good
economic results.

In Ecuador, President Jose Maria Velasco Ibarra
declared himself dictator in 1970, and then studied
the Peruvian liberal system with the idea of imposing
a similar system in Ecuador.  As a result, Velasco
redistributed land and nationalized industries and the
economy declined as U.S. investments declined.  A coup
placed General Guillermo Rodriguez Lara in power, and
he continued the anti-U.S. nationalist policy.  Inflation ran rampant to a rate of over 80% in 1974.  By
1977, a junta ruled and there was a return to private
enterprise and more friendly relations with the U.S.
Foreign companies were invited in, and, by the end of
the decade, economic conditions had improved, and
relations with the U.S. had greatly improved.

The 1960s in Bolivia were a time of troubles.
Strongmen ruled guerillas attacked.  U.S. aid was

substantial, and in 1967 the revolutionary, Che
Guevara, was killed in Bolivia as he led rebels
against the government. The next decade saw many
regimes and coups, as Left and Right jockeyed for
position. Some reform was carried out, and at times
Bolivia was ruled by a Communist-Socialist coalition.
But by the mid-1970s, Rightists were in power.
Soviets were expelled, and the economy was in terrible shape. Finally in the late 1970s, the pendulum
came to rest in the middle, as President Hugo Banzer
Suarez, moderated his ultra-right position, and dealt
with Russia and the Leftists. Reforms were carried
out, and the economy began to turn around. A coup in
1978 overthrew Banzer and as the decade ended, Bolivian
politics were unstable.

Paraguay continued to have problems after 1960 as
Stroessner continued to rule. Argentina was unfriendly
and served as a base for anti-Stroessner exiles, and
the Church, especially the Jesuits, allied with the
Leftists and the peasants. By 1970, some real reforms
had been made, and economic progress was realized with
Brazilian and American aid. Paraguay's problems lessened in the late 1970s, but politically, there was
instability. Stroessner's death or overthrow could
mean chaos in Paraguay. A similar chaos was seen in
Uruguay in the 1960s when the National Council was put
aside in favor of General Oscar Daniel Gestido. The
Tupamaros continued to cause problems as they killed
an American official, Daniel A. Mitrione, in 1970. But
this also served to lessen guerilla activity, for the
Tupamaros lost their popular appeal. In 1973, the
army staged a coup, and conditions improved, especially
in the control of political violence. As the economy
improved, the central government became more conservative, more repressive, and many Leftist leaders fled
into exile. Uruguay was one of the countries criticized by the Carter administration, and Uruguay refused U.S. aid completely. By 1980, relations with
the U.S. were still strained.

Partisan politics continued to be the main feature of Argentina in the 1960s. Three presidents between 1962 and 1963 could do little to help the economy
or the political system. A coup by the military put
General Juan Carlos Ongania in power in 1966; he had
good ideas for improving the situation, but little
positive was done. General strikes and Leftist violence led to a declaration of martial law in 1969, and
by the 1970s it appeared that a revival of the

Peronists could unite the factions. Alejandro Lanusse
headed a junta in 1971 which promoted a sort of mystical Peronist union.  Peron was allowed to return in
1972, but he refused to run for president.  In 1973,
with violence and turmoil at a peak, Peron ran for
president with his wife "Isabelita" running for vice
president, and they won.  Violence lessened as the
various Peronist and liberal parties united.  Cuba was
recognized, and the Peron regime turned away from U.S.
aid and monies.  Peron, however, was dead within a
year, and despite attempts to promote "Isabelita" as
the new "Evita", chaos followed.  Inflation ran over
100% per year and hundreds of deaths were reported.
Even in the late 1970s things were only mildly improved as President Jorge Rafael Videla continued in
power.  Leftist guerillas, the Monteneros, carried
out numerous assassinations, but many, many violent
groups were checked by an increasingly repressive
policy.  The economy continued to be a severe problem
as inflation exceeded 1100% for six traight years.
Labor unrest and strikes did nothing to help the situation, and U.S. relations were strained by Carter's
accusations of human rights violations.  As the decade
ended the most promising area was the economy as over
370 companies were denationalized, and private and
foreign investment increased greatly.

    Most Latin nations experimented with various
types of governments in the period from 1960 to 1980.
No one type seems to have truly worked, for violence
could emerge from Right or Left, but in general,
Leftist experiments failed, the exceptions being Cuba,
and possibly Nicaragua.  In three cases, U.S. relations were almost the whole story of the nation during this period.  These three were Chile, Cuba, and
Mexico.  Interestingly, one each from South America,
the Caribbean, and Middle America.  And, from the
history and culture of each has come an important
literary voice, each of which points, in its own way,
to the future of the hemisphere, and what America can
learn from its past actions.

    In Chile, the election of 1964 features a moderate
reform candidate, Eduardo Frei, and a radical candidate,
Salvador Allende.  The former won, and his six year
term was marked by some progress.  Agrarian reforms
were carried out, and many companies were nationalized.
But financial problems led to Leftist violence by the
1970 elections, and Allende got the most votes.  He
was proclaimed president, making him the "first ever"

freely-elected Marxist-Neninist ruler anywhere.  He
was violently anti-Yankee, and in his first year of
rule he nationalized most American companies.  Allende
then undertook an ill-advised socialist program.  He
took lands from the wealthy and gave them to the poor.
He raised wages 40% across the board and froze prices.
He recognized all Communist countries and began trade
with them.  By 1971, foreign investment was nonexist-
ent, industrial production had plummeted, and economic
conditions were worse than ever.  The middle class was
becoming restless, and they called a general strike in
1972.  Allende blamed the situation on the U.S., but
the populace rapidly turned on him, and Allende was
overthrown in 1973 by a military coalition.  There's
no doubt that U.S. aid had helped engineer the coup,[8]
which led renowned Chilean author Fernando Alegria to
write:

> If tradesman consider what was lost
> with Allende and decide to brutally
> recoup; if industrialists want the
> gringos to return - the good gringos,
> then - and credit to be opened and
> start negotiation; if professionals
> ask for the heads of the Marxists and
> that the bums be cleaned out and
> stopped from screwing.  Abundancy of
> the middle class alien here, partic-
> ularly in the first groups.  Then,
> check the presence of another dif-
> ficult sector, difficult to define,
> but not to recognize: upper class,
> foreign education, clean and hard
> ideology, tactic of immediate action
> that constitutes the civilian manage-
> ment behind, not under, and sometimes
> in front of the armada of the dicta-
> torial offensive.  Its terrorism,
> complex and efficient, is of a
> sophisticated nature.  First and
> foremost, the CIA.  But at the very
> end when the chips are down, they
> have to disdain equally the Brazilian
> and the Yankee; one for racial motives
> and the other for class reasons, the
> North American can never be elegant,
> no matter what; he might be powerful
> and wise, but never polished.[9]

216

Tens of thousands were arrested by the new administration of General Augusto Pinochet Ugarte, and thousands were killed. Allende was found dead in his palace. Industry was denationalized and the middle class was strengthened. Relations with the U.S. improved, but other trade and aid sources were established. The economy began to show signs of recovery, and by 1978 some of the repressive measures were relaxed. As the decade ended, relations with the U.S. were strained, for the Carter presidency had placed too many conditions on aid. Moreover, an Allende official, Orlando Letelier, and several others were killed in Washington in 1976 with aid from Chileans. Chile cooperated little and slowly, and the U.S. withdrew its ambassador. Chile under Pinochet had become too reactionary as shown not only by problems with the U.S., but also by poor relations with Argentina and Bolivia.

One of Allende's chief allies, and the seat of most Latin revolutionary activity was Castro's Cuba. Fidel Castro announced that Cuba was a socialist state on May 1, 1961. Land was collectivized, and a Communist Party was established. By the mid-1960s, Castro was training and financing revolutionaries throughout Latin America, and his aid, Che Guevara, was in Bolivia training guerillas. Politically, Castro faced several crises, most importantly the Bay of Pigs invasion, in which a CIA-backed operation attempted to invade the island and overthrow Castro, and the Cuban missile crisis, in which the Kennedy administration effectively kept Soviet missiles out of Cuba with a blockade. Castro's Cuba was a failure in its first decade. By 1969, the economy had declined, illiteracy had risen, and crime and juvenile delinquency were very high. Only Mexico and Jamaica of the Latin American nations recognized Cuba. Russia had helped a great deal with trade agreements and aid, but many Cubans were disenchanted with socialism and Castro. In fact, many thousands left the island until Castro cut off the flight in 1971. The U.S. relazed its anti-Castro policies in the early 1970s, and Castro desocialized his economic policies to some extent. Free elections were allowed, and some private enterprise was encouraged. In 1976 and 1977, Cuba became involved in Angola, and Castro vowed that he would back revolutionary activity anywhere in the world. The greatest strides which Cuba made in these years seemed to be due to their athletic programs, while Cuban troops in Africa led to opposition by most countries, even

217

Communist countries such as Yugoslavia.  By 1978 and
1979, Castro said that he had done all that he could
to normalize relations with the U.S.  But as seen in
his introduction to The Diary of Che Guevara, Castro
will always be determined to support the "Revolution";
and this type of philosophy on America's border will
never allow for truly normal relations.  Castro has
also voiced, many times, his feelings that the CIA has
tried to kill him, to invade his country, and has even
blown up Cuban airliners.  Given this feeling, Castro
is unlikely to ever be friendly toward the U.S.[10]

Only one ally of both Allende and Castro remains
to be discussed - Mexico.  As already analyzed, Mexico
has perhaps been the Latin nation most poorly treated
by the U.S.  The Guadalupe-Hidalgo Treaty of the mid-
19th century took much of Mexico, which is today the
American Southwest.  And as we shall see, Mexico is
still unhappy about these events.  The "revolution"
which began in the early part of this century, continued into the 1960s and lands were redistributed, the
government became more involved in industry and social
programs were extended.  A great event for Mexico was
the 1968 Olympics held in Mexico City.  This boosted
the economy, but led to a decline after the Olympiad.
The new president in 1970, Luis Echevarria, was a
liberal reformer, but he faced opposition from both
Left and Right.  He was forced to a more conservative
stand when a Soviet plot to overthrow the government
was uncovered in 1971.  He did, however, carry out
some reforms including the redistribution of land.  He
was no friend of the U.S. and considered himself a
champion of the "Third World" countries; as such he
travelled throughout the world to seek trade agreements with other underdeveloped nations.  He also
recognized the Allende government and attacked U.S.
policies on many occasions, including at a session of
the U.S. Congress.  By the mid-1970s, the oil industry was booming, tourism was on the rise, but terrorism was also increasing drastically.  The new president, Jose Lopez Portillo (1976-1982), moved in to
this situation, and he was more pro-U.S. and less
"Third World" oriented.  His problems continued as
Left and Right were violent in their protests.  The
U.S. began to make demands on Mexico - that drug
traffic be checked, that illegal immigrants be stopped,
and that Mexican oil be made available.  Relations grew
cool, until 1979 Lopez Portillo was maintaining a
neutral position with regard to the U.S.  A Mexican
oil spill in the Gulf of Mexico also strained relations

218

as the decade came to a close.

Perhaps one of the most deep-seated problems regarding Mexico is something that has been little discussed, and that is the treatment which the original Indo-Hispanic peoples have received at the hands of the U.S. The U.S. agreed in the 1950s to recognize Spanish and Mexican land grants in those lands lost by Mexico, but by 1900 the terms of the treaty had been forgotten (see chapter 1). U.S. citizens of Mexican ancestry in the American Southwest have been ruthlessly robbed of their land. And especially to Indo-Hispanic peoples, this family land is extremely important. The plight of these dispossessed peoples has been dealt with in several books, but never with more passion than in the writings of Reies Lopez Tijerina. In several articles and in his very convincing biographical book, "My Struggle for the Land, Tijerina explains how Washington has unfairly treated these Indo-Hispanic people. He has travelled in Spain studying archives of Seville, learning the old Spanish writings, and talking to the press. He also spent much time furthering his cause before the Spanish Parliament and King Juan Carlos I to have Mexican lands restored to their rightful owners.[11]

Tijerina began his struggle in the 1950s, as he realized that over 100,000,000 acres of land had been taken from the rightful owners with the approval of the U.S. government. Despite the fact that the U.S. Constitution supported the terms of the Guadalupe-Hidalgo Treaty,[12] after 110 years, the Mexican-Americans still did not have their lands. Tijerina wrote to Eisenhower and Johnson to solve the problem peacefully. He was treated coldly and received no acceptable explanation, so that in 1967 he occupied the courthouse of Tierra Amarilla in order to publicize his cause. Tijerina did two things which he hoped would help his cause. He formed a society which vowed to live as the Mexicans had when they owned the land, and he documented his case, which claimed that Mexican and Spanish land grants could be used to restore lands to their rightful owners. He traced the ownership documents to the "Laws of the Indies" of the 16th and 17th centuries.[13] He also proved that the town of San Joaquin de Canon de Chama was given to the citizens by a grant of King Charles IV of Spain in 1806. Despite this sound evidence, however, Tijerina was pretty much ignored. But with a spirit which borders on the mystical, he continues to fight - a fight which he feels is representative of the conflict between Indo-Hispanic races and the Anglo imperialistic race - that is, the U.S. government.[14]

One sees in Tijerina, as in Castro, and Allende, and Trujillo, and the Sandinistas, that the actions of the U.S. in 1840, and 1850, and 1898, and 1910, and 1914, cannot be forgotten. The history of the American domination of the Latin peoples cannot be forgotten. The U.S. has lost the Canal, and Cuba, and many of its industrial holdings. It is threatened today with the loss of many allies, and Tijerina has even brought the threat within the boundaries of the U.S., as he continues to fight for the restoration of lands to the Latin peoples of the Southwest. The U.S. is paying for its role as Colossus, and it will perhaps always be paying for the Latin American resentment and fear of the U.S. continues to this day. As the excepts in this entire book have shown, the Latin peoples will never forget the wrongs that they have perceived, and anti-Yankeeism has become a part of their national literature.

In the cultural realm, one sees no pronounced movement or school. In literature, as in music and the visual arts, there were many renowned individuals, and they must be viewed as just that - individuals. Jorge Luis Borges, Carlos Fuentes, and Julio Cortazar continued to flourish in the period from 1960 to 1980. All three of these men are best known for their surrealist fiction and have been discussed in the last chapter. Also of importance during this period were a number of writers not previously discussed. From Mexico, Octavio Paz has distinguished himself with books of poetry and essays, and Rosario Castellano has produced many works in a modern style based upon Mexican regionalism. A somewhat similar style was also seen in Julio Cartazar of Argentina, but unlike Castellano, he turned in the 1960s to what is called "magical realism". Vargas Llosa of Peru and Roa Bastos of Paraguay also produced fiction in a modern style. The one author of many who varied from the modernist fictional trend was Garcia Marques of Colombia, who is best known for his violent literary attacks upon the Colombian dictatorship. This literature of protest also emerged from the pen of the Chilean writer Fernando Alegria, whose Chilean Spring presents an excellent view of the fall of the Allende government.

It is important to note that the most important Latin authors of this period did not produce a literature of protest against North America. In fact, the "Modern", or "Surrealist" styles do not lend themselves to political or social matters. Even Alegria, who is a well-known literary figure, shows little blatent anti-Yankeeism. But this does not mean that no one was writing anti-American works in this period. One has only to look at the Diary of Che Guevara. This work by the Cuban revolutionary has become a world-wide best-seller, and the introduction to this violently anti-American work has been written by another man whose politics far outdistance his literary talents; Fidel Castro. In Castro and Guevara, as well as Arevalo, the attacks upon the U.S. are obvious, but in writers such as the first two, we are not dealing with great literary talent. We see that once again in the 1960s and 1970s, as in the period to 1890, that the great literary figures have generally abandoned political and social matters for the obscure topics of surrealism and for literature for its own sake.

As the last two decades of the 20th century approach, anti-Yankee writings appear with a strong dose of Communism, or with Messianic imagery, and they do not come from the pens of great writers. The two most important figures are Castro and Tijerina. As already discussed, Castro came to power as a popular leader, and he turned to a Marxist-Leninist orientation. As such, his view of America is strongly influenced by these political philosophies. Tijerina is also a man of the people, for he represents the depressed and dispossessed Indo-Hispanic of the U.S. Southwest. His words lack eloquence and the stule of a Neruda or an Alegria, but his meaning is clear. He is interested in reviving a culture which has been lost, and he is demanding that the U.S. live up to its promises of 100 years ago. The following sections deal with the contemporary words of these two champions of the people.

# FIDEL CASTRO

*Cuba*

(1927-19   )


Fidel Castro was born in Oriente province on August 13, 1927. He was educated in Santiago and Havana and received his law degree from the University of Havana in 1950.

He was active in student agitation and in political ventures, both national and international. On July 26, 1953, intending to overthrow the regime of Fulgencio Batista, he led an unsuccessful attack on a Santiago army barracks. In 1955, Castro was freed by amnesty, and he went to Mexico and organized a force of 82 Cuban exiles, who invaded Cuba on December 2, 1956. This attack was also unsuccessful, resulting in the death or capture of most of the invading force.

In the Sierra Maestra mountains, Castro began a guerilla campaign against Batista, who fled on January 1, 1959. Castro became Cuba's prime minister in February of 1959. He chose Manuel Urrutia as president, but in mid-1959, Castro forced Urrutia out and replaced him with Osvaldo Dorticos.

Castro undertook dramatic and extreme programs of social and economic reform, executing followers of Batista and undertaking a tremendous hatred of foreigners, particularly against the U.S. As his relations with the U.S. cooled, relations with Russia improved.

Castro, in the beginning, had the support of Latin America and Cuba. However, when, in 1961, Castro announced his Leninist leanings, and declared there would be no more elections in Cuba, Latin American nations were less warm toward him.

In 1963, Castro visited Russia and was received with acclaim. In 1965, Castro signed trade pacts with Russia and Red China, but as Castro supported Latin American revolutionaries, even Cuba's Russian relations deteriorated. The O.A.S., in 1954, condemned him for aggression against Venezuela. In 1965, the Communist Party of Cuba was created.

Cuban relations with Communist China deteriorated in 1966, with Castro attacking Chinese officials and policies, whereupon China reduced trade with Cuba.

Five Cubans were arrested and sentenced to extensive prison terms for plotting against Castro's life, in what was alleged to be an American C.I.A. plan.

Although Castro announced in 1966 that the first congress of the Communist Party of Cuba would be held the following year, it was not. In 1967, Castro relinquished all offices except prime minister and first secretary of the Communist Party.

"A NECESSARY INTRODUCTION"

From The

DIARY OF CHE GUEVARA

It was Che's habit during his life as a guerilla
fighter to annotate meticulously in a personal diary
his daily observations.  In the long marches through
abrupt and difficult terrains, in the midst of humid
forests, when the rows of men, always stooped under
the weight of their backpacks, ammunitions and weapons,
stopped for an instant to rest, or when the column
received the order to stop to camp at the end of a
tiring journey, one could see Che - as he was affec-
tionately named by the Cubans from the beginning -
extracting a small notebook and with his minute and
almost illegible writing of a doctor, write down all
his notes.

Whatever he was able to conserve from these notes
enabled him to write later his magnificent historic
accounts of the revolutionary war in Cuba, full of
revolutionary, pedagogic and human content.

This time, thanks to that invariable habit of
his annotating the main events of each day, we have
at our command, detailed information, rigorously
exact and priceless, of those heroic final months
of his life in Bolivia.

Those annotations, which were not necessarily
written for publication, were used by him as an
instrument of work for the constant evaluation of
the events, situations, and men, at the same time
it gave way to his profoundly observant and analytic
spirit, very often blended with subtle humor.  They
are moderately edited and possess uninterrupted co-
herence from beginning to end.

Take into account that they were written in the
limited moments of rest, in the midst of an epic and
superhuman physical effort and in his exhausting
obligations as leader of a (guerrilla-like) military
detachment in the difficult stage, at the beginnings
of a struggle of this nature, which was unfolding in
incredibly hard physical material conditions, which
reveals once more his style of work and his iron will.

In this diary, upon analyzing in detail the daily incidents, it becomes evident that there are faults, criticisms, and recriminations which are proper and unavoidable in the development of a revolutionary guerrilla.

In the heart of a military detachment those criticisms must be made continuously, above all during the stage in which it is formed only by a small group, confronted with adverse material conditions and by an enemy infinitely superior in number, when the slightest error or the most insignificant defect can be fatal and the leader must be exhaustively demanding, and at the same time utilizing each event or episode, no matter how insignificant it seems, to educate the combatants and future cuadros (troops) of the new military detachments.

The formation process of the guerrilla is an incessant calling to the conscience and honor of each man. Che knew how to touch the most sensitive fibers of the revolutionists. When Marcos, admonished separately by Che, was warned that he could be dishonorably discharged from the guerrillas, he answered, 'I'd rather be executed!' Later on he gave his life heroically. Similar was the conduct of all the men on whom Che put his trust and those to whom he saw the need to admonish for one reason or another in the course of the struggle. A fraternal and human chief, he knew also how to be demanding and at times severe; but first of all, and to a greater degree, he was so with himself. Che based discipline on the moral conscience of the guerrilla fighter and in the tremendous power of his own example.

The diary also contains numerous references to Regis Debray and makes evident the enormous preoccupation caused by the arrest and imprisonment of the revolutionary writer whom Che had charged with a mission in Europe although deep inside Che would have wished that Debray remained in the guerrillas. That is why Che shows certain nonconformity, and on occasion, some doubts over his conduct.

Che did not have the possibility of knowing the odyssey experienced by Debray in the wars of the repressive elements and the firm and valiant posture he maintained before his captors and torturers.

Nevertheless, the enormous political importance

226

of the process prevailed, and on October 3, six days
before his death, in the midst of bitter and tense
events, wrote: 'A valiant interview was heard between Debray and a student provocator'. This is his
last reference to the writer.

Since in this diary the Cuban Revolution and its
relation with the guerrilla movement appear distantly
pointed out, some might interpret that its publication on our part constitutes an act of provocation
which would give arguments to the enemies of the
Revolution and to the Yankee imperialists and their
allies, the oligarchies of Latin America, to double
their plans of blockade, isolation, and aggression
against Cuba.

To those who judge the events in this manner, it
is good to remind them that Yankee imperialism has
never needed excuses to perpetrate its misdeeds in
any part of the world and that its efforts to crush
the Cuban Revolution were begun since the first
revolutionary law was proclaimed in our country, by
the obvious and well-known fact that this imperialism
is the policeman of world reaction, systematic pro-
moter of the counter-revolution and protector of the
most retrograded and inhuman social structures that
subsist in the world.

The solidarity with the revolutionary movement
can be taken as a pretext, but it will never be the
cause of the Yankee aggressions. Denying the solidarity, to deny the pretext, is the ridiculous politic
of an ostrich, which has nothing to do with the international character of the contemporary social revolutions. To leave the solidarity with the revolutionary
movement is not to deny it a pretext, but in fact to
seek solidarity with the Yankee imperialism and its
politics of dominance and slavery of the world.

Cuba is a small country with an under-developed
economy, as were all those that were for centuries
dominated and exploited by colonialism and imperialism,
situated only 90 miles from the coast of the United
States, with a Yankee naval base in its own territory,
confronted by numerous obstacles to carry out its
socio-economic development. Great dangers have sifted
over our nation since the triumph of the revolution.
But even so, imperialism will not achieve its submis-
sion because the importance of the difficulties of a
consequent revolutionary line, to us, have no importance.

From the revolutionary point of view, the publication of Che's diary in Bolivia does not allow for an alternative. Che's diary was left in the hands of Barrientos who immediately delivered a copy to the CIA, the Pentagon, and the government of the United States. Journalists partisan to the CIA had access to the document even in Bolivia and had photostats made of the same, although they had the option of abstaining, for the moment, from publishing it.

The government of Barrientos and the top ranking officers have enough reason not to publish the diary, in which is evident the immense incapacity of its army and the innumerable defeats they suffered at the hands of a handful of persistent guerrilla warriors who, within a few weeks, snatched away in combat, nearly two-hundred arms.

Furthermore, Che describes Barrientos and his regime in deserving terms with words that can never be erased from history.

On the other hand, imperialism also had its reasons: Che and his extraordinary example gain more and more strength in the world. His ideas, his portraits, his name, are banners of war against the injustices among the oppressed and the exploited and raise passionate interest among the students and the intellectuals of the whole world.

Even in the United States, the black movement and progressive students, who are increasing in number, have adopted the figure of Che as their own. In the more belligerent manifestations for civil rights and against the aggression in Vietnam, Che's portraits are brandished as emblems of struggle. Very few times in history, or perhaps never, has there been a figure, a man, an example which has been universalized with such swiftness and passionate force. It is just that Che incarnates in its purest and most selfless form the internationalist spirit that characterizes the world of today and more each day the world of tomorrow.

From a continent that was oppressed by the colonial powers yesterday, exploited and kept in a backward and underdeveloped state by Yankee imperialism, today rises a singular figure which becomes the universal breath of revolutionary struggle even in the imperialists' and colonialists' metropolises.

228

The Yankee imperialists fear the power of that
example and anything that might contribute to spread
it. It is the intrinsic value of the Diary, vivid
expression of an extraordinary personality, martial
lesson written under the heat and tension of each day,
inflammable gunpowder, real demonstration that Latin
American man is not impotent when confronted by the
enslavers of nations and their mercenary armies, that
has impeded its publicity to this day.

It would be of great interest, if this Diary had
never been made known, to the pseudo-revolutionists,
opportunists, and charlatans of every kind, who, thinking themselves Marxists, Communists, and other such
titles, have not hesitated in considering Che a mistaken man, adventurer, and more mildly, an idealist,
whose death is the song of the swan of the armed
revolutionary struggle in Latin America. 'If Che',
they exclaim, 'maximum exponent of those ideas and an
experienced warrior, died in the guerrilla struggle
and his movement did not liberate Bolivia, that
demonstrates how mistaken he was!' How many of these
miserable men were gladdened by the death of Che,
without blushing in thinking that their position and
reasons coincide entirely with those of the more reactionary oligarchies and imperialism!

Thus they justify themselves or the treacherous
leaders who in a decisive moment did not hesitate to
play in the armed struggle with the real purpose - as
was seen later - of destroying the military detachments, halt the revolutionary action and impose their
shameful and ridiculous political compromises, because
they were absolutely incapable of any other line; or
those who don't want to fight, nor will they ever
fight, for the people and their freedom and have
caricaturized athe revolutionary ideas making them
a dogmatic opium without content or message to the
masses, and converted the organizations of struggle
for the people into instruments of conciliation with
the internal and external exploiters and proponents
of politics which have nothing to do with the real
interests of the exploited people of this continent.

# Reies López Tijerina

*Unites States*

(1926-19  )

Born in Texas to a sharecropping family in 1926, Reies Lopez Tijerina has spent most of his life spotlighted in dazzling contrast to his obscure and dirt-poor beginnings. At the age of seven he was already working the fields. Three of his siblings (there were ten in all) died in infancy. His mother, Herlinda, died when he was still a young child. Poverty was part of his inheritance, but so was pride, and aspirations on a grand scale. Antonio Tijerina, his father, set an example for him throughout his childhood. The elder Tijerina coupled back-breaking work with unrelenting protest against the landowners whose exploitation of workers finally drove the family to new lives as migrant workers. Neither lowly occupation could stifle the father's claim that he was an heir to a Spanish land grant near Laredo, Texas.

Reies Tijerina followed in his father's footsteps at an early age. While still in his early teens, despite an erratic formal education, he became known among migrant workers as the "abogado sin libros" (lawyer without books). Another element in his childhood was a strong religious faith nurtured in him by his mother. Although his early religious training was Roman Catholic, he elected to study at a Bible college sponsored by the Latin American Council of the Assemblies of God Church. This fundamentalist, pentecostal training added another ingredient to an already colorful unfolding of his character. It was during this time that he lived in a cave and experienced what he termed "great illuminations". The personal drive and determination that would emerge in his later life as charismatic was present in his personality during his college years.

231

During this time he walked from Illinois to
Texas to see his dying grandfather.  Soon afterward,
he accepted his first position in the ministry.  But
his role as a clergyman for the Assemblies of God
Church were short-lived.  Conflict with his superiors
led to his becoming a non-denominational pastor within
three years.

As such, he worked as an itinerant preacher,
living on the charity of whatever followers he could
inspire.  He had given up all his worldly possessions,
an act which would inspire his next foray into the
realm of leadership.  By the early 1950s he decided to
form a utopian society and convinced seventeen Spanish-
American families to pool their resources to buy 160
acres of land in the desert in Pinal County, Arizona.
The community thrived for a short time, but was ultimately destroyed by neighbors who violently opposed
their communal endeavor.

By 1957, Tijerina's penchant for conflict brought
him into legal difficulties.  He was charged with grand
theft at this time.  The charges were dismissed because of insufficient evidence, but within the same
year he ran afoul of the law again for abetting the
jailbreak of his brother, Margarito.  A timely
"messianic vision" inspired him to go to Mexico to
fight the cause of land grant claims.  He returned to
Albuquerque in 1960, living and working in secret until
the statute of limitations on his Arizona charges had
expired.  In 1963 he founded (with thirty-seven sup-
porters) the Alianza Federal de Mercedes.  Once incorporated, he attacked the land-grant issue with the
same religious fervor that characterized his earlier
commitments to fundamentalism and utopianism.

By 1966, having exhausted the means available to
him in pageantry and legal maneuvers, Tijerina and his
followers became activists in the most radical sense.
They took over the Echo Amphitheatre of the Kit Carson
National Forest, proclaimed it as the re-established
Pueblo de San Joaquin del Rio de Chama (a nineteenth
century land-grant), arrested two forest rangers, put
them on trial, and established a government that was
subsequently dismantled by state and federal officers.

Having attracted attention on a much larger scale
at this point, Tijerina danced in an out of legal con-
frontations until the spring of 1967 when, fearing
arrest, he resigned as president and temporarily

disbanded the Alianza. He then reorganized as the Alianza Federal de los Pueblos Libres, and was arrested for unlawful assembly that summer. On June 5, 1967, the conflict between the Alianza and the law blossomed into open warfare. Armed Alianza members occupied the Rio Arriba County Courthouse and Jail. In an exchange of gunfire, the jailer and a state policeman were wounded. A newspaper reporter and a deputy sheriff became Alianza hostages. This led to what was called the largest manhunt in New Mexico's history.

Tijerina was arrested on June 10. After being released on bond, he participated in the National Conference for New Politics in Chicago. Following his trial, while he was free on bail, after being found guilty, he participated in the Poor People's Campaign in Washington, D. C. Here, he came into conflict with black leaders when he accused them of ignoring the rights of non-black minorities, and of squandering money that was earmarked for campaigns to further the cause.

By the summer of 1968, Tijerina created the People's Constitutional Party and ran for governor. He was disqualified because of his felony charge. Following acquittal on three major charges, he was still faced with minor offenses at the end of that year. Trying a new ploy, he attempted a citizen's arrest of U.S. Supreme Court appointee, Warren E. Burger, for "decisions detrimental to the civil rights of minority groups". He also tried arresting Los Alamos Laboratory Director, Norris Bradbury and the Governor of the state. Another run-in with Forest Service officers finally netted him a two-year prison term for aiding in the destruction of government property. The remaining charges from the courthouse raid added another two concurrent sentences.

Tijerina presently lives in Albuquerque with his second wife and their children and is once again active with the Alianza organization. He has also returned to the Roman Catholic Church, because, he says, "my people expect it".

# MY STRUGGLE FOR THE LAND

That morning very early, I began to listen to
the news. The danger of war in the Middle East was
the chief news and the failure of the Alliance in
Coyote was the next most important. Alfonso Sanchez
was boasting that he had avoided a revolution in
Coyote, and was showing to all the reporters the gas
masks and ammunition that had been confiscated from
the Reies' "lieutenants".

This was his main justification for what he had
done in Coyote with 35 police cars. Later that same
morning on the radio we heard that eleven officials
of the Alliance would be indicted that morning in
Tierra Amarilla. Already Tobias Leyva's ranch could
not accommodate the people who were arriving. Suddenly, the place seemed like a huge encampment. All
came with the news that in Canjilon we were going to
bring about the people's convention that the "Anglos"
disrupted in Coyote. And Tobias had promised me that
if we did that in his ranch, he would donate four
young lambs so that everyone could eat. And because
of the lambs, the story spread around that there would
be a picnic in Canjilon.

Before breakfast, I heard on the radio that
Alfonso Sanchez would be in Tierra Amarilla that day
at two in the afternoon. When I heard the news, my
heart took a leap, and I felt an electric current run
through my blood and the organs of my body. Like a
stab wound, an idea that I least expected struck me:
to go to Tierra Amarilla and to arrest the symbol of
"Anglo-Saxon justice", Alfonso Sanchez. Without having lunch, I joined the various heads of the families,
and I proposed to them my idea. All were so enraged
by what happened in Coyote that they didn't even question me. We immediately put the idea to a vote, and
no one voted against it. The valiant kept all that to
themselves, and we did not reveal it to our families.

Patricia suspected something. But she didn't
know what it was about. Finally, Tobias' wife sent
for an alarmed Patricia, and she came to the place
where we were preparing the strategy for arriving in
Tierra Amarilla. Before she could open her mouth, I
told her to leave. She did just that and she never
knew what we were scheming until she learned about it
on the radio.

We all knew that the State Police would be in
Tierra Amarilla in full force, because they were
going to have to deal with eleven officials of the
Alliance.  Thus, the problem was to diminish the
Anglos's power without wounding or killing people.

I sent Moses Morales to visit the courthouse
and to make a report on the size of the police force
in Tierra Amarilla.  Minutes later Moses telephoned:
"Quite a few", he said.  And immediately, we carried
out the plans which we had made.

Rosita, my 18-year-old daughter, offered voluntarily to enter the courthouse at the front of the
first group.  We wanted to do that in order not to
alarm the police or all would have ended in disorder.
The main things was to avoid failure at all costs and
the second thing was to prevent the seizure from
spreading outside of police headquarters.  For that
reason, Rosita's role was very important.

With already half the day passed in Canjilon, I
had scarcely eaten.  The people gathered the guns
which the police had not confiscated in Coyote.  As
two p.m. approached, everyone was ready.  A one ton
pickup truck, three cars, and a medium size pickup.
I told Juan Valdez to cover his truck with a thick
blanket, because we had to pass by the office of the
forest wardens, who had a telephone, and he would
warn the police in Tierra Amarilla.  In Coyote, the
wardens had participated in a conspiracy to crush the
people's convention.  Above all, several of our brave
ones told me that they had seen James Evans with an
automatic rifle with a 30 bullet loader.  This James
Evans had no business to be in Coyote.  But, since
the Anglos were true executioners who wanted to wipe
out the Alliance, they went around inciting Alfonso
Sanchez, that idiot foreman, as the people called him,
from that day onwards.  I never forgot that it was
Evans who struck terror in the people that day in
Coyote.

This was what I hoped to avoid:  I didn't want
the wardens to alarm the state police nor to join them,
as they had done in Coyote.

I gave orders to those in cars that, on passing by
the wardens' offices they crouch down in their seats,
leaving only the young men to show their faces.  Besides, I arranged that the vehicles not pass by one

after the other so that the guards would not be suspicious.

Scarcely at 2 p.m., the first car left for Tierra Amarilla; three minutes later, we sent the second one. In this way, we all left Tobias' ranch. The women remained cooking beans in the open air and tossing tortillas in the frying pans. The women and children did not know where we were going. Among the guns which we were carrying were four or five automatic weapons, rifles, pistols, and some 22-calibre guns.

The people did not know how I felt in my heart, as I spoke to them about the arrest of Alfonso Sanchez. I never said even to my most faithful companions what I was thinking on that long morning of June 5th. My whole life opened like a book. My years as an excapee appeared to me; they helped me to think that the angels of justice and truth were with me. That whole day I had asked for a sign. Not to tell me what I should do. I wanted rather a sign that might prevent the trip to Tierra Amarilla. But, on the other hand, I felt that it was my duty to set an example of courage for the people. The Anglo wanted to wipe me out so that I would not arouse the people. I knew that ever since I began to fight for land in 1956. I felt that this was the moment of truth, in a fight against those who had robbed my people of their land and their culture. All the power of the Anglos had challenged me in Coyote. They had one plan: to draw us out in the open: me and the loyal men of the Alliance. So stated the Albuquerque Journal. According to the propaganda media, Reies and his followers were not courageous; they only were full of air, and accordingly, in Coyote, they knocked the air ou- of us. I personally was furious. By around 2 p.m., I had already decided to go with twenty of my loyal companions with canvas in Juan Valdez' truck.

The guards did not suspect our plans. The plan was (and so it was carried out) that several vehicles arrive from one side of the square and others from the other, to insure that there would be no more police than Moses Morales had said. Cristobal, my brother, and other Alliance officials had just left the courthouse under bail, five minutes before our arrival. Thus, not one of them was present.

The police, seeing that the friends of the Alliance did not apear, withdrew, leaving only four

in the area. The square was very bare. When we arrived, Rosita and those who accompanied her entered
first.

Through a small opening, I saw and awaited the
signal from Rosita. Before I gave the order to jump
the truck, a shot was heard. At the same time, Rosita
appeared and gave the signal to all to descend and to
hurry.

From the cars and pickups people emerged; and
from the big truck, twenty people, among them my son,
Daniel, only thirteen years old, who didn't want to
stay in the fields of Canjilon, and David, the oldest
of my family. All surrounded the courthouse, seat of
"English" power and the instrument of those who would
put an end to our sacred right of property.

We came for Alfonso Sanchez, but Alfonso didn't
have the courage to go in person to Tierra Amarilla.
The radio announced that he would be there. But they
really took the wind out of his sails. The people became angry when a state policeman resisted. Even when
I entered, the townspeople were still accusing him of
being stupid for having done what he did. Someone was
saying to him: "Two days ago, you gave me a slap in
the face in Coyote. Now let's see the courage that
you showed there." The trooper was panicked and feared
for his life.

Most people do not know the story of this officer
nor that he came from Magdalena, New Mexico, and they
removed him from there when a minor accused him of
violating her. Tobias Leyva also was very angry. He
snatched the pistol from the officer and discharged it
on the floor of the courthouse. The commotion of 40
people angered by what the government of the "Anglos"
had done to the people of Coyote was difficult to
imagine.

When the first shot was heard, we all jumped down
from the trucks; before entering the room of the crime,
we all saw an old friend escaping from a window. Since
everyone had orders that no one should leave the courthouse so that news of the attack would not spread, many
shouted to Eulogio Salazar not to go out and that no
one was going to hurt him. But from what I could see
and undoubtedly others, Eulogio was terrified to see
a state trooper shouting. When he put his left foot
on the windowsill to jump down, he did not look outside

and apparently did not listen to the shouts that he not jump. Of the group that had not yet entered the courthouse, three were carrying automatic weapons. One of them, wanting to warn Eulogio with shots aimed at the floor in order not to wound him, ended up by hitting him. But, the opinion that I had of that, while walking in the mountains, was that Eulogio fell out of the window, and much faster than we expected. Because of the fall, the unaimed bullets hit him in the air before he hit the ground.

I saw that and it shook me up. Not because of the blood and its consequences, but because Eulogio Salazar was a faithful friend and the Anglo ranchers and the police knew it. Baltazar, another man, and I ran for him; as soon as he hit the ground, he was dragged towards his car that was about 30 meters away without looking in any direction. The blood did not appear immediately. I wanted to explain to him our mission, telling him that we were not looking for him. We reached him and we explained it to him, adding that an ambulance would arrive immediately, that he should wait, because he was badly wounded and that they couldn't take of him in the house. Also, I asked him: "Why did you run, didn't you hear the shouts?" He answered in the negative. We carried him to another car, and I told Baltazar and David to call an ambulance. Scarcely had I left Eulogio when I ran into the courthouse, fearful also that blood had been shed there. Upon entering, I saw what I just described. A youngster stepped up and said to the trooper: "Say your prayers because you are going to die." And the policeman, terrified, thinking that the young man was going to shoot him, answered: "I'm already saying my prayers."

After the short conversation between the youth and the trooper, the young man disappeared inside the courthouse. Juan, Ventura, and I went together to look for Alfonso Sanchez in the second floor rooms. Many were empty. When we arrived at one of them, the door would not open. We tried to force it, and immediately, from within, a shot was fired, piercing the door, and missing us miraculously. That irritated us even more. The people came in a legitimate mission to arrest a felon, and one of them fires a shot at us to obstruct our mission.

One of the automatics aimed at the metal shield of the door, and in a split second, the whole door

shattered in the air.  Daniel Rivera, assistant to
Sheriff Benny Naranjo, was hiding in the room.  When
he heard the shot from the automatic, he became terrified and put his pistol back in his cartridge belt.

So we saw him, upon opening the door.  One companion, infuriated by the shot that Daniel had made
at the door, entered the room, raised the handle of
his automatic and shot the assistant in the face.
Daniel did not fall.  Blood appeared immediately.  At
that moment, I learned that Alfonso wasn't there and
that he - not Reyes - was the one who had hidden himself.  Already, by that time, the whole state of New
Mexico knew what was happening in Tierra Amarilla.
But we didn't know that.  The courtroom was empty, nor
did we ever see the judge.  That seemed suspicious to
me, but there was still time to get away.

"Let's go", I said to Juan and to Ventura as we
came down from the second floor.  Again I said to the
people:  "Let's go.  Alfonso Sanchez is not here."
Everyone immediately headed for the cars.  Baltazar
Martinez was not around and didn't hear me.  That day,
June 5th, Baltazar Martinez moved like a cyclone.  He
did so many things that it is almost impossible to
describe them.

Upon leaving the courthouse, I saw two state
police cars approaching.

"If they come this far, they as well as ourselves
will be obliged to confront each other with guns and
it is better that they stay back", I thought.  Immediately, we fired from afar when they were still
about 100 meters away.  The windshield of the police
car shattered and the car stopped instantly.  The
driver crouched in his seat, backing the car up until
he hit a large old truck.  There, the cops in his car
got out and dispersed in the field which bordered the
Tierra Amarilla school.  Another police car, seeing
what happened to their companions, made an about face,
to return home, not without hitting a lamp post, next
to the sidewalk, and denting the police car.  In that
way, we avoided that day a confrontation between the
police and the town.

Why did the Anglos train the police to act blindly,
like dogs, and to protect only the landowners?  An Anglo
never spoke to the police about civil rights while
making civil arrests.  If the Anglos had educated the

240

police properly in Tierra Amarilla, there would not
have been anyone shot on June 5th. But, the Anglo,
in New Mexico, has this complex which always pursues
him: that the people took his land and are putting
his culture to an end. Because of this fear in his
conscience, he has no trust in the Indo-Hispanic
people. Instead of showing a spirit of democracy,
all powers of arrest have been given to the police that
the Anglo chooses through his chain of police influence.
Intentionally, all power of civil arrest have been de-
prived of the original natives. We were still in possession of the courthouse when the ambulance arrived
for the wounded. We looked for Eulogio Salazar in
order to put him in first, but we didn't find him. He
had already disappeared. Somebody I didn't know came
up and said that Tito Salazar, a brother of Eulogio,
had already taken him to the Espanola Hospital. That
calmed my fears for Eulogio.

At this point must get ahead of my story a bit.

When Salazar left the place where we left him, he
went to the home of Oralia M. Olivas and Rose Mary O.
Mercure.

Oralia, Rose Mary, and her husband were in a
restaurant when they heard the shots; they went outside and saw Eulogio still standing but weak. The
three men put him in their house, and took care of
him. Each one asked Eulogio: "Who shot you?" and
each time Eulogio answered: "Los Tijerinas". That
testimony appears in the record of Robert Gilliland
and Thomas Richardson, two state troopers of New
Mexico.

Eulogio said that on June 5th, Oralia Olivas,
Rose Mary, her daughter, and the god-daughter of
Eulogio and Mercure, Rose Mary's husband, so testi-
fied on June 9th of the same year.

Eulogio Salazar told his story on June 21st to
Robert Gilliland. In the same testimony, Eulogio repeated what he had said to his daughter-in-law,
Oralia, his god-daughter, Rose, and to Placido Mercure
to the effect that "Los Tijerinas" had shot him. Robert
Gilliland, after interrogating Eulogio and signing himself the testimony, later made a resume of the record
of Salazar in which he drastically changed what
Salazar said. Salazar said that "Los Tijerinas" shot
him while Gilliland corrected that to say just one

Tijerina shot him.

Since it was five in the afternoon, we boarded our vehicles and returned to Canjilon. On the way, we met many police cars; so, it was already known that a large number of people had been offended by what took place in Coyote.

An incident that should not go unnoticed is that while the people were seizing the courthouse, there was present an Anglo reporter from UPI by the name of Larry Calloway. He was in a phone booth talking with UPI headquarters concerning the trial that had taken place that afternoon at 1 p.m. As he was doing this, before his eyes, the state policeman was shot. Larry was afraid as soon he passed the news over all the national media which crossed the Mexican border and into Latin America. From New York the news went worldwide. That same day, The New York Times sent a special reporter to Tierra Amarilla, Canjilon, and Coyote.

Baltazar was so busy that he did not hear my voice nor that of the people when we decided to return to Canjilon. On the way, we saw a police car well hidden behind some pines. This time, the famous National Park Wardens were caught sleeping on the job. By the time we returned to Canjilon, our wives were alarmed. All radio stations and the television had interrupted their programs and were only giving special news bulletins. The first that I heard were the orders of General Jolly, giving an emergency call to the National Guard. That was on all radio and TV stations.

I met with the leaders of the village and explained to them what had happened in Tierra Amarilla; I spoke of the mobilization of the National Guard. Meanwhile, I ordered that the women prepare food for three days for six or seven people, a portable radio, binoculars, and rain gear, because it had been raining for five days without stopping. Then, I told them that victory and the benefits of that June 5th were so great that years would pass before we would see the true results. I told them: "Blessed is true justice, the three angels of justice and judgment who will look over us." We carried outomatic weapons.

I told Patricia not to be afraid and to take care of Isabel who was only about six months and 25 days old.

242

Patricia never knew what happened in Tierra Amarilla; she only knew what she heard on the radio.

Juan Valdez and Moses Morales knew the mountains like their hands; they knew each plain, peak, mountain, and valley by name.

We withdrew into the mountains as the sun set. It was around 7 p.m. when we left the village. From Tobias' ranch, one could see part of the square in Canjilon. We saw a long wall made of state police cars. But, the natives of the region knew the terrain very well; so, we left camp without the police seeing us. Already in the mountains, we listened to whatever news or comment as we fled.

The voices of the Anglos had changed. No longer were they making fun of me or of the people that I had assembled in the Alliance. Another rare act of fate: at the same time when we took Tierra Amarilla, Israel seized Jerusalem. After about 25 minutes of walking in the mountains, we heard the first "choppers" of helicopters. Shortly, the second and then a third arrived. The pine forests were not thick, and the helicopter went wherever the police indicated. They suspected that we had headed for the mountains behind Tobias' ranch. We had no other way to escape. Thus, they gave us a real fright. However, we moved like deer. My seven years as a fugitive served me well now to control my nerves and to calm those of my companions. Besides the helicopters, there were three light search planes and a four-engine plane flying overhead, taking photos of the whole area.


THE END...

or maybe the beginning.

NOTES

Introduction

[1]Victor Petit Perez, Rodo su vida su obra
(Montevideo, Uruguray: Claudio Garcia y Cia, 1918),
p. 151.

[2]"American Antiquarium Society," 1914, Volume 24,
p.77.

Chapter 1

[1]Jean-Jaques Rousseau, Social Contract, Everyman's
Library, 1949.

[2]The Spanish Crown sold the rights to trade in
specific goods and in specific areas to trade companies.
This grant was called an asiento, and was often given
to non-Spanish companies. For more information, see
Salvador de Madariaga, The Rise of the Spanish American
Empire (New York: Free Press, 1965).

[3]Foremost among Romantic works were the following:
Jorge Isaacs, Columbia (1837-1895), Maria (1867); Jose
Marmol (1817-1871), Amalia (1855); Esteban Echeverria,
Argentina (1805-1831), El Matadero (1838); Domingo
Faustino Sarmiento, Argentina (1811-1888), Facundo
Quiroga (1845); and Ricardo Palma, Peru (1833-1919),
Tradiciones Peruanas (1872).

[4]Bernard Moses, South America on the Eve of Emancipation (New York: Cooper Square, 1906).

[5]Lucas Alaman, Semblanzas e ideario.

[6]Francisco Bilbao, La America en peligro (Santiago
de Chile: 1856).

[7]See the Doctrine as presented in the appendix.
Also see Dexter Perkins, A History of the Monroe
Doctrine (New York: Little, 1955).

[8]See appendix.

[9]The Gadsden Purchase took place on December 30,
1853 and completed the American territory in the
Southwest. The area purchased was located just north

of the Rio Grande River.

[10]Fortunately, we have an excellent source for these matters as Walker wrote a book of his exploits entitled The War in Nicaragua (Mobile, Al: S.H. Goetzel, 1860).

## Chapter 2

[1]For Clayton-**Bulwer** Treaty, see appendix.

[2]On Napoleon III see James M. Thompson, Louis Napoleon and the Second Empire (London: Blackwell, 1954). And for more information on his Mexican fiasco see the work by E.C. Corti, Maximilian and Charlotte of Mexico (New York: Knopf, 1929).

[3]The United States had demanded the withdrawal of the French, which had led to Napoleon's abandonment of Maximilian. They also promised full support for Juarez in overthrowing the emperor. Actual U.S. troop involvement was never needed, as Juarez' troops easily handled the matter.

[4]For Hay-Pauncefort see appendix.

[5]For Panama Canal Treaty, see appendix.

[6]This document caused problems for President Franklin Pierce; for, when the Manifesto was made public, his administration was attacked as pro-slavery.

[7]Frank B. Friedel, The Splendid Little War, (New York: Little, 1958).

[8]For Platt Amendment, see appendix.

[9]Richard Hofstadter, Social Darwinism in American Thought (Boston: Beacon, 1955). Social Darwinists applied the principles of natural selection and "survival of the fittest" of Darwin to society. As such they saw the Anglo-Saxon race as the "natural" superior race.

[10]The Roosevelt Corollary was the strongest position for the superiority of the U.S. with regard to Latin America.

[11]Heredia's and Bello's most important works include: from Andres Bello, Venezuela (1781-1865) Alocucion a la Poesia, Filosofia del Entendimiento, and Estudios Sobre el Peoma del Cid; from Jose Maria Heredia, Cuba (1803-1839) Al Salto del Niagara, and En el Teocalli de Cholula.

[12]Allison William Bunkley, The Life of Sarmiento (Princeton: Princeton University Press, 1952).

[13]Jose Marti, Nuestra America (Havana, Cuba: Editorial Ley, 1953).

[14]Selected analytical work on these 19th-century movements is: Crane Brinton, Ideas and Men (New York: Prentice-Hall, 1963, 2d ed.).

[15]Ruben Dario, Prosas Profanas, 1896.

[16]Jose Asuncion Silva, Poisias, 1908.

[17]This "New Worldism" emphasized the distinctive qualities of the civilization of America and marked a true split with the traditions of the "Old World."

[18]Ruben Dario, Songs of Life and Hope (Madrid: 1905).

[19]Ibid.

[20]Jose Santos Chocano, Alma America, 1906.


Chapter 3


[1]See note on Social Darwinism in last chapter. This new liberalism assumed the superiority of Democratic institutions especially as seen in the U.S. Although the intent was to "make the world safe for democracy," it tended to be all too similar to Roosevelt's view of the world.

[2]S.R. Ross, Francisco I Madero, Apostle of Mexican Democracy (New York: Columbia, 1955); R.E. Quirk, The Mexican Revolution, 1914-1915 (Bloomington: Indiana University 1960).

[3]Robert E. Quirk, An Affair of Honor (Lexington: University of Kentucky Press, 1962).

[4]Ibid.

[5]The importance attributed to these incidents by the United States is further shown by the awarding of the Congressional Medal of Honor to Admiral Fletcher; "For distinguished conduct in battle engagements of Vera Cruz, April 21-22, 1914. Under fire, he was senior officer present at Vera Cruz, and the landing and the operations of the landing force were carried out under his orders and directions." Karl Schuon, U.S. Navy Biographical Dictionary, (New York: Watts, 1964).

[6]Robert E. Quirk, An Affair of Honor (Lexington: University of Kentucky Press 1962).

[7]Frank Tannenbaum, Mexico: The Struggle for Peace and Bread (New York: Knopf, 1950).

[8]Dara G. Munro, Intervention and Dollar Diplomacy in the Caribbean (Princeton: Princeton University Press, 1964).

[9]Philippe Bunan-Varilla, The Great Adventure of Panama (New York: Doubleday, 1920).

[10]Earl Harding, The Untold Story of Panama (New York: Athene Press, 1959).

[11]Mario Rodriguez, Central America (New York: Prentice-Hall, 1965).

[12]J.D.Martz, Central America: The Crisis and the Challenge (Chapel Hill: University of North Carolina Press, 1959).

[13]Good guides to these nations are: Vincent Checchi, et al, Honduras: A Problem in Economic Development (Westport; Conn: Greenwood Press, 1977); Vera Kelsey and Lilly de Jongh Osborne, Four Keys to Guatemala, rev. ed. (New York: Funk & Wagnalls, 1961); Lilly de Jongh Osborne, Four Keys to El Salvador (New York: Funk & Wagnalls, 1956).

[14]R.F. Smith, The U.S. and Cuba: Business and Diplomacy, 1917-1960 (New York: Bookman Associates, 1961).

[15]Selden Rodman, Haiti: The Black Republic (New York: Devin, 1963).

[16]John E. Fagg, Cuba, Haiti, and the Dominican Republic (New York: Prentice-Hall, 1965).

[17]A.C. Wilgus, ed., The Caribbean, British, Dutch, French, United States (Gainesville, Fl: Univ. of Florida Press, 1958).

[18]A good guide for 20th-century -isms is: William Ebenstein, Today's Isms: Communism, Fascism, Capitalism, Socialism (New York: Prentice, 1967).

[19]Gilbert J. Butland, Chile (London: Royal Institute of International Affairs, 1953).

[20]F.B. Pike, Chile and the U.S., 1881-1962 (South Bend: University of Notre Dame Press, 1963).

[21]George Pendle, Uruguay (London: Oxford, 2d. ed., 1957).

[22]A selected reference on this period is: Thomas Rourke, Gomez, Tyrant of the Andes (New York: Morrow, 1936).

[23]A selected work is: Ysabel Fisk Rennie, The Argentine Republic (New York: Macmillan, 1945).

[24]George Pendle, Paraguay, A Riverside Nation (London: Institute of International Affairs, 1956).

[25]No good scholarly books are available on Peruvian events, but the following gives a pleasant view: T.R. Ford, Man and Land in Peru (1955).

[26]G.I. Blankston, Ecuador, Constitutions and Candillos (Berkley: University of California Press, 1951).

[27]Harold Osborne, Bolivia, 3d. ed. (Oxford: Oxford University Press, 1964).

[28]Some selected books on Latin American consciousness are the following: Leopoldo Zes, Latin American Mind (Norman, Ok: University of Oklahoma Press, 1963); Carlton Beals, et al, What South Americans Think of U.S. - A Symposium (New York: McBride, 1945).

[29]Pedro Henriquez-Urena, Literary Currents in Hispanic America (Cambridge, Mass: Harvard University Press, 1945).

249

[30]Gabriela Mistral, *Paginas en Prosa* (Kapelusz, S.A.: Buenos Aires, 1962).

[31]Jose Enrique Rodo, *Ariel* (Porrua, Mexico: 1972).

[32]Baldomero Lillo, *Sub Terra* (Nascimiento, Santiago, Chile: 1966).

[33]Romulo Gallegos, *Dona Barbara* (Espasa Calpe, Buenos Aires, Argentina: 1969).

[34]Manuel Ugarte, *The Future of Latin America* (Valencia: 1910).

## Chapter 4

[1]An excellent work on this period and on the Marshall Plan is Howard S. Ellis, *The Economics of Freedom* (New York: Harper, 1950).

[2]On inter-American conferences see Samuel G. Inman, *Inter-American Conferences 1826-1954* (Washington, D.C.: 1965); and G. Connell-Smith, *The Inter-American System* (New York: 1966).

[3]Howard F. Cline, *Mexico, Revolution to Evolution, 1940-1960* (London: Oxford, 1962).

[4]An excellent work on Panama is David A. Howarth, *Panama: Four Hundred Years of Dreams and Cruelty* (New York: 1966); the last third deals with this period.

[5]A good overview of this area is presented in Thomas L. Karnes' *The Failure of Union: Central America 1824-1960* (Chapel Hill: Univ. of North Carolina Press, 1961).

[6]Many books are available on Cuba and the Revolution. One good one is Ramon E. Ruiz, *Cuba: The Making of a Revolution* (Amherst, Mass: 1968).

[7]A brief survey with a strong pro-U.S. bias is R.J. Hunter, *Puerto Rico: A Survey of Historical Economic and Political Affairs* (Washington, D.C.: GPO, 1960).

[8]J.P.Harrison, The Caribbean: Peoples, Problems, and Prospects (Gainesville: Univ. of Florida, 1952). Most useful works deal with specific countries and can be found in the Bibliography.

[9]J.D. Martz, Colombia: A Contemporary Political Survey (Chapel Hill: Univ. of North Carolina Press, 1962); and A. Curtis Wilans and Raul e'Eca, Latin American History (New York: Barnes & Noble, 1963).

[10]Glen L. Kold, Democracy and Dictatorship in Venezuela, 1945-1958 (Hamden, Conn.: 1974).

[11]John D. Martz, Ecuador: Conflicting Political Culture and the Quest for Progress (Boston: 1972); Jorge Basadre, Historia de la Republica del Peru, 5th ed. (Lima: 1963).

[12]James W. Wilkie, The Bolivian Revolution and U.S. Aid Since 1952 (Los Angeles, Ca: 1969).

[13]Jay Kinsbruner, Chile: A Historical Interpretation (New York: 1973).

[14]Thousands of books have been written dealing with Argentina in the 1940's and 1950's. One accurate one is Marvin Goldwert, Democracy, Militarism, and Nationalism in Argentina, 1930-1966 (Austin: Univ. of Texas, 1972).

[15]George Pendle, Uruguay, 3rd ed., (London: Oxford, 1963). A very brief analysis of this area and time period is included in J.H. Ferguson, The River Plate Republics (New York: 1965).

[16]Simon G. Hanson, Dollar Diplomacy Modern Style: Chapters on the Failure of the Alliance for Progress (Washington D.C.: 1970); Harvey S. Perloff, Alliance for Progress: A Social Invention in the Making (Baltimore, Md: 1969).

[17]Enrique Anderson Imbert, Spanish American Literature (Detroit: Wayne State University Press, 1953).

[18]Juan Jose Arevalo, The Shark and the Sardines, trans. J. Cobb and R. Osegueda (New York: Lyle Stuart, 1961).

251

[19]Enrique Anderson Imbert, Spanish American Literature (Detroit: Wayne State University Press, 1953).


Chapter 5


[1]Simon G. Hanson, Dollar Diplomacy Modern Style: Chapters on the Failure of the Alliance for Progress (Washington DC: 1970).

[2]Nelson A. Rockefeller, The Rockefeller Report on the Americas (Chicago: 1969).

[3]Lakas became the first chief of state of a Latin American nation to be of Greek ancestry.

[4]U.S. - Panama Treaty Concerning the Panama Canal (Washington, DC: USGPO, 1977).

[5]The term Sandinista is often not fully understood. The name was taken by the Leftist revolutionaries in tribute to the Nicaraguan guerilla leader, Augusto Cesar Sandino, who was a violent anti-Yankee and who was treacherously murdered by the National Guard under the direction of Anastasio Somoza in the early 1930's.

[6]U.S. public opinion was strongly opposed to the right-wing guards due to the death of several American nuns, and this may have kept U.S. troops out of El Salvador.

[7]Johnson and his aids admitted this some years after the fact.

[8]CIA director William Colby testified before a congressional hearing that the Nixon administration had authorized over $8 million to help overthrow Allende between 1970 and 1973. It was also revealed that the CIA worked to defeat Allende as far back as 1964.

[9]Fernando Alegria, El Paso de los Gansos (New York: Ediciones Puelch: 1975).

[10]Fidel Castro, "Introduction," to Che Guevara, The Diary of Che Guevara (Radio Habana Cuba, 1967).

252

[11]R.L. Tijerina, *Mi Lucha por la Tierra* (Fonde de Cultura Economica: Mexico, 1978).

[12]Signed in 1848 at the Mexico City suburb of Guadelupe-Hidalgo, and explained in Chapter 1. See appendix for relevant sections.

[13]"Las Leyes de los Reinos de las Indias"

[14]There has been much written of Tijerina, but he rejects much of it as inaccurate. The authors have discussed these matters with him, and Tijerina has advised that the only true story of his struggle is that told in his book.

# ❧ APPENDIX ❧

## THE MONROE DOCTRINE

The political system of the allied powers is essentially different from that of America.... We owe it, therefore, to candor and to the amicable relationships existing between the United States and those powers to declare that we should consider any attempt on their part to extend their system to any portion of this hemisphere as dangerous to our peace and safety....with the governments who have declared their independence...we could not view any interposition for the purpose of oppressing them, or controlling in any manner their destiny, by any European power in any other light than as the manifestation of an unfriendly disposition toward the United States....

In the wars of the European powers in matters relating to themselves we have never taken any part, nor does it comport with our policy so to do. It is only when our rights are invaded or seriously menaced that we resent injuries or make preparations for our defense....Our policy in regard to Europe,... remains the same, which is, not to interfere in the internal concerns of any of its powers;...

With the existing colonies of dependencies of any European power we have not interfered and shall not interfere.

## ROOSEVELT COROLLARY TO THE MONROE DOCTRINE
### December 6, 1904

"...If a nation shows that it knows how to act with reasonable efficiency and decency in social and political matters, if it keeps order and pays its obligations, it need fear no interference from the United States. Chronic wrongdoing, or an impotence

which results in a general loosening of the ties of
civilized society, may in America, as elsewhere, ultimately require intervention by some civilized nation, and the Western Hemisphere the adherence of the
United States to the Monroe Doctrine may force the
United States, however reluctantly, in flagrant cases
of such wrongdoing or impotence, to the exercise of
an international police power...."

## TREATY OF GUADALUPE HIDALGO
### Signed February 2, 1848; Ratified May 30, 1848

Art. I.    There shall be firm and universal peace
between the United States of America and the Mexican
Republic, and between their respective countries,
territories, cities, towns, and people, without exception of place or persons....

Art. V.    The boundary line between the two Republics shall commence in the Gulf of Mexico, three
leagues from land, opposite the mouth of the Rio
Grande, otherwise called Rio Bravo del Norte, or
opposite the mouth of its deepest branch, if it
should have more than one branch emptying directly
into the sea; from thence up the middle of that
river, following the deepest channel, where it has
more than one, to the point where it strikes the
southern boundary of New Mexico; thence, westwardly,
along the whole southern boundary of New Mexico
(which runs north of the town called Paso) to its
western termination; thence, northward along the
western line of New Mexico, until it intersects the
first branch of the River Gila; (or if it should not
intersect any branch of that river, then to the point
on the said line nearest to such branch, and thence
in a direct line to the same;) thence down the middle of the said branch and of the said river, until
it empties into the Rio Colorado; thence across the
Rio Colorado, following the division line between
Upper and Lower California, to the Pacific Ocean....

Art. VII.    The River Gila, and the part of the Rio
Bravo del Norte lying below the southern boundary of
New Mexico, being agreeably to the fifth article,
divided in the middle between the two republics, the
navigation of the Gila and of the Bravo below said
boundary shall be free and common to the vessels and
citizens of both countries; and neither shall, without the consent of the other, construct any work that

may impede or interrupt, in whole or in part, the exercise of this right; not even for the purpose of favoring new methods of navigation....

Art. VIII. Mexicans now established in territories previously belonging to Mexico, and which remain for the future within the limits of the United States, as defined by the present treaty, shall be free to continue where they now reside, or to remove at any time to the Mexican republic, retaining the property which they possess in the said territories, or disposing thereof, and removing the proceeds wherever they please, without their being subjected, on this account, to any contribution tax, or charge whatever....

Art. IX. The Mexicans who, in the territories aforesaid, shall not preserve the character of citizens of the Mexican republic conformably with what is stipulated in the preceding article...shall be incorporated into the Union of the United States, and admitted as soon as possible, according to the principles of the federal constitution, to the enjoyment of all the rights of citizens of the United States. In the meantime they shall be maintained and protected in the enjoyment of their liberty, their property, and the civil rights now vested in them according to the Mexican laws. With respect to political rights, their condition shall be in an equality with that of the inhabitants of Louisiana and the Floridas, when these provinces, by transfer from the French republic and the crown of Spain, became territories of the United States.

The same most ample garanty shall be enjoyed by all ecclesiastics and religious corporations or communities, as well in the discharge of the offices of their ministry, as in the enjoyment of their property of every kind, whether individual or corporate. This guaranty shall embrace all temples, houses, and edifices dedicated to the Roman catholic worship; as well as all property destined to its support; or to that of schools, hospitals, and other foundations for charitable or beneficent purposes. No property of this nature shall be considered as having become the property of the American government, or as subject to be by it disposed of, or diverted to other uses.

Finally, the relations and communication between the Catholics living in the territories aforesaid, and their respective ecclesiastical authorities, shall be

257

open, free, and exempt all hinderance whatever, even although such authorities should reside within the limits of the Mexican republic, as defined by this treaty; and this freedom shall continue, so long as a new demarkation of ecclesiastical districts shall not have been made, conformable with the laws of the Roman Catholic church.

Art. X. All grants of land made by the Mexican government or by the competent authorities, in territories previously appertaining to Mexico, and remaining for the future within the limits of the United States, shall be respected as valid, to the same extent that the same grants would be valid if the said territories had remained within the limits of Mexico. But the grantees of lands in Texas, put in possession thereof, who by reason of the circumstances of the country since the beginning of the troubles between Texas and the Mexican government, may have been prevented from fulfilling all the conditions of their grants, shall be under the obligation to fulfill the said conditions within the periods limited in the same respectively; such periods to be now counted from the date of the exchange of ratifications of this treaty; in default of which, the said grants shall not be obligatory upon the State of Texas, in virtue of the stipulations contained in this article.

The foregoing stipulation in regard to grantees of land in Texas is extended to all grantees of land in territories aforesaid, elsewhere than in Texas, put in possession under such grants; and, in default of the fulfillment of the conditions of any such grant, within the new period, which, as is above stipulated, begins with the day of the exchange of ratifications of this treaty, the same shall be null and void.

The Mexican government declares that no grant whatever of lands in Texas has been made since the second day of March, one thousand eight hundred and thirty-six; and that no grant whatever of land, in any of the territories aforesaid, has been made since the thirteenth day of May, one thousand eight hundred and forty-six.

Art. XII In consideration of the extension acquired by the boundaries of the United States, as defined in the fifth article of the present treaty, the Government of the United States engages to pay to that of the Mexican Republic the sum of fifteen

258

millions of dollars....

Art. XIII.   The United States engage,moreover, to
assume and pay to the claimants all the amounts now
due them, and those hereafter to become due, by reason of the claims already liquidated and decided a-
gainst the Mexican Republic, under the conventions
between the two republics severally concluded on the
eleventh day of April, eighteen hundred and thirty-
nine, and on the thirtieth day of January, eighteen
hundred and forty three; so that the Mexican Republic
shall be absolutely exempt, for the future, from all
expense whatever on account of the said claims.

Art.XIV.   The United States do furthermore discharge the Mexican Republic from all claims of citizens of the United States not heretofore decided
against the Mexican Government, which may have arisen
previously to the date of the signature of this treaty;
which discharge shall be final and perpetual, whether
the said claims be rejected or be allowed by the board
of commissioners provided for in the following article,
and whatever shall be the total amount of those allowed....

Art. XV.   The United States, exonerating Mexico
from all demands on account of the claims of their
citizens mentioned in the preceding article, and
considering them entirely and forever cancelled, whatever their amount may be, undertake to make satis-
faction for the same, to an amount not exceeding
three and one quarter millions of dollars....

Art. XXI.   If unhappily any disagreement should
hereafter arise between the governments of the two
republics, whether with respect to the interpretation
of any stipulation in this treaty, or with respect to
any other particular concerning the political or commercial relations of the two nations, the said governments, in the name of those nations, do promise
to each other that they will endeavor, in the most
sincere and earnest manner, to settle the differences
so arising and to preserve the state of peace and
friendship in which the two countries are now placing
themselves; using, for this end, mutual representations
and pacific negotiations.   And if, by these means,
they should not be enabled to come to an agreement,
a resort shall not, on this account, be had to reprisals, agression, or hostility of any kind, by the
one republic against the other, until the Government

of that which deems itself aggrieved shall have mature-
ly considered, in the spirit of peace and good neigh-
borship, whether it would not be better that such
difference should be settled by the arbitration
of comissioners appointed on each side, or by that of
a friendly nation.  And should such course be proposed by either party, it shall be acceded to by the
other, unless deemed by it altogether incompatible
with the nature of the difference, or circumstances
of the case.


## PANAMA CANAL TREATIES


### CLAYTON - BULWER TREATY
### April 19, 1850

   Art. I.  The governments of the United States and
Great Britain hereby declare that neither the one nor
the other will ever obtain or maintain for itself any
exclusive control over the said ship canal, agreeing
that neither will ever erect or maintain any fortifications commanding the same or in the vicinity thereof, or occupy, or fortify, or colonise, or assume,
or exercise any dominion over Nicaragua, Costa Rica,
the Mosquito Coast, or any part of Central America;
nor will either make use of any protection which
either affords or may afford, or any alliance which
either has or may have to or with any state or people,
forthe purpose of erecting or maintaining any such
fortifications, or of occupying, fortifying, or
colonising Nicaragua, Costa Rica, the Mosquito Coast,
or any part of Central America, or of assuming or
exercising dominion over the same; nor will the United
States or Great Britain take advantage of any intimacy,
or use any alliance, connection, or influence that
either may possess with any state or government
through whose territory the said canal may pass, for
the purpose of acquiring or holding, directly or indirectly, for the citizens or subjects of the one,
any rights or advantages in regard to commerce or
navigation through the said canal which shall not be
offered on the same terms to the citizens or subjects of the other.

   Art. II.  Vessels of the United States or Great
Britain, traversing the said canal, shall, in case of
war between the contracting parties, be exempted from
blockade, detention, or capture, by either of the

belligerents; and this provision shall extend to such a distance from the two ends of the said canal, as may hereafter be found expedient to establish.

Art. III.   In order to secure the construction of the said canal, the contracting parties engage that, if any such canal shall be undertaken upon fair and equitable terms by any parties having the authority of the local government or governments, through whose territory the same may pass, then the persons employed in making the canal, and their property used, for that object, shall be protected, from the commencement of the said canal to its completion, by the government of the United States and Great Britain, from unjust detention, confiscation, seizure, or any violence whatsoever.

Art. IV.   The contracting parties will use whatever influence they respectively exercise, with any state, states, or governments possessing or claiming to possess any jurisdiction or right over the territory which the said canal will traverse, or which shall be near the waters applicable thereto, in order to induce such states or governments to facilitate the construction of the said canal by every means in their power.   And furthermore, the United States and Great Britain agree to use their good offices, wherever or however it may be most expedient, in order to procure the establishment of two free ports, one at each end of the said canal.

Art. V.   The contracting parties further engage that, when the said canal shall have been completed, they will protect it from interruption, seizure, or unjust confiscation, and that they will guarantee the neutrality thereof, so that the said canal for ever will be open and free, and the capital invested therein, secure.   Nevertheless the governments of the United States and Great Britain, in according their protection to the construction of the said canal, and guaranteeing its neutrality and security when completed, always understand that this protection and guarantee are granted conditionally, and may be withdrawn by both governments, or either government, if both governments, or either government, should deem that the persons or company undertaking or managing the same adopt or establish such regulations concerning the traffic thereupon as are contrary to the spirit and intention of this convention, either by making unfair discriminations in favour of the commerce

of one of the contracting praties over the commerce
of the other, or by imposing oppressive exactions
or unreasonable tolls upon passengers, vessels, goods,
wares, merchandise, or other articles.  Neither party,
however, shall withdraw the aforesaid protection and
guarantee without first giving six months' notice
to the other.

Art. VI.  The contracting parties in this convention engage to invite every state with which both or
either have friendly intercourse, to enter into stipulations with them similar to those which they have
entered into with each other; to the end that all
other states may share in the honour and advantage of
having contributed to a work of such general interest
and impottance as the canal herein contemplated.  And
the contracting parties likewise agree, that each shall
enter into treaty stipulations with such of the Central American States as they may deem advisable, for
the purpose of more effectively carrying out the great
design of this convention, namely, that of constructing and maintaining the said canal as a ship communication between the two oceans for the benefit of mankind, on equal terms to all, and of protecting the
same; and they also agree that the good offices of
either shall be employed, when requested by the other,
in aiding and assisting the negotiation of such treaty
stipulations; and should any difference arise as to
the right or property through which the said canal
shall pass between the states or governments of Central America, and such differences should in any way
impede or obstruct the execution of the said canal,
the governments of the United States and Great Britain
will use their good offices to settle such differences
in a manner best suited to promote the interests of
the said canal, and to strengthen the bonds of friendship and alliance that exist between the contracting
parties.

Art. VII. It being desirable that no time should
be unnecessarily lost in commencing and constructing
the said canal, the governments of the United States
and Great Britain determine to give their support
and encouragement to such persons or company as may
first offer to commence the same, with the necessary
capital, the consent of the local authorities, and
on such principles as accord with the spirit and intention of this convention; and if any person or company should already have, with any state through which
the proposed ship canal may pass, a contract for the

construction of such a canal as that specified in this convention, to the stipulations of which contract neither of the contracting parties in this convention have any just cause to object; and the said persons or company shall, moreover, have made preparations, and expended time, money, or trouble on the faith of such contract, it is hereby agreed that such persons or company shall have a priority of claim over every other person, persons, or company, to the protection of the governments of the United States and Great Britain, and be allowed a year from the date of the exchange of the ratifications of this convention, for concluding their arrangements, and presenting evidence of sufficient capital subscribed to accomplish the contemplated undertaking; it being understood that if, at the expiration of the aforesaid period, such persons or company be not able to commence and carry out the proposed enterprise, then the governmnets of the United States and Great Britain shall be free to afford their protection to any other persons or company that shall be prepared to commence and proceed with the construction of the canal in question.

Art. VIII.   The governments of the United States and Great Britain having not only desired, in entering into this convention, to accomplish a particular object, but also to establish a general principle, they hereby agree to extend their protection, by treaty stipulations, to any other practicable communications, whether by canal or railway, across the isthmus which connects North and South America; and especially to the interoceanic communications, should the same prove to be practicable, whether by canal or railway, which are now proposed to be established by way of Tehuantepec or Panama.   In granting, however, their joint protection to any such canals or railways as are by this article specified, it is always understood by the United States and Great Britain that the parties constructing or owning the same shall impose no other charges of conditions of traffic thereupon than the aforesaid governments shall approve of as just and equitable; and that the said canals or railways, being open to the citizens or subjects of the United States and Great Britain on equal terms, shall also be open on like terms to the citizens and subjects of every other state which is willing to grant thereto such protection   as the United States and Great Britain engage to afford.

Art. IX. The ratifications of this convention shall be exchanged at Washington within six months from this day, or sooner if possible.

In faith thereof, we, the respective plenipotentiaries, have signed this convention, and have hereunto affixed our seals.

Done at Washington, the nineteenth day of April, Anno Domini one thousand eight hundred and fifty.

## HAY - PAUNCEFOTE TREATY
### November 18, 1901

Art.I. The high contracting parties agree that the present treaty shall supersede the afore-mentioned convention of the 19th April, 1850.

Art. II. It is agreed that the canal may be constructed under the auspices of the government of the United States, either directly at its own cost, or by gift or loan of money to individuals or corporations, or through subscription to or purchase of stock and shares, and that, subject to the provisions of the present treaty, the said government shall have and enjoy all the rights incident to such construction, as well as the exclusive right of providing for the regulation and management of the canal.

Art. III. The United States adopts, as the basis of the neutralisation of such ship canal, the following rules, substantially embodied in the convention of Canstantinople, signed the 29 of October, 1888 for the free navigation of the Suez Canal, that is to say:-

1. The canal shall be free and open to the vessels of commerce and of war of all nations observing these rules, on terms of entire equality, so that there shall be no discrimination against any such nation, or its citizens or subjects, in respect of the conditions of the charges of traffic, or otherwise. Such conditions and charges of traffic shall be just and equitable.

2. The canal shall never be blockaded, nor shall any right of war be exercised nor any act of hostility be committed within it. The United States, however, shall be at liberty to maintain such military police along the canal as may be necessary to protect it

against lawlessness and disorder.

3. Vessels of war of a belligerent shall not re-
victual nor take any stores in the canal except so far
as may be strictly necessary; and the transit of such
vessels through the canal shall be effected with the
least possible delay in accordance with the regulations
in force, and with only such intermission as may result from the necessities of the service.
Prizes shall be in all respects subject to the
same rules as vessels of war of the belligerents.

4. No belligerent shall embark or disembark
troops, munitions of war, or warlike materials in the
canal, except in case of accidental hindrance of the
transit, and in such case the transit shall be resumed
with all possible dispatch.

5. The provisions of this article shall apply to
waters adjacent to the canal, within three miles at
either end. Vessels of war of a belligerent shall not
remain in such waters longer than twenty-four hours at
any one time, except in case of distress, and in such
case shall depart as soon as possible; but a vessel of
war of one belligerent shall not depart within twenty-
four hours from the departure of a vessel of war of
the other belligerent.

6. The plant, establishments, buildings, and all
work necessary to the construction, maintenance, and
operation of the canal shall be deemed to be part thereof, for the purposes of this treaty, and in time of
war, as in time of peace, shall enjoy complete immunity
from attack or injury by belligerents, and from acts
calculated to impair their usefulness as part of the
canal.

Art. IV. It is agreed that no change of territorial sovereighty or of the international relations of
the country or countries traversed by the before-men-
tioned canal shall affect the general principle of
neutralisation or the obligation of the high contracting parties under the present treaty.

Art. V. The present treaty shall be ratified by
the President of the United States, by and with the
consent of the Senate thereof, and by His Britannic
Majesty; and the ratifications shall be exchanged at
Washington or London at the earliest possible time
within six months from the date hereof.

In faith whereof the respective plenipotentiaries
have signed this treaty and thereunto affixed their
seals.

Done in duplicate at Washington, the 18th day
of November, in the year of our Lord one thousand
nine hundred and one.

HAY - BUNAN - VARILLA TREATY
November 18, 1903

Art.I.   The United States guarantees and will
maintain the independence of the Republic of Panama.

Art. II.   The Republic of Panama grants to the
United States in perpetuity the use, occupation, and
control of a zone of land and land under water for the
construction, maintenance, operation, sanitation, and
protection of said canal, of the width of ten miles
extending to the distance of five miles on each side
of the centre line of the route of the canal to be
constructed; the said zone beginning in the Caribbean
Sea three marine miles from mean water mark, and extending to a distance of three miles from mean low
water mark, with the proviso that the cities of
Panama and Colon and the harbours adjacent to said
cities, which are included within the boundaries of
the zone above described, shall not be included with
this grant.   The Republic of Panama further grants to
the United States in perpetuity the use, occupation,
and control of any other lands and waters outside of
the zone above described which may be necessary and
convenient for the construction, maintenance, sanitation, and protection of the said canal or of any
auxiliary canals or other works necessary and convenient for the construction, maintenance, operation,
and protection of the said enterprise.

The Republic of Panama further grants in like
manner to the United States in perpetuity all islands
within the limits of the zone above described and in
addition thereto the group of small islands in the
Bay of Panama, named Perico, Naos, Culebra, and
Flamenco.

Art. III.   The Republic of Panama grants to the
United States all the rights, power and authority
within the zone mentioned and described in Article II.
of this agreement, and within the limits of all auxiliary lands and waters mentioned and described in

said Article II. which the United States would possess and exercise if it were the sovereign of the territory within which said lands and waters are located, to the entire exclusion of the exercise by the Republic of Panama of any such sovereign rights, power, and authority.

Art. IV. As rights subsidiary to the above grants, the Republic of Panama grants in perpetuity to the United States the right to use the rivers, streams, lakes, and other bodies of water within its limits for its navigation, the supply of water or water-power or other purposes, so far as the use of said rivers, streams, lakes, and bodies of water and the waters thereof may be necessary and convenient for the construction, maintenance, operation, sanitation, and protection of the said canal.

Art. V. The Republic of Panama grants to the United States in perpetuity a monopoly for the construction, maintenance, and operation of any system of communication by means of canal or railroad across its territory between the Caribbean Sea and the Pacific Ocean.

Art. VI. The grants, herein contained shall in no manner invalidate the title rights of private land-holders or owners of private property in the said zone or in or to any of the lands or waters granted to the United States by the provisions of any article of this treaty, nor shall they interfere with the rights of way over the public roads passing through the said zone or over any of the said lands or waters unless said rights of way or private rights shall conflict with rights herein granted to the United States, in which case the rights of the United States shall be superior. All damages to the owners of private lands or private property of any kind by reason of the grants contained in this treaty or by reason of the operations of the United States, its agents or employees, or by reason of the construction, maintenance, operation, sanitation, and protection of the said canal or of the works of sanitation and protection herein provided for, shall be appraised and settled by a joint commission appointed by the governments of the United States and the Republic of Panama, whose decisions as to such damages shall be final, and whose awards as to damages shall be paid solely by the United States. No part of the works on said canal or the Panama railroad or any auxiliary works relating thereto and authorised by the terms of this treaty shall be prevented, delayed of impeded by or pending such proceedings to ascertain such damages. The appraisal of said private lands and private property and the assessment of damages to them shall be based upon their value before the date of this convention.

Art. VII. THe Republic of Panama grants to the United States within the limits of the cities of Panama and Colon and their adjacent harbours, and within the territory adjacent thereto, the right to acquire by purchase or by the exercise of the right of eminent domain, any lands, buildings, water rights or other properties necessary and convenient foʈ the construction, maintenance, operation, and protection of the canal and of any works of sanitation, such as the collection and disposition of sewage and the dis-tribution of water in the said cities of Panama and Colon, which, in the discretion of the United States may be necessary and convenient for the construction, maintenance, operation, sanitation, and protection of the said canal and railroad....

Art. VIII. The Republic of Panama grants to the United States all rights which it now has or hereaftet may acquire to the property of the New Panama Canal Company as a result of the transfer of sovereignty from the Republic of Colombia to the Republic of Panama over the Istumus of Panama, and authorises the New Panama Canal Company to sell and transfer to the United States its rights, privileges, properties, and concessions as well as the Panama Railroad and all the shares or part of the shares of that company;....

Art. IX. The United States agrees that the ports at either entrance of the canal and the waters thereof, and the Republic of Panama agrees that the towns of Panama and Colon shall be free for all time, so that there shall not be imposed or collected custom-house tolls, tonnage, anchorage, lighthouse, wharf, pilot, or quarantine dues, or any other charges or taxes of any kind upon any vessel using or passing through the canal or belonging to or employed by the United States, directly or indirectly, in connection with the con-struction, maintenance, operation, sanitation, and protection of the main canal, or auxiliary works, or upon the cargꙩ, officers, crew, or passengers of any such vessels, except any such tolls and charges as may be imposed by the United States for the use of the canal and other works, and except tolls and charges imposed by the Republic of Panama upon merchandise destined to be introduced for the consumption of the rest of the Republic, and upon vessels touching at the ports of Colon and Panama and which do not cross the canal....

Art. X. The Republic of Panama agrees that there shall not be imposed any taxes, national, municipal, departmental, or of any other class, upon the canal, the railways and auxiliary works, tugs and other vessels employed in the service of the canal, storehouses, workshops, offices, quarters for labourers, factories of all kinds, warehouses, wharves, machinery and other works, property, and effects appertaining to the canal or railroad and auxiliary works, or their officers or employees, situated within the cities of Panama and Colon, and that there shall not be imposed contributions or charges of a personal character of any kind upon officers, employees, labourers, and other individuals in the service of the canal and railroad and auxiliary works.

Art. XI. The United States agree that the official dispatches of the government of the Republic of Panama shall be transmitted over any telegraph and telephone lines established for canal purposes and used for public and private business, at rates not higher than those required from officials in the service of the United States.

Art. XII. The government of the Republic of Panama shall permit the immigration and free access to the lands and workshops of the canal and its auxiliary works, of all employees and workmen of whatever nationality under contract to work upon or seeking employment upon, or in anywise connected with the said canal and its auxiliary works, with their respective families, and all such persons shall be free and exempt from the military service of the Republic of Panama.

Art. XIII. The United States may import at any time into the said zone and auxiliary lands, free of custom duties, imposts, taxes, or other charges, and without any restrictions, any and all vessels, dredges, engines, cars, machinery, tools, explosives, materials, supplies, and other articles necessary and convenient in the construction, maintenance, operation, sanitation, and protection of the canal and auxiliary works, and all provisions, medicines, clothing, supplies and other things necessary and convenient for the officers, employees, workmen, and labourers in the service and employ of the United States and for their families....

Art.XIV.   As the price or compensation for the rights, powers, and privileges granted in this convention by the Republic of Panama to the United States, the government of the United States agrees to pay to the Republic of Panama the sum of ten million dollars ($10,000,000) in gold coin of the United States on the exchange of the ratification of this convention, and also an annual payment during the life of this convention of two hundred and fifty thousand dollars ($250,000) in like gold coin, beginning nine years after the date aforesaid.

The provisions of this article shall be in addition to all other benefits assured to the Republic of Panama under this convention.

But no delay of difference of opinion under this article or any other provisions of this treaty shall affect or interrupt the full operation and effect of this convention in all other respects.

Art. XV.   The joint commission referred to in Article VI.  shall be established as follows:-

The President of the United States shall nominate two persons and the President of the Republic of Panama shall nominate two persons, and they shall proceed to a decision; but in case of disagreement of the commission (by reason of their being equally divided in conclusion) an umpire shall be appointed by the two governments, who shall render the decision. In the event of death, absence, or incapacity of a commissioner or umpire, or of his omitting, declining, or ceasing to act, his place shall be filled by the appointment of another person in the manner above indicated.  All decisions by the majority of the commission or by the umpire shall be final.

Art. XVI.   The two governments shall make adequate provisions by future agreement for the pursuit, capture, imprisonment, detention, and delivery within said zone and auxiliary lands to the authorities of the Republic of Panama, of persons charged with the commitment of crimes, felonies, or misdemeanours without said zone, and for the pursuit, capture, imprisonment, detention, delivery without said zone to the authorities of the United States, of persons charged with the commitment of crimes, felonies, and misdemeanours within said zone and auxiliary lands.

Art. XVII.   The Republic of Panama grants to the United States the use of all ports of the Republic open to commerce as places of refuge for any vessels employed in the canal enterprise, and for all vessels passing or bound to pass through the canal which may be in distress and be driven to seek refuge in said ports.   Such vessels shall be exempt from anchorage and tonnage dues on the part of the Republic of Panama.

Art. XVIII.   The canal, when constructed, and the entrances thereto shall be neutral in perpetuity, and shall be open upon the terms provided for by section 1 of Article III. of, and in conformity with all the stipulations of, the treaty entered into by the governments of the United States and Great Britain on November 18, 1901.

Art. XIX.   The government of the Republic of Panama shall have the right to transport over the canal its vessels and its troops and munitions of war in such vessels at all times without paying charges of any kind.   This exemption is to be extended to the auxiliary railway for the transportation of the police force charged with the preservation of public order outside of said zone, as well as to their baggage, munitions of war, and supplies.

Art. XX.   If by virtue of any existing treaty in relation to the territory of the Isthmus of Panama, whereof the obligation shall descend or be assumed by the Republic of Panama, there may be any privilege or concession in favour of the government or the citizens and subjects of a third power relative to an inter-oceanic means of communication which in any of its terms may be incompatible with the terms of the present convention, and in case the existing treaty contains no clause permitting its modification or annulment, the Republic of Panama agrees to procure its modification or annulment in such form that there shall not exist any conflict with the stipulations of the present convention.

Art. XXI.   The rights and privileges granted by the Republic of Panama to the United States in the preceding articles are understood to be free of all anterior debts, liens, trusts, or liabilities or concessions or privileges to other governments, corporations, syndicates or individuals, and consequently, if there should arise any claims on account of the present concessions or privileges or otherwise, the claimants shall resort to the government of the Republic of Panama and not to the United States for any indemnity or compormise which may be required....

Art. XXIII.   If it should become necessary at any time to employ armed forces for the safety and protection of the canal, or of the ships that make use of the same, or the railways and auxiliary works, the United States shall have the right, at all times and in its discretion, to use its police and its land naval forces or to establish fortifications for these purposes.

Art. XXIV.   No change either in the government or in the laws and treaties of the Republic of Panama shall without the consent of the United States, affect any right of the United States under the present convention, or under any treaty stipulations between the two countries that now exist touching the subject matter of this convention.

If the Republic of Panama shall hereafter enter as a constituent into any other government or into any union or confederation of states, so as to merge her sovereignty or indepencence in such government, union or confederation, the rights of the United States under this convention shall not be in any respect lessened or impaired.

Art. XXV.   For the better performance of this convention and to the end of the efficient protection of the canal and the preservation of its neutrality, the government of the Republic of Panama will sell or lease to the United States lands adequate and necessary for naval and coaling stations on the Pacific coast and on the western Caribbean coast of the Republic at certain points to be agreed upon with the President of the United States.

PANAMA CANAL TREATY
September 7, 1977

The United States of America and the Republic
of Panama,
Acting in the spirit of the Joint Declatation of
April 3, 1964, by the Representatives of the Governments of the United States of America and the Republic
of Panama, and of the Joint Statement of Principles
of February 7, 1974, initialed by the Secretary of
State of the United States of America and the Foreign
Minister of the Republic of Panama, and
Acknowledging the Republic of Panama's sovereignty
over its territory,
Have decided to terminate the prior Treaties
pertaining to the Panama Canal and to conclude a new
Treaty to serve as the basis for a new relationship
between them, and accordingly, have agreed upon the
following:

Art. I.   Abrogation of Prior Treaties and
Establishment of a New Relationship

1.   Upon its entry into force, this Treaty ter-
minates and supercedes:
(a)   The Isthmian Canal Convention between the
United States of America and the Republic of Panama,
signed at Washington, November 18, 1903.
(b)   The Treaty of Friendship and Cooperation
signed at Washington, March 2, 1936, and the Treaty
of Mutual Understandings Reached, signed at Panama,
January 25, 1955, between the United States of America
and the Republic of Panama.
(c)   All other treaties, conventions, agreements
and exchanges of notes between the United States of
America and the Republic of Panama concerning the
Panama Canal which were in force prior to the entry
into force of this Treaty; and
(d)   Provisions concerning the Panama Canal which
appear in other treaties, conventions, agreements, and
exchanges of notes between the United States of America
and the Republic of Panama which were in force prior
to the entry into force of this Treaty.

2.   In accordance with the terms of this Treaty
and related agreements, the Republic of Panama, as
territorial sovereigh, grants to the United States of
America, for the duration of this Treaty, the rights
necessary to regulate the transit of ships through the
Panama Canal, and to manage, operate, maintain, improve,

protect and defend the Canal. The Republic of Panama guarantees to the United States of America the peaceful use of the land and water areas which it has been granted the rights to use for such purposes pursuant to this Treaty and related agreements.

3. The Republic of Panama shall participate increasingly in the management and protection and defense of the Canal, as provided in this Treaty.

4. In view of the special relationship established by this Treaty, the United States of America and the Republic of Panama shall cooperate to assure the uninterrupted and efficient operation of the Panama Canal.

Art. III. Canal Operation and Management

1. The Republic of Panama, as territorial sovereign, grants to the United States of America the rights to manage, operate, and maintain the Panama Canal, its complementary works, installations and equipment and provide for the orderly transit of vessels through the Panama Canal....

4. An illustrative description of the activities the Panama Canal Commission will perform in carrying out the responsibilities and rights of the United States of America under this Article is set forth at the Annex. Also set forth in the Annex are procedures for the discontinuance or transfer of those activities performed prior to the entry into force of this Treaty by the Panama Canal Company or the Canal Zone Government which are not to be carried out by the Panama Canal Commission.

5. The Panama Canal Commission shall reimburse the Republic of Panama for the costs incurred by the Republic of Panama in providing the following public services in the Canal operating areas and in housing areas set forth in the Agreement in Implementation of Article III of this Treaty and occupied by both the United States and Panamanian citizen employees of the Panama Canal Commission: police, fire protection street maintenance, street lighting, street cleaning, traffic management and garbage collection. The Panama Canal Commission shall pay the Republic of Panama the sum of ten million United States dollars ($10,000,000) per annum for the foregoing services. It is agreed that every three years from the date

that this Treaty enters into force, the costs involved
in furnishing said services shall be re-examined to
determine whether adjustment of the annual payment
should be made because of inflation and other relevant
factors affecting the cost of such services.

6.  The Republic of Panama shall be responsible
for providing, in all areas comprising the former
Canal Zone, services of a general jurisdictional
nature such as customs and immigration, postal services. courts and licensing, in accordance with this
Treaty and related agreements.

7.  The United States of America and the Republic
of Panama shall establish a Panama Canal Consultative
Committee, composed of an equal number of high-level
representatives of the United States of America and
the Republic of Panama, and which may appoint such
sub-committees as it may deem appropriate.  This
committee shall advise the United States of America
and the Republic of Panama on matters of policy
affecting the Canal's operation.  In view of both
parties' special interest in the continuity and efficiency of the Canal operation in the future, the
Committee shall advise on matters such as general
tolls policy, employment and training policies to
increase the participation of Panamanian nationals in
the operation of the Canal.  The Committee's recommendations shall be transmitted to the two governments, which shall give such recommendations full
consideration in the formulation of such policy
decisions.

8.  In addition to the participation of Panamanian
nationals at high management levels of the Panama
Canal Commission, as provided for in paragraph 3 of
this Article, there shall be growing participation of
Panamanian nationalsᴝat all other levels and areas of
employment in the aforesaid commission, with the
objective of preparing, in an orderly and efficient
fashion, for the assumption by the Republic of Panama
of full responsibility for the management, operation,
and maintenance of the Canal upon the termination of
this Treaty.

9.  The use of the areas, waters and installations
with respect to which the United States of America is
granted rights pursuant to this Article, and the rights
and legal status of United States Government agencies
and employees operating in the Republic of Panama

pursuant to this Article, shall be governed by the Agreement in Implementation of this Article, signed this date.

10.  Upon entry into force of this Treaty, the United States Government agencies known as the Panama Canal Company and the Canal Zone Government shall cease to operate within the territory of the Republic of Panama that formerly constituted the Canal Zone.

Art. IV.  Protection and Defense

1.  The United States of America and the Republic of Panama commit themselves to protect and defend the Panama Canal.  Each Party shall act, in accordance with its constitutional processes, to meet the danger resulting from an armed attack or other actions which threaten the security of the Panama Canal or of ships transiting it.

2.  For the duration of this Treaty, the United States of America shall have primary responsibility to protect and defend the Canal.  The rights of the United States of America to station, train, and move military forces within the Republic of Panama are described in the Agreement in Implementation of this Article signed this date.  The use of areas and installations and the legal status of the armed forces of the United States of America in the Republic of Panama shall be governed by the aforesaid Agreement.

3.  In order to facilitate the participation and cooperation of the armed forces of both Parties in the protection and defense of the Canal, the United States of America and the Republic of Panama shall establish a Combined Board comprised of an equal number of senior military representatives of each Party.  These representatives shall be charged by their respective governments with consulting and cooperating on all matters pertaining to the protection and defense of the Canal, and with planning for actions to be taken in concert for that purpose.  Such combined protection and defense arrangements shall not inhibit the identity or lines of authority of the armed forces of the United States of America or the Republic of Panama.  The Combined Board shall provide for coordination and cooperation concerning such matters as:

(a)  The preparation of contingency plans for the protection and defense of the Canal based upon the

cooperative efforts of the armed forces of both
Parties;
(b)   The planning and conduct of combined military exercises; and
(c)   The conduct of United States and Panamanian
military operations with respect to the protection and
defense of the Canal.


4.   The Combined Board shall, at five-year inter-
vals throughout the duration of this Treaty, review
the resources being made available by the two Parties
for the protection and defense of the Canal.   Also,
the Combined Board shall make appropriate recommendations to the two Governments respecting projected
requirements, the efficient utilization of available
resources of the two Parties, and other matters of
mutual interest with respect to the protection and
defense of the Canal.

5.   To the extent possible consistent with its
primary responsibility for the protection and defense
of the Panama Canal, the United States of America
will endeavor to maintain its armed forces in the
Republic of Panama in normal times at a level not in
excess of that of the armed forces of the United
States of America in the territory of the former
Canal Zone immediately prior to the entry into force
of this Treaty.

Art. V.   Principle of Non- Intervention

Employees of the Panama Canal Commission, their
dependents and designated contractors of the Panama
Canal Commission, who are nationals of the United
States of America, shall respect the laws of the
Republic of Panama and shall abstain from any activity
incompatible with the spirit of this Treaty.   Accordingly, they shall abstain from any political activity
in the Republic of Panama as well as from any intervention in the internal affairs of the Republic of
Panama.   The United States of America shall take all
measures within its authority to ensure that the
provisions of this Article are fulfilled.

Art. VI.   Protection of the Environment

1.   The United States of America and the Republic
of Panama commit themselves to implement this Treaty
in a manner consistent with the protection of the

natural environment of the Republic of Panama.   To
this end, they shall consult and cooperate with each
other in all appropriate ways to ensure that they
shall give due regard to the protection and conserva-
tion of the environment.

2.   A Joint Commission on the Environment shall
be established with equal representation from the
United States of America and the Republic of Panama,
which shall periodically review the implementation of
this Treaty and shall recommend as appropriate to the
two Governments ways to avoid or, should this not be
possible, to mitigate the adverse environmental im-
pacts which might result from their respective actions
pursuant to the Treaty.

3.   The United States of America and the Republic
of Panama shall furnish the Joint Commission on the
Environment complete information on any action taken
in accordance with this Treaty which in the judgement
of both, might have a significant effect of the environment.   Such information shall be made available to
the Commission as far in advance of the contemplated
action as possible to facilitate the study by the
Commission of any potential environmental problems
and to allow for consideration of the recommendation
of the Commission before the contemplated action is
carried out.

Art. VII.   Flags

1.   The entire territory of the Republic of
Panama, including the areas the use of which the
Republic of Panama makes available to the United States
of America pursuant to this Treaty and related agreements, shall be under the flag of the Republic of
Panama, and consequently such flag always shall occupy
the position of honor.

2.   The flag of the United States of America may
be displayed, together with the flag of the Republic
of Panama, at the headquarters of the Panama Canal
Commission, at the site of the Combined Board, and
as provided in the Agreement in Implementation of
Article IV of this Treaty.

3.   The flag of the United States of America also
may be displayed at other places and on some occasions,
as agreed by both Parties.

Art. VIII.  Privileges and Immunities

1.  The installations owned or used by the
agencies or instrumentalities of the United States of
America operating in the Republic of Panama pursuant
to this Treaty and related agreements, and their official archives and documents, shall be inviolable.
The two Parties shall agree on procedures to be followed in the conduct of any criminal investigation at
such locations by the Republic of Panama.

2.  Agencies and instrumentalities of the Government of the United States of America operating in the
Republic of Panama pursuant to this Treaty and related
agreements shall be immune from the jurisdiction of
the Republic of Panama.

3.  In addition to such other privileges and immunities as are afforded to employees of the United
States Government and their dependents pursuant to this
Treaty, the United States of America may designate up
to twenty officials of the Panama Canal Commission who,
along with their dependents, shall enjoy the privileges
and immunities accorded to diplomatic agents and their
dependents under international law and practice.  The
United States of America shall furnish to the Republic
of Panama a list of the names of said officials and
their dependents, identifying the positions they occupy in the Government of the United States of America,
and shall keep such list current at all times...

Art. XI.  Provisions for the Transition Period

1.  The Republic of Panama shall reassume plenary
jurisdiction over the former Canal Zone upon entry
into force of this Treaty and in accordance with its
terms.  In order to provide for an orderly transition
to the full application of the jurisdictional arrangements established by this Treaty and related agreements,
the provisions of this Article shall become applicable
upon the date this Treaty enters into force, and shall
remain in effect for thirty calendar months.  The
authority granted in this Article to the United States
of America for this transition period shall supplement,
and is not intended to limit, the full application and
effect of the rights and authority granted to the
United States of America elsewhere in this Treaty and
in related agreements.

2.  During this transition period, the criminal

and civil laws of the United States of America shall
apply concurrently with those of the Republic of Panama
in certain of the areas and installations made available
for the use of the United States of America pursuant
to this Treaty, in accordance with the following
provisions:

The Republic of Panama permits the authorities of
the United States of America to have the primary right
to exercise criminal jurisdiction over United States
citizen employees of the Panama Canal Commission and
their dependents, and members of the United States
Forces and civilian component and their dependents, in
the following cases:
(i)   for any offense committed during the transition period within such areas and installations, and
(ii)   for any offense committed prior to that
period in the former Canal Zone.

The Republic of Panama shall have the primary right
to exercise jurisdiction over all other offenses committed by such persons, except as otherwise provided
in this Treaty and related agreements or as may be
otherwise agreed.
(a)   either Party may waive its primary right
to exercise jurisdiction in a specific case or category
of cases.

3.   The United States of America shall retain the
right to exercise jurisdiction in criminal cases relating to offences committed prior to the entry into
force of this Treaty in violation of the laws applicable in the former Canal Zone.

4. For the transition period, the United States of
America shall retain police authority and maintain a
police force in the aforementioned areas and installations.   In such areas, the police authorities of the
United States of America may take into custody any
person not subject to their jurisdiction if such
person is believed to have committed or to be commit-
ting an offense against applicable laws or regulations,
and shall promptly transfer custody to the police
authorities of the Republic of Panama.   The United
States of America and the Republic of Panama shall
establish joint policy patrols in agreed areas.   Any
arrests conducted by a joint patrol shall be the
responsibility of the patrol member or members repre-
senting the Party having primary jurisdiction over
the person or persons arrested.

5. The courts of the United States of America and related personnel, functioning in the former Canal Zone immediately prior to the entry into force of this Treaty, may continue to function during the transition period for the judicial enforcement of the jurisdiction to be exercised by the United States of America in accordancy with this Article.

6. In civil cases, the civilian courts of the United States of America in the Republic of Panama shall have no jurisdiction over new cases of a private civil nature, but shall retain full jurisdiction during the transition period to dispose of any civil cases, including admiralty cases, already instituted and pending before the courts prior to the entry into force of this Treaty.

7. The laws, regulations, and administrative authority of the United States of America applicable in the former Canal Zone immediately prior to the entry into force of this Treaty, shall, to the extent not inconsistent with this Treaty and related agreements, continue in force for the purpose of the exercise by the United States of America of law enforcement and judicial jurisdiction only during the transition period. The United States of America may amend, repeal or otherwise change such laws, regulations, and administrative authority. The two Parties shall consult concerning procedural and substantive matters relative to the implementation of this Article including the disposition of cases pending at the end of the transition period, and, in this respect, may enter into appropriate agreements by an exchange of notes or other instrument.

8. During this transition period, the United States of America may continue to incarcerate individuals in the areas and installations made available for the use of the United States of America by the Republic of Panama pursuant to this Treaty and related agreements, or to transfer them to penal facilities in the United States of America to serve their sentences....

Art. XIII. Property Transfer and Economic Participation by the Republic of Panama

1. Upon termination of this Treaty, the Republic of Panama shall assume total responsibility for the management, operation, and maintenance of the Panama

Canal, which shall be turned over in operating condition and free of liens and debts, except as the two Parties may otherwise agree.

2. The United States of America transfers without charge, to the Republic of Panama all right, title, and interest the United States of America may have with respect to all real property, including non-removable improvements thereon, as set forth below:

(a) upon the entry into force of this Treaty, the Panama Railroad and such property that was located in the former Canal Zone but that is not within the land and water areas the use of which is made available to the United States of America pursuant to this Treaty. However, it is agreed that the transfer on such date shall not include buildings and other facilities, except housing, the use of which is retained by the United States of America pursuant to this Treaty and related agreements, outside such areas;

(b) such property located in an area or portion thereof at such time as the use by the United States of America if such area or portion thereof ceases pursuant to agreement between the two Parties.

(c) housing units made available for occupancy by members of the Armed Forces of the Republic of Panama in accordance with paragraph 5(b) of Annex B to the Agreement in Implementation of Article IV of this Treaty at such time as such units are made available to the Republic of Panama.

(d) upon termination of this Treaty, all real property and non-removable improvements that were used by the United States of America for the purposes of this Treaty and relaged agreements and equipment related to the management, operation and maintenance of the Canal remaining in the Republic of Panama.

3. The Republic of Panama agrees to hold the United States of America harmless with respect to any claims which may be made by third parties relating to rights, titles and interest in such property.

4. The Republic of Panama shall receive, in addition, from the Panama Canal Commission a just and equitable return on the national resources which it has dedicated to the efficient management, operation, maintenance, protection and defense of the Panama Canal in accordance with the following:

(a) An annual amount to be paid out of Canal operating revenues computed at a rate of thirty hundredths of a United States dollar ($0.30) per

Panama Canal net ton, or its equivalency, for each
vessel transiting the Canal after the entry into force
of this Treaty, for which tolls are charged.  The rate
of thirty hundredths of a United States dollar ($0.30)
per Canal net ton, or its equivalency, will be adjusted
to reflect changes in the United States wholesale
price index for total manufactured goods during biennial periods.  The first adjustment shall take place
five years after entry into force of this Treaty,
taking into account the changes that occurred in such
price index during the preceding two years.  Thereafter, successive adjustments shall take place at the
end of each biennial period.  In the United States of
America should decide that another indexing method is
preferable, such method shall be proposed to the Republic of Panama and applied if mutually agreed.
   (b)  A fixed annuity of ten million United States
dollars ($10,000,000) per year, to be paid out of
Canal operating revenues to the extent that such revenues exceed expenditures of the Panama Canal Commission including amounts paid pursuant to this Treaty.
In the event Canal operating revenues in any year do
not produce a surplus sufficient to cover this payment,
the unpaid balance shall be paid from operating sur-
pluses in future years in a manner to be mutually
agreed.

   Art. XIV.   Settlement of Disputes

   In the event that any question should arise between
the Parties concerning the interpretation of this
Treaty or related agreements, they shall make every
effort to resolve the matter through consultation in
the appropriate committees established pursuant to
this Treaty and related agreements, or, if appropriate,
through diplomatic channels.  In the event the Parties
are unable to resolve a particular matter through
such means, they may, in appropriate cases, agree to
submit the matter to conciliation, mediation, arbitration, or such other procedure for the peaceful
settlement of the dispute as they may mutually deem
appropriate....

   Treaty Concerning the Permanent Neutrality and
      Operation of the Panama Canal

   The United States of America and the Republic of
Panama have agreed upon the following:

   Art. I.   The Republic of Panama declares that the

Canal, as an international transit waterway, shall be permanently neutral in accordance with the regime established in this Treaty. The same regime of neutrality shall apply to any other international waterway that may be build either partially or wholly in the territory of the Republic of Panama.

Art. II. The Republic of Panama declares the neutrality of the Canal in order that both in time of peace and in time of war it shall remain secure and open to peaceful transit by the vessels of all nations on terms of entire equality, so that there will be no discrimination against any nation, or its citizens or subjects, concerning the conditions or charges of transit, or for any other reason, and so that the Canal, and therefore the Isthmus of Panama, shall not be the target of reprisals in any armed conflict between other nations of the world. The foregoing shall be subject to the following requirements:

(a) Payment of tolls and other charges for transit and ancillary services, provided they have been fixed in conformity with the provisions of Article III (c);

(b) Compliancy with applicable rules and regulations, provided such rules and regulations are applied in conformity with the provisions of Article III;

(c) The requirement that transiting vessels commit no acts of hostility while in the Canal;

(d) Such other conditions and restrictions as are established by this Treaty.

Art. III. 1. For purposes of the security, efficiency and proper maintenance of the Canal the following rules shall apply:

(a) The Canal shall be operated efficiently in accordance with conditions of transit through the Canal, and rules and regulations that shall be just, equitable and reasonable, and limited to those necessary for safe navigation and efficient, sanitary operation of the Canal;

(b) Ancillary services necessary for transit through the Canal shall be provided;

(c) Tolls and other charges for transit and ancillary services shall be just, reasonable equitable and consistent with the principles of international law;

(d) As a pre-condition of transit, vessels may be required to establish clearly the financial responsibility and guarantees for payment of reasonable and adequate indemnification, consistent with international practice and standards, for damages resulting from acts or omissions of such vessels when passing through the Canal. In the case of vessels owned or operated by a State or for which it has acknowledged responsibility, a certification by that State that it shall observe its obligations under international law to pay for damages resulting fron the act or omission of such vessels when passing through the Canal shall be deemed sufficient to establish such financial responsibility;

(e) Vessels of war and auxiliary vessels of all nations shall at all times be entitled to transit through the Canal, irrespective of their internal operation, means of propulsion, origin, destination, or armament, without being subjected, as a condition of transit, to inspection, search or surveillance. However, such vessels may be required to certify that they have complied with applicable health, sanitation, and quarantine regulations. In addition, such vessels shall be entitled to refuse to disclose their internal operation, origin, armament, cargo or destination. However, auxiliary vessels may be required to present written assurances, certified by an official at a high level of the government of the State requesting the exemption that they are owned or operated by that government and in this case are being used only on government non-commercial service.

2. For the purposes of this Treaty, the terms "Canal," "vessel of war," "auxiliary vessel," "internal operation," "armament," and "inspection" shall have the meanings assigned to them in Annex A to this Treaty.

Art. IV. The United States of America and the Repbulic of Panama agree to maintain the regime of neutrality established in this Treaty, which shall be maintained in order that the Canal shall remain permanently neutral, notwithstanding the termination of any other treaties entered into by the two Contracting Parties.

Art. V. After the termination of the Panama Canal Treaty, only the Republic of Panama shall operate the Canal and maintain military forces, defense sites, and military installations within its national territory.

Art. VI. 1. In recognition of the important contributions of the United States of America and of the Republic of Panama to the construction, operation, maintenance and protection and defense of the Canal, vessels of war and auxiliary vessels of those nations shall, notwithstanding any other provisions of this Treaty, be entitled to transit the Canal irrespective of their internal operation, means of propulsion, origin, destination, armament or cargo carried. Such vessels of war and auxiliary vessels will be entitled to transit the Canal expeditiously.

2.  The United States of America, so long as it has responsibility for the operation of the Canal, may continue to provide the Republic of Colombia toll-free transit through the Canal for its troops, vessels and materials of war.  Thereafter, the Republic of Panama may provide the Republic of Colombia and the Republic of Costa Rica with the right of toll-free transit.

Art. VII.  1.  The United States of America and the Republic of Panama shall jointly sponsor a re-solution in the Organization of American States opening to accession by all nations of the world the Protocol to this Treaty whereby all the signatories will adhere to the objectives of this Treaty, agreeing to respect the regime of neutrality set forth herein.
2.  The Organization of American States shall act as the depositary for this Treaty and related instruments.

Art. VIII.  This Treaty shall be subject to rati-fication in accordance with the constitutional pro-cedures of the two Parties.  The instruments of rati-fication of this Treaty shall be exchanged at Panama at the same time as the instruments of ratification of the Panama Canal Treaty, signed this date, are exchanged.  This Treaty shall enter into force, simultaneously with the Panama Canal Treaty, six calendar months from the date of the exchange of the instruments of ratification.

Done at Washington, this 7th day of September, 1977, in the English and Spanish languages, both texts being equally authentic.

# PLATT AMENDMENT
## March 2, 1901

...Provided further, That in fulfillment of the declaration contained in the joint resolution approved April twentieth, eighteen hundred and ninety-eight, entitled, "For the recognition of the independence of the people of Cuba, demanding that the Government of Spain relinquish its authority and government in the island of Cuba and to withdraw its land and naval forces from Cuba and Cuban waters, and directing the President of the United States to use the land and naval forces of the United States to carry these resolutions into effect," the President is hereby authorized to "leave the government and control of the island of Cuba to its people" so soon as a government shall have been established in said island under a constitution which, either as a part thereof or in an ordinance appended thereto, shall define the future relations of the United States with Cuba, substantially as follows:

I.   That the Government of Cuba shall never enter into any treaty or other compact with any foreign power or powers which will impair or tend to impair the independence of Cuba, nor in any manner authorize or permit any foreign power or powers to obtain by colonization or for military or naval purposes or otherwise, lodgement in or control over any portion of said island.

II.   That said Government shall not assume or contract any public debt, to pay the interest upon which, and to make reasonable sinking-fund provision for the ultimate discharge of which, the ordinary revenues of the island, after defraying the current expenses of Government shall be inadequate.

III.   That the Government of Cuba consents that the United States may exercise the right to intervene for the preservation of Cuban independence, the maintenance of a government adequate for the protection of life, property, and individual liberty, and for discharging the obligations with respect to Cuba imposed by the treaty of Paris on the United States, now to be assumed and undertaken by the Government of Cuba.

IV.   That all acts of the United States in Cuba

during its military occupancy thereof are ratified and validated, and all lawful rights acquired thereunder shall be maintained and protected.

V. That the Government of Cuba will execute, and as far as necessary, extend, the plans already devised or other plans to be mutually agreed upon, for the sanitation of the cities of the island, to the end that a recurrence of epidemic and infectious diseases may be prevented thereby assuring protection to the people and commerce of Cuba, as well as the commerce of the Southern ports of the United States and the people residing therein.

VI. That the Isle of Pines shall be omitted from the proposed constitutional boundaries of Cuba, the title thereto being left to future adjustment by treaty.

VII. That to enable the United States to maintain the independence of Cuba, and to portect the people thereof, as well as for its own defense, the Government of Cuba will sell or lease to the United States lands necessary for coaling or naval stations at certain specified points, to be agreed upon with the President of the United States.

VIII. That by way of further assurance the Government of Cuba will embody the foregoing provisions in a permanent treaty with the United States. . . .

# BIBLIOGRAPHY

Alba, Victor. The Mexicans: The Making of a Nation.
    New York: Praeger, 1967.

Alegria, Fernando. El Paso de los Gansos. Ediciones
    Puelche. 1975.

Alexander, Robert J. The Peron Era. New York:
    Columbia, 1951.

Alisky, Marvin. Uruguay: A Contemporary Survey.
    New York, 1969.

Altamira, y Crevea, Rafael. Historia de Espana y de la
    Civilacion Espanola. Vols. 2,3,4. Barcelona:
    1900-1911.

Arevalo, Juan Jose. The Shark and the Sardines. Trans.
    J. Cobb and R. Osegueda. New York: Lyle Stuart,
    1961.

Arnade, C.W. The Emergence of the Republic of Bolivia.
    Gainesville: University of Florida, 1957.

Asturia, Miguel A. Hombres de Maiz. Buenos Aires:
    Editorial Losada, 1970.

_____. El Papa Verde. Buenos Aires: Editorial
    Losada, 1973.

_____. Viento Fuerte. Buenos Aires: Editorial
    Losada, 1976.

Basadre, Jorge. Historia de la Republica del Peru.
    Lima. 1963.

Beals, Carleton. What the South Americans Think of Us.
    New York: McBride, 1945.

Bemis, Samuel F. The Latin American Policy of the
    United States. New York: Harcourt Brace, 1943.

Bilbao, Francisco. La America en Peligro. Santiago:
    1856.

Blankston, G.I. Ecuador: Constitutions and Caudillos.
    Berkley: University of California, 1951.

Brenner, Anita. The Wind That Swept Mexico: The History of the Mexican Revolution, 1910-1942. New York: Harper, 1943.

Brinton, Crane. Ideas and Men. New York: Prentice-Hall, 1963.

Briones, Valbuena. Literatura Hispanoamericana. Barcelona: Gustavo Gili, 1967.

Bunan-Varilla, Philippe. The Great Adventure of Panama. New York: Doubleday, 1920.

Bunkley, Allison W. The Life of Sarmiento. Princeton: Princeton University Press, 1952.

Butland, Gilbert J. Chile. London: Royal Institute of International Affairs, 1953.

Callcott, W.H. The Caribbean Policy of the United States: 1890-1920. Baltimore: Johns Hopkins University Press, 1942.

Canovas, Agustin Cue. Los Estados Unidos y el Mexico Olividado. Mexico: Costa-Amic, 1970.

Cespedes, del Castillo, Guillermo. Latin America: The Early Years. New York, 1974.

Checchi, Vincent, et al. Honduras: A Problem in Economic Development. Westport, Conn.: Greenwood Press, 1977.

Chocano, Jose Santos. Alma America. 1906.

Cline, Howard F. Mexico: Revolution to Evolution,1940-1960. London: Oxford, 1962.

Coester, Alfred. Literary History of Spanish America. New York: Macmillan, 1928.

Connell-Smith, G. The Inter-American System. New York: 1966.

Corti, E.C. Maximillian and Charlotte of Mexico. New York: Knopf, 1929.

Dario, Ruben. Prosas Profanas. 1896.

290

Dario, Ruben. Songs of Life and Hope. Madrid: Espasa
    Calpe, 1967.

de Castro, Jose and John Gerassi. Latin American
    Radicalism. New York: Vintage Books, 1969.

de Madariaga, Salvador. The Fall of the Spanish
    American Empire. London. 1947.

_____. The Rise of the Spanish American Empire. New
    York: Free Press, 1965.

Dyer, J.M. United States-Latin American Trade and
    Financial Relations. 1961.

Ebenstein, William. Today's Isms: Communism, Fascism,
    Capitalism, and Socialism. New York: Prentice,
    1967.

Ellis, Howard S. The Economics of Freedom. New York:
    Harper, 1950.

Fagg, John E. Cuba, Haiti, and the Dominican Republic.
    New York: Prentice-Hall, 1956.

Fallas, Carlos L. Mamita Yunai. Mexico: Fondo de
    Cultura Popular, 1957.

Ferguson, J.H. The River Plate Republics. New York.
    1965.

Ford, T.R. Man and Land in Peru. 1955.

Friedel, Frank B. The Splendid Little War. New York:
    Little, 1958.

Galbraith, W.O. Colombia. London: Oxford, 1966.

Galdames, Luis. A History of Chile. Chapel Hill:
    University of North Carolina, 1941.

Gallegos, Romulo. Dona Barbara. Espasa Calpe, 1969.

Goldwert, Marvin. Democracy, Militarism, and Nation-
    alism in Argentina, 1930-1966. Austin: University
    of Texas, 1972.

Graham, Richard. Independence in Latin America: A
    Contemporary Approach. New York. 1972.

Guevara, Che. El Diario de Che in Bolivia. Cuba:
Radio Havana, 1967.

Hanson, Simon G.G. Dollar Diplomacy Modern Style:
Chapters on the Failure of the Alliance for
Progress. Washington, 1970.

Harding, Earl. The Untold Story of Panama. New York:
Athene Press, 1959.

Haring, C.M. The Spanish Empire in America. New York:
Harcourt Brace, 1863.

Harrison, J.P. The Caribbean: Peoples, Problems, and
Prospects. Gainesville: University of Florida
Press, 1952.

Henriquez Urena, Pedro. Literary Currents in Latin
America. Cambridge, Mass.: Harvard, 1935.

Hofstadter, Richard. Social Darwinism in American
Thought. Boston: Bacon, 1955.

Howarth, David A. Panama: Four Hundred Years of
Dreams and Cruelty. New York. 1966.

Hunter, R.J. Puerto Rico: A Survey of Historical,
Economic, and Political Affairs. Washington:
GPO, 1960.

Imbert, Enrique Anderson. Spanish American Literature.
Detroit: Wayne State University Press, 1953.

Inman, Samuel G. Inter-American Conferences: 1826-
1954. Washington, 1965.

Kalijarvi, T.M.V. Central America: Land of Lords and
Lizards. New York: VanNostrand, 1962.

Karnes, Thomas L. The Failure of Union: Central
America, 1824-1900. Chapel Hill: University of
North Carolina, 1961.

Keen, Benjamin. Latin American Civilization. Boston:
Houghton, 1955.

Kelsey, Vera and Lilly de Jongh Osborne. Four Keys to
Guatemala. New York: Funk & Wagnalls, 1961.

Kennan, George. American Diplomacy: 1900-1950. New
York: Mentor Books, 1951.

Kinsbruner, J. Chile: A Historical Interpretation.
New York. 1973.

Kold, Glen. L. Democracy and Dictatorahip in Venezuela;
1945-1958. Hamden, Conn. 1974.

Levene, Ricardo. A History of Argentina. New York:
Russell & Russell, 1963.

Lillo, Baldomero. Sub Terra. Santiago: Nascimiento,
1966.

Linke, Leo. Ecuador: Country of Contrasts. London:
Oxford, 1960.

Litt, John. Urban Guerilla Warfare in Latin America.
Cambridge: Harvard, 1974.

Lynch, John. Spanish Colonial Administration; 1782-
1810. London: University of London, 1958.

McCann, Thomas. An American Company. New York:
Crown Publishers, 1976.

Manross. L.M. Development of the Good Neighbor Policy.
1945.

Marti, Jose. Inside the Monster. New York: Monthly
Review Press, 1975.

_____. Nuestra America. Cuba: Editorial Ley, 1953.
Barcelona; Editorial Ariel, 1973.

Martz, J.D. Central America: The Crisis and the
Challenge. Chapel Hill: University of North
Carolina Press, 1959.

_____. Colombia: A Contemporary Political Survey.
Chapel Hill: University of North Carolina Press,
1962.

_____. Ecuador: Conflicting Political Culture and the
Quest for Progress. Boston. 1972.

Mecham, J.L. Church and State in Latin America. Chapel
Hill: University of North Carolina Press, 1934.

Mistral, Gabriela. *Paginas en Prosa*. Kapelusz: Buenos Aires, 1962.

Moses, Bernard. *The Intellectual Background of the Revolution in South America*. New York: Hispanic Society, 1926.

_____. *South America on the Eve of Emancipation*. New York: Cooper Square, 1966.

_____. *Spanish Colonial Literature in South America*. New York: Hispanic Society, 1922.

Munro, Dara G. *Intervention and Dollar Diplomacy in the Caribbean*. Princeton: Princeton University Press, 1964.

Nehemkis, Peter R. *Latin America: Myth and Reality*. New York: New American Library, 1966.

Osborne, Harold. *Bolivia*. London: Oxford, 1964.

Osborne, Lilly de Jongh. *Four Keys to El Salvador*. New York, 1956.

Padgett, Vincent. *The Mexican Political System.* Boston: Houghton, 1966.

Pendle, George. *Argentina*. London: Royal Institute of International Affairs, 1956.

_____. *Paraguay: A Riverside Nation.* London: Institute of International Affairs, 1956.

_____. *Uruguay*. London: Oxford University Press, 1957.

Perez, Victor Petit. *Rodo su Vida su Obra*. Montevideo: Claudio Garcia y Cia, 1918.

Perkins, Dexter. *A History of the Monroe Doctrine*. Boston: Little-Brown, 1955.

Perloff, Harvey S. *Alliance for Progress: A Social Invention in the Making.* Baltimore. 1969.

Pike, F.B. *Chile and the U.S.; 1881-1962*. South Bend: University of Notre Dame Press, 1963.

Quintanilla, Luis. *A Latin American Speaks*. New York:

Mac Millan, 1959.

Quirk, Robert E. *An Affair of Honor*. Lexington: University of Kentucky Press, 1962.

Rennie, Ysabel Fish. *The Argentine Republic*. New York: MacMillan, 1945.

Rockefeller, Nelson. *The Rockefeller Report on Americas* Chicago. 1969.

Rodman, Seldon. *Haiti: The Black Republic*. New York: Devon, 1963.

Rodo, Jose Enrique. *Ariel* Mexico: Porrua, 1972.

_____. *Ariel Liberalismo y Jacobinismo Ensayos*. Mexico: Porrua, 1977.

Rodriguez, Mario. *Central America.* New York: Prentice-Hall, 1965.

Rosenthal, Mario. *Guatemala: The Story of an Emergent Latin American Democracy*. New York: Twayne, 1962.

Ross, S.R. *Francisco I Medero, Apostle of Mexican Democracy*. New York: Columbia, 1955.

Rourke, Thomas. *Gomez, Tyrant of the Andes*. New York: Morrow, 1936.

Rousseau, Jean-Jacques. *The Social Contract*. Everyman's Library, 1949.

Ruiz, Ramon Eduarto. *Cuba: The Making of a Revolution*. Amherst, Mass. 1968.

Schuon, Carl. *U.S. Naval Biographical Dictionary*. New York: Watts, 1964.

Shapiro, Samuel. *Invisible Latin America*. Boston: Beacon, 1963.

Silva, Jose Asuncion. *Poesias*. 1908.

Smith, R.F. *The U.S. and Cuba: Business and Diplomacy*; 1917-1960. New York: Bookman Associates, 1961.

Tannenbaum, Frank. *Mexico: The Struggle for Peace and Bread*. New York: Knopf, 1950.

Thompson, James. Louis Napoleon and the Second Empire. London: Blackwell, 1954.

Tijerina, Reies Lopez. Mi Lucha por la Tierra. Mexico: Fondo de Cultura Economica, 1978.

Torres, -Rioseco, Arturo. New World Litereture. Berkley: University of California Press, 1949.

Toscano, Filippo. El Sentimiento Anti-Yanqui en el Ariel y en La Raza Cosmica. Faculty Journal of Delaware State College, 1976-1977.

Ugarte, Manuel. The Future of Latin America. Valencia. 1910.

U.S.-Panama Treaty Concerning the Panama Canal. Washington: USGPO, 1977.

Veliz, Claudio, ed. Obstacles to Change in Latin America. London: Oxford, 1969.

Vallejo, Cesar. Tungsteno. Lima: Moncloa Campodonico, 1970.

Vasconcelos, Jose. La Raza Cosmica. Mexico: Espasa Calpe, 1976.

_____. Ulises Criollo. Boston: D.C. Heath, 1960.

Walker, William. The War in Nicaragua. Mobile: S.H. Goetzel, 1860.

Whitaker, Arthur P. Latin America and the Enlightenment Ithaca, N.Y.: Cornell, 1961.

_____. Nationalism in Latin America. Gainesville: University of Florida, 1962.

_____. The U.S. and Argentina. Cambridge: Harvard, 1955.

_____. The U.S. and the Independence of Latin America; 1800-1830. Baltimore: John's Hopkins, 1962.

White, Alistair. El Salvador. New York. 1973.

Wilgus, A.C. and Raul e'Eca. Latin American History. New York: Barnes & Noble, 1963.

296

Wilgus, A.C., ed.   The Caribbean, British, Dutch, French, United States. Gainesville: University of Florida, 1958.

Wilkie, James E.   The Bolivian Revolution and U.S. Aid Since 1952.   Los Angeles. 1969.

Worchester, Donald E. and Wendell Schaeffer.   The Growth and Culture of Latin America. New York: Oxford, 1956.

Zea, Leopoldo.   Latin American Mind.   Norman: University of Oklahoma, 1963.